I Touched
Freedom

DAY NGUYEN

ISBN 978-1-68197-117-9 (paperback)
ISBN 978-1-68197-118-6 (digital)

Christian Faith Publishing, Inc.
296 Chestnut Street
Meadville, PA 16335
www.christianfaithpublishing.com

Printed in the United States of America

CONTENTS

Introduction 5

Chapter 1   Geneva Accords of 1954 7

Chapter 2   Communists Kidnapped My Brother, Tan 14

Chapter 3   Game of Dice Rolling 29

Chapter 4   The Collapse of the South Vietnamese
             Government 41

Chapter 5   My First Journey 63

Chapter 6   Engine Installation 147

Chapter 7   Testing the Boat's Endurance 157

Chapter 8   Gift Giving 188

Chapter 9   Final Preparations 204

Chapter 10   Coffee for the Manager 210

Chapter 11   Gathering at a Secret Location to be Picked Up 229

Chapter 12   Party at the Gas Station 236

Chapter 13   God Listening to Our Prayers 254

Chapter 14   Rescued by the United States Navy 266

Chapter 15   Fired from My First Job 286

Chapter 16   America—A Great Country 295

Book Summary 307

INTRODUCTION

I want to live in a free country. I want to raise my children in a country where they can go to school and learn the truth about the world. Where they can choose to be a clerk, a farmer, or a lawyer. In a country where they don't have to bribe Communist officials to do business, a country where they can be free to write a book or speak their mind critical of the government and not be beaten up, imprisoned, or killed. A country where they can own a home that the government cannot claim the right to enter at any time.

Vietnam is not free; the people of Vietnam are not free. Choosing where to live, choosing a career, locking the door of our home and being safe is not possible. Nor is traveling to another country on vacation.

Vietnam, under Communism, is no longer my beloved country. Risking my life and the lives of my family just to get away from Communism was preferable to raising my children in such a harsh authoritarian state.

After much poverty and hardship, as well as a long stressful time of paranoia keeping our departure a secret, we are now living our dream in America.

There were a series of circumstances I had experienced from childhood, and later in 1975 in particular when the Communists took over all of Vietnam and made life miserable, which placed me into a situation where I had to make a drastic decision. Finally, I felt I could make no other choice. I would have to expose my family to danger and a treacherous journey in our quest for freedom.

CHAPTER 1

Geneva Accords of 1954

The first Indochina war lasted for almost nine years till the French and Allied troops were defeated in the battle of Dien Bien Phu in 1954. The Geneva Accords were then signed to divide Vietnam at the seventeenth parallel into two halves. That area became the demilitarized zone. More than a million North Vietnamese civilians hastily immigrated to the South, leaving everything behind. At that time, I had a difficult time understanding why they left their homeland and relatives with nothing on their back. According to the accords, all the Communist troops and agents in the South had to resettle to the North. However, many agents still remained in the South, though this was in blatant violation of the accords. The Communist leaders already had a plan to invade South Vietnam even before they signed the Geneva Accords. They therefore ordered the Communist cadres to hide all their weapons. They even encouraged the cadres who were to move to the North to have intimate relations with the women in the South and to impregnate them.

A few years later, in 1960, the Communist leaders began to move the Southern Communist agents and also sent a large number of North Vietnamese regular troops with heavy weapons to the South via the Ho Chi Minh trail, preparing for an invasion of South Vietnam. The Communist leaders knew clearly that the South Vietnamese people weren't sympathetic to Communism. So that same year, they established a political organization called the National Liberation Front to foment an insurgency to fight the South Vietnamese government and US forces. The Communists consistently argued that the insurgent forces were indigenous to the South and were struggling to liberate the people from the puppet government and US imperialism. With this deceptive tactic, they were able to win support from a few left-wing scholars of the world community and the naïve Vietnamese nationalists.

We had several years of peace after the signing of the Geneva Accord, and most people in my hamlet worked for the public works department of the province or some had a small piece of land to grow vegetables or fruit. We were poor people, but we lived together harmoniously. We helped each other to build houses, to dig wells, and to care for the burying of the dead and other social affairs.

I went to the elementary school of our hamlet, but we were too poor to support the teacher's salary and the building structure for the fourth and fifth grade. As a result, by the time I got to fourth grade, I had to walk about four kilometers to school on the muddy road during the rainy season. I hated school. I wanted to quit, but my parents didn't let me. Walking on the muddy road didn't bother me much, but I was not good in school so the teacher kept twisting and pinching my ears, striking my fingertips with a ruler, and even using the dehydrated tail of a stingray to beat our bottoms when we couldn't answer his questions. I was his frequent victim. We called him a maniac. I hated my fourth-grade teacher. Going to school we had to walk uphill, and on the way back we had to walk downhill on the sloping, slippery road. I loved the way home from school because I was able to let my feet slide down the road when it was muddy after a heavy rain. I didn't have a pair of shoes; I always walked barefoot so the skin at the bottoms of my feet became very thick.

When it came to protecting my books, I was smarter than other kids. I wrapped a thick sheet of used plastic around my books and then used many rubber bands to hold the plastic in place. They didn't get wet when it was rainy and they didn't get dirty when I fell down on the muddy road.

One day, my dad praised me for keeping my books clean, and when I told him how I did it. He said, "You are genius."

I was proud of myself. However, since my parents didn't know how to read and write but still survived to raise the four of us, I couldn't understand why they forced me to go to school.

I skipped school many times to go to the woods with friends, picking wild fruits and trapping birds. When my parents found out about it, they called my brother who was in the military home to give me a good lecture. My brother not only lectured me, he also administered very tough punishment. He told me to lie face down on the wooden board, and each time he asked me a question, he hit my bottom with a bamboo stick. I wondered why he became so cruel to me, and whether the military had taught him this way.

"Are you going to skip school again?"

"No brother…no brother," I implored.

"Sir, not brother. Do you understand?" my brother commanded.

"Yes, sir. Yes, sir," I said.

"You need to remember this," he said then hit my bottom with the bamboo stick. I tried to cover my bottom with my hands, but when he hit my hands, it was even more painful. He hit me so hard that I felt like my skin was split and my bottom was swollen. I was so skinny; my butt didn't have any flesh, so anytime he hit I throbbed with excruciating pain.

"Mom! Mom! Help me!" I was crying and screaming.

My mother asked him to stop, but he didn't listen; instead, he pushed her aside.

"Mom, leave me alone, I have to teach him a lesson," he said.

"I did teach a lesson…no, I meant I did learn a lesson. No more skipping school, no more, sir," I said, writhing in pain.

After beating me up for ten minutes, he told me to ask for his forgiveness. It didn't make any sense, but I didn't want to get hurt again.

"Please forgive me, sir, no more skipping school, I promise, sir," I said through my tears.

My mother took me aside and put some kind of eucalyptus oil on my wounds. She cried and expressed her resentment.

I had skipped school for many days, so my dad had to walk me to school and turn me over to the teacher. This maniac didn't let me go to class but ordered me to stay in the headmaster's office. He ordered me to stay after school for almost two hours to write only one sentence for ten pages: I will not skip school again. My bottom hurt so badly. I couldn't sit properly for several days.

After that, I didn't skip school anymore and I paid more attention to my homework to avoid punishment by the teacher and my sadistic brother. I wasn't stupid, but I didn't think school was important. As much as I resented my brother, Tan, at the time for the beating me, it kept me in school, and I eventually excelled at my studies enough to stay in school of my own accord and even get a bachelor's degree in law from a university. This achievement was unheard of in my small farming hamlet. My education not only helped me to get a better job in the city, but also taught me to think for myself and to solve problems using logic. My college education and white-collar job would later set me apart as a threat to the Communists, but the skills I learned in school would also help me to outwit them.

During my youth, our hamlet was very remote and was surrounded by thick woods and mountains. The Communists used this area to hide troops during the day and invade the hamlet at night to collect foodstuffs from people. It was dangerous for the government troops to go into the hamlet at night. We, however, had not seen any fights between the Communist agents and government troops in the last few years.

The Communist troops, however, appeared more often at night and went right into the houses of people who they suspected of having some kind of relationship with the government and killed them. They used different tactics now; it became blunter with no abduction or kidnapping but rather murder on the spot.

I didn't hate the Communists initially because I didn't know much about them, but I gradually saw that their activities were not helping the poor people like us. After my brother Tan's run in with the Communists, I paid much more attention to their actions than their words. What I saw was that while they talked about helping the common man, their actions consisted of sabotage. That included the blowing up of bridges, setting up roadblocks, blowing up civilian buses, shelling schools and marketplaces with mortars, all to kill innocent people. I looked at them more or less as a group of terrorists who destroyed the peaceful lives of our people.

One thing that caught my attention in particular happened when the government was bringing in the machinery and equipment to pave our muddy road with gravel and asphalt. The Communist guerillas moved in at night, blowing up all the machinery and equipment, with the result that only the first half of the road was paved and the other half was still mud. The separation line was right in front of my house. It took another six months before the government could bring in the replacements to fix the road with the protection of the military forces, and the equipment had to be withdrawn from the hamlet each night. I was now already nine years old, and my mind was as clear and impressionable as a blank sheet of paper; this event inked a permanent bad image of Communism in my mind.

Returning to the South, the Communist agents received support from an organized group of people that consisted of Communist cadres disguised as civilians who had remained and mingled with the population as well as their wives, lovers, and children who were left behind. These agents were trained in the North on how to conduct an effective guerilla war before returning to the South.

The majority of the Vietnamese people were poor farmers, and Vietnam's topography consisted mostly of hills and densely forested mountains. Vietnam, therefore, had many factors suitable for a guerilla war. The Communists' strategy was to use the rural areas to choke cities around the country. After several years of conducting guerilla war, the Communist leaders didn't believe that the guerilla tactic could win the war decisively and quickly. They also wanted to quickly take advantage of the political situation, where in South Vietnam there were many regime changes and in America there was eroding support for the Vietnam War. The Communists were also enticed by the huge amount of weaponry they received from the Communist bloc, so they eventually changed their tactics from hiding in tunnels, schools, churches, and pagodas to a more conventional form of warfare, fighting directly with the Republic of Vietnam Army and their American allies.

The war escalated to a level where the Communists of the North blatantly violated the Geneva Accords by moving their best regular troops and heavy weaponry to the South through the Ho Chi Minh trail to attack the South Vietnamese and American troops. Many conventional battles were conducted by the Communist troops with the intention of annihilating the Army of the Republic of Vietnam. Using Chinese and Russian weaponry, they first targeted the small military headquarters of a province or district to demolish the facilities and spirit of the ARVN troops. Next, they used the human sea tactic to overrun the installation. In return, the American and South Vietnamese troops, with the support of B-52 bomber strikes and the heavy weapons provided by their allies, were effective enough to either defend themselves or defeat the Communist troops. Millions of Vietnamese civilians and hundreds of thousands of troops on both sides were killed or injured in the war.

The Communist leaders showed their treachery and deceit in the spring of 1968. They wanted to show the world and the Vietnamese people that they were the leaders who were humane, nationalist, legitimate, and cared for people by proposing a three-day truce with the Saigon regime in order to honor the sacred national holidays called Tet. The Saigon government agreed and signed a three-day truce agreement. Trusting the Communists, the Saigon government released the curfew hours and allowed more than fifty percent of the troops home furloughs.

Taking advantage of the unpreparedness and naivety of the Saigon regime, the Communists launched a military campaign to attack all the cities throughout South Vietnam on the first day of the Tet holiday. The Communist troops were brainwashed into believing that the urban populations of South Vietnam would rise up against the Saigon government as soon as they arrived. The reality was in stark contrast. People tried to run away from them. In so many instances the Communists shelled with mortars to stop people from fleeing. As a result, tens of thousands of people were killed in the provinces lying close to the demilitarized zone such as Quang Tri, Hue, and Da Nang.

The Communist troops couldn't take the major military or government facilities of South Vietnam, but they were able to occupy some small buildings in Saigon for a short period of time. Some of the guerrillas even successfully entered the American Embassy in Saigon by blowing a hole through the outer wall of this building using dynamite. At the American Embassy, the US Marines killed all the Communist infiltrators on the same day of the attack. The rest were all killed or flushed out by the American and South Vietnamese troops after a few weeks of fighting.

The Communist troops failed to capture any residential areas from the military forces of South Vietnam except the city of Hue, where they retained control for two months. While occupying the city, the Communist troops committed heinous atrocities by executing many South Vietnamese government officials, police officers, and civilians. However, after a long and fierce battle with the ARVN and American troops, they were pushed out of Hue after suffering heavy losses.

The Communists, who had hoped for an uprising from the people in support of their actions, had met with stiff resistance instead. As a result of this military defeat, the Communist infrastructure in the south of Vietnam was very much shattered; it took them a long time to recuperate. They, however, achieved some political gain in that the American people and the world believed that they were strong and had the support of the people because they were able to launch a large-scale military campaign throughout South Vietnam. The Communist Tet offensive of 1968 vividly brought back to my memory a major event that our family had gone through, which brought horrendous suffering in our lifetime.

2

Communists Kidnapped
My Brother, Tan

It was the end of the lunar calendar year of 1952 when people of my hamlet prepared for celebrating the New Year. Men were still working, and only women were on their way home from a shopping trip to buy food. The bus carrying them home was an old French Renault model. It traveled through one of the most beautiful streets of Dalat, a city in the highlands of South Vietnam. Homes, many designed in the French style, lined both sides. These buildings had magnificent front and backyards. A majority of the buildings were located on the lush rolling hills far away from the street, or on top of private hills surrounded by pines, shady tropical trees, and exotic plants imported from France. The trees were thick, making it very secluded, and each yard was a unique little world. Most of these buildings were owned by either the French or high-ranking Vietnamese officials, and they were located on asphalt-paved roads.

After thirty minutes, the bus stopped at a place where the asphalt road changed to dirt. The passengers, mostly women, prepared to disembark, their bulky bamboo baskets full of banana leaves, fruits, pork belly meat, and other goods needed for celebrating the most important Vietnamese holiday of the year, Tet. Some of them were small vendors carrying necessities to sell to people unable to get to the market at the last minute.

The road going down to the hamlet where these people lived was very steep, and the heavy rain over the last few days had made it muddy and slippery as well. The bus driver refused to drive down this road because he knew that his bus would either end up in a ditch or tumbling down the bank into the valley, so the women had to walk home on this muddy road. They rolled their pant legs above their knees and slowly descended the road. These women were familiar with the condition of the road after rain, so they walked very carefully, using their toes to stop themselves from sliding down while balancing the baskets of food on their heads.

Though they had to struggle to walk down this slippery road, they still shared laughter and friendly chatter, talking about how happy they were that their children and other relatives were coming home this holiday. Poverty was widespread in this area, and these women had worked all year to make ends meet. A very simple thing such as saving enough money to buy new clothes for their children or being able to make a few extra pieces of rice cake for the New Year brought great joy to them.

Regardless of whether they were rich or poor, all families took the first three days of the New Year off from work to celebrate Tet. Traditionally, this was an occasion for all members of the family to be together.

Children wore new clothes and received gifts from their parents or adults in the form of small red envelopes with some cash inside. In return, children paid respect to their parents and wished them a healthy and prosperous New Year.

Young and old, rich and poor, people wanted to have a happy, peaceful time in which to enjoy the New Year. They tried to avoid trouble at all costs during these three sacred days. Adults got together to talk and drink rice wine and eat carrots, leeks, shallot pickles, and rice cakes. They also used the time off to play cards and roll dice with friends and family members. Children had their own animal dice game set up in the public places.

Because there had been many years of peace, the government allowed people to light up firecrackers for this special occasion. It is believed that firecrackers would chase away the evil spirit of the old year and welcome the good luck of the New Year. At midnight of the last day of the year, they set off long strings of firecrackers that left tattered red residue throughout the holidays to scare away evil and show how wealthy they were.

I was eight years old at this time and had a brother, Tan, who was fifteen years older than me. He had graduated from the elementary school but couldn't go any higher because we didn't have a high school close to home and our family was not wealthy enough to send him away. Elementary education alone was significant then for us because Tan was one of a very few people in our hamlet who had this diploma, enabling him to communicate in French. He got an entry-level job at the print shop for the National Geographical Directorate. The office building of this agency was located about four kilometers from our home. Tan had to walk there using a shortcut until he saved enough money to buy an inexpensive bike.

My brother loved sports, especially soccer, so he invited young men of his age or younger to set up a soccer team for the hamlet, and they usually practiced over the weekend. He put up the bulk of his money. With contributions from the other team members, they bought uniforms and a ball. However, they didn't have soccer shoes because they were so expensive and not popular in the field. Actually, no team had shoes, so they all played with bare feet when they had a meet, and that way they didn't face too much risk of injury. Before the game, they usually gathered at our house to discuss strategy and tactics on how to play and win the game; statistically they won more than lost. I was only eight years old but I loved listening to their talk about the sport. I always stood at a corner of the room or at one side of the door for hours, sticking my head in so I could listen to them. They didn't ever talk about politics; all they wanted was to have some fun over the weekend because the hamlet didn't have any other activities for them to enjoy.

I paid close attention to one team member, Do, who often came to the house alone and talked to my brother. He was the goalie and he was good at it. He was thin and short, but he was quick and could jump very high. He spent time talking to Tan regularly, but many times he skipped practice. Often, the team had to beg him play when they had a game.

Preparations for Tet presented another opportunity for me to tag along with my brother. There were only two more days until Tet, and we still had not yet started to cook the rice cakes. It was a delicious and traditional item for this festival. I was older now, if just one year older than last year, so I asked my parents for permission to stay up late with my brother to help him with the rice cake cooking. I was ecstatic just thinking about the prospect of sitting next to the campfire, listening to the popping noise of the wood logs, roasting a fresh ear of corn on the hot coals, enjoying the warm, cozy heat of the fire when the temperature outside was dropping down to forty or fifty degrees Celsius. I just couldn't wait!

This was the first time I was allowed to accompany my brother on this wonderful occasion, so I didn't really know how it was going to be yet, but I was already exhilarated. For the last many months, I had carried wood logs with my brother's help from a creek at the bottom of a deep valley just about a kilometer from my house and now I had the opportunity to set them on fire myself. It was so exciting.

Since we had to use two huge cauldrons and big logs for cooking, we had to set up campfires outside the house. We planned to use six large pieces of rock as a base for the logs, but they were too heavy so I suggested to my brother that we use bricks instead. We drew a round circle and placed three groups of bricks evenly on the circle, each stacked three layers high. Then we placed the cauldrons on top and filled them with water to see if the bricks were strong enough to withstand the weight. Two fires were necessary, one for cooking and one for boiling the water that would be used to replenish the other.

At around seven o'clock in the evening, while we were busy moving the logs and pouring water into the two cauldrons, Do, my brother's friend, suddenly appeared. He kept clinging to my brother like a leech; wherever my brother went, he went. Instead of helping us to do the work, he was trying to talk to Tan about something that he didn't want me to hear. I knew it would take many hours—at least six—to get the cake fully cooked on high heat; we had a lot of work ahead of us to do. Do kept interrupting Tan, demanding his attention. The two left me struggling with moving the wood logs and lighting the fire alone. Tan had never behaved like this before; he always gave me a hand when I needed help. The topic discussed had to be very interesting to him.

I was a little upset, but on the other hand, I was also excited since I now had a chance to light up the logs, the kind of work I had never been allowed to do. Even though the wood had been cut into logs about one meter long, it still took me quite a bit of effort to move them to the fire pit. I laid them flat on the ground underneath of the cauldrons with each log pointing to the center of the pit. The hard part was over; all I had to do now was to set them on fire. My heart was jumping with joy at the idea of roasting my corn in the fire.

I dumped a basketful of wood shavings on top of the logs, and when I realized that I didn't have a lighter or matches to light them up, I asked Tan, "Where can I get some matches?"

He, however, continued talking to Do without even looking at me; it seemed as if he didn't hear my question. I yelled louder, and Tan turned toward me, asking, "What do you want?"

"Matches," I said.

"In the kitchen," he said inattentively.

I immediately ran into the kitchen, looking for a book of matches. It had only five sticks left. I struck the first match a couple of times and I meticulously lit up the wood shavings. It worked beautifully and all the shavings bloomed into small flames, but it didn't last long. Finally it died out, and only a few dots of fire remained. The wood logs hadn't caught fire, and there was no popping noise as I expected. The logs lay quietly on the ground like nothing had happened. I was kind of disappointed but I didn't give up as yet. I then collected all the twigs in the surrounding area, some pine roots in the kitchen, pine straw, and the remaining wood shavings, and I dumped them all on top of the wood logs. The entire kindling lit up! I hoped that the wood logs would catch the fire this time. The fire lasted much longer, making me hopeful, but though the logs were singed the outside, there was still no flame. I struggled to blow at the fire for more than five minutes to no avail, and my eyes were full of tears from the smoke. I was tired and stressed out.

I was so desperate that I didn't know what else to do, while Tan was still talking to his friend and ignoring what I was doing. In my eyes, it seemed as if he was hypnotized by his unwelcomed friend.

I had to rely on a bold last resort, kerosene. I had seen people pour this type of liquid on wood to start a fire before. I took out a kerosene lamp from the house and dumped all the remaining liquid in the lamp container on the wood logs, but instead of reviving the fire, it smothered all the flames on the logs completely and more smoke started spewing out of the logs. Regardless, I struck a match and threw it at the wood logs, and the entire fire pit burst into flame and lighted up the entire area. The sudden, hot flames threw me back a few steps.

This caught the attention of my brother. He screamed at the top of his lungs, "What in the world are you doing?" I couldn't answer because I was so shocked and scared.

Thank God this stopped him from ignoring me, and he stood and walked over next to me. I was afraid that he would slap me so I bit my teeth hard to be ready for it. He instead slightly tapped on my right shoulder and gently asked, "What did you do?"

"I poured kerosene on the logs," I admitted timidly, noting the flames hadn't died yet.

Tan told me, "The fire needs air to burn." He then removed all the logs from the fire pit and evenly positioned four pieces of brick under the cauldron. Then he placed the logs on top of the bricks and arranged them so one log rested on top of another. He asked me to get him some pine roots; he split them into small sticks and stacked them in the same manner under the logs. He was able to get the fire started. I was impressed.

Finally, Tan sat on a log at the other side of the fire across from me. Do was right next to him, and he was fearful that Tan would reject his request, so he whispered in Tan's ear.

"No, I can't give you the map!" Tan said disagreeably.

"Why?" he asked, a worried tone in his voice.

"It is the company property. I can't take it out. I will be fired if I take anything that belongs to the company out," said Tan.

"I will pay if you want money," Do quickly suggested.

"Honestly, I would give it to you for free if I could. You are my friend," Tan said.

Do didn't leave; instead, he sat next to Tan, nagging, trying to convince him to give in. I wanted him to go home and leave my brother alone. I did not just resent the time and attention of my brother that he took away, but also I had to do all the work alone while he was chatting with my brother! In the flickering light of the campfire, I saw his face and studied him closely for the first time. He had a long, pointed chin and sharp, protruding cheekbones. His slanted eyes resembled a thin thread with more white than black. He never looked at anyone straight in the eyes when he talked, and his severe overbite lent his smile an almost evil, deceptive cast. I felt very uncomfortable looking at his eyes. Moreover, his crude, impolite manner toward Tan was so out of place. It seemed as if he had spent most of his life in the jungle away from civilized people. I knew I shouldn't ask him to leave since it would be disrespectful of me, but I was upset seeing him nagging my brother.

"Mr. Do, go home...it is getting late now," I said, getting really agitated.

"Quiet, you go to sleep," my brother scolded, but it wasn't easy for him to chase me away.

"Well, Mom gave me permission to stay late with you tonight," I insisted.

"Then sit there quietly," Tan said.

After my brother's reprimand, there was little I could do except lapse into sulky silence. The long-awaited rice cooking expedition had lost much of its allure, and I was bitterly disappointed at having lost to Do in the competition for my beloved brother's attention. I would have been even more sullen had I known that I would be seeing Do again very soon.

Several days later, on the second day of Tet, we all sat around eating at the wooden table in our kitchen. My brother and sisters were laughing because I had put a big piece of rice cake in my mouth and couldn't chew. The cake was made from glutinous rice, which was very sticky, making it difficult to chew and swallow. They enjoyed making fun of me.

"Piggy, you should only bite off what you can chew," my brother said with a smirk.

"If I don't eat quickly enough, then nothing would be left. I guess I know who the pigs are," I retorted, my mouth still full.

"You are a naughty boy," my sister chided, her voice very gentle.

Although my back faced the door, I felt a sudden draft coming from behind me, making my neck cold. I turned around and saw Do slipping in. My mood immediately soured. Do was wearing a worn black jacket, trousers, a pair of old shoes, and a cap. I had never ever seen him wearing a cap before; it made him look strangely different. It was four in the afternoon already, so what he was doing here and why he kept pestering us eluded me. I fretted over his unwelcome presence.

"Hope everyone has a Happy New Year," Do said with a smile.

My brother shook his hand and wished a happy New Year to him also.

With an unpleasant smile that showed his overbite, Do patted me on the shoulder, handed me a small red envelope and said, "Well, I have some New Year money for this young man. You should eat a lot and grow fast. Okay."

"Thank you," I said indifferently. Given the culture and the importance of the Tet holidays, I thought he should have arrived at our house in a proper way, by entering the front door. He should have met my parents first, wishing them good health instead of slipping through the back kitchen door. I was not superstitious, but I had a premonition that this man would not bring any luck to my family this year. However, I didn't dare to share my thoughts with anyone else in the family.

Do then quickly turned and approached my brother, who was sitting on a wooden bench, and said abruptly, "Tan, let's go for a game of dice. One of the neighbors is hosting the game at his house.

We worked hard all year round, and we have only three days to enjoy ourselves. Let's go."

"Good idea, but it is rather cold tonight. I need to put on a jacket and a pair of shoes, and I have to be home before ten," my brother said.

"Hurry up, then," Do said.

After my brother put on the jacket, he couldn't find a pair of socks. He asked me to go get them for him.

"I don't know where you keep them," I said, indignant because I didn't want my brother to go.

"In the right corner of my wooden chest in our room."

Do appeared to be antsy and he behaved as if he wanted to leave immediately. I, on the other hand, just wanted to drag it out, so I walked slowly and heavily and took my time to search for the socks.

While putting on his socks, my brother informed my parents that he would go for a game of dice and would be back before ten, in time for the family dinner.

"It gets dark very early this time of the year and it is quite cold at night, so try to get home as soon as you can," my mom reminded Tan affectionately.

"Good-bye, see you all later," Do said as they quickly left. I watched them disappear down the muddy road.

By seven thirty that evening, my mother and sisters had prepared all the wonderful foods and treats for the gathering. The artistic spread was a feast we looked forward to all year and included all of my favorite foods, which were sometimes scarce the year round. I couldn't take my eyes off the enticingly aromatic rice cakes, which were arranged with tantalizing artistry on a large, round plate. The light-green exterior promised the sweet flavor of banana leaves, but my favorite part was the perfectly cooked meat at the center of each slice. Competing for my attention was a platter of steamed pork shoulder sliced thinly and arrayed on a shallow plate among a wealth of herbs. At the center of the table was a bowl of meticulously prepared fish sauce. My mother made the best fish sauce in our hamlet, putting just enough sugar, lemon juice, and red hot peppers picked from our backyard. At each corner of the table was a stack of rice paper, which was used to wrap the pork and herbs. The roll would then be dipped into the fish sauce. However, we couldn't eat until Tan returned home. All the special dishes made my mouth water, and the longer I had to wait for my brother, the more I resented Do.

My parents, sisters, and a few close relatives were sitting without eating around the table in the kitchen, trying to get some heat from the cooking pit. They smoked, drank tea, and talked about the work that they would plan for the New Year. They were also anxious to know why Tan wasn't yet home. It was already nine thirty. My mother even suggested we go to Do's house to find out if he was home yet.

It was very dark and cold outside. Do's house wasn't too far, only one kilometer from our house, but the road was muddy and slippery. It was hard to walk on this mud road during the day and much more difficult to walk on it at night, but my sister and I still volunteered to go.

Mom put a warm jacket and an old wool hat on me and lit a wooden torch made from pine roots. Surrounding our village were thick woods that made the night even darker, and we had very rarely gone out at night. It was scary because of the darkness. I stayed very close behind my older sister; my fist clenching the hem of her sweater. The road was very slippery and steep, and I had to carry my slippers; otherwise, they would be stuck in the mud. The mud was so cold that my feet started to feel numb. Although it was only a short distance, it still took us almost twenty minutes to get to his house. The house was lit from within by an oil lamp on top of the table. We knocked on the door and left the torch outside when we were asked in. Do was already in a different outfit than when he had come to our house in the afternoon, and his parents had already gone to bed.

"What is happening? Why are you out here so late?" he asked.

"My brother is not home yet, and since he went out with you to the dice game, we need to know if you know his whereabouts," my sister explained.

"Well, we left the last game at about nine thirty, and your brother told me that he would go directly home, so I don't have any idea where he went after we left," Do replied with a baleful look.

"Was my brother with someone else?" I piped up.

"After he left, I don't really know," Do said, seeming very sure of it.

On the way home, I told my sister that I didn't believe what this man said. If Do had left the game at nine thirty, then it would have been impossible for him to get home before we arrived unless he ran.

"Did he wear shoes when he was at our house this afternoon?" my sister asked.

"Yes, he did, and since the road is so muddy, I don't think he would be able to run that quickly," I said then added with all of the authority an eight-year-old could summon, "I know where the game was held, and the distance from that location to Do's house is actually longer than from our house to his. You probably noticed that he was in a clean outfit, different than what he had on when he was at our house. He had to be at home for quite a while. Something is very wrong."

"I was busy with all the cooking and preparation so I didn't pay attention to him when he was at our house this afternoon," she said.

"And he was also at our house for only a short time. He was so pushy even our brother Tan was annoyed with his behavior," I remembered, a strange chill running up my spine.

My sister was dismayed and frightened. She told me we needed to get home soon because our parents were waiting for us. My whole body was shaking uncontrollably, because of nervousness, the bitter cold, and my feeling that something awfully wrong had happened to Tan. But regardless of how hard I tried, I couldn't walk any faster because the road was so slippery. It had rained heavily the last few days, and after a heavy rain, this road was almost impassable. Ironically, when there was no rain for a few weeks, conditions were still terrible. Then, all the trees and houses along both sides of the road would be covered with a thick layer of yellow dust.

Back home there was an ominous silence. All of our relatives had already gone home. The food was uneaten and getting cold on the table in our kitchen. My mother, sitting alone and motionless at the wooden table, stared sadly out into space under the dim wavering light of the oil lamp. She begged for news about my brother, so we explained to her what had happened according to Do. She sighed, and in a toneless voice she said, "Your brother is not yet home."

The memory of the death of a young man three weeks earlier in the hamlet added to stress on our family. He was decapitated, and his body left at the edge of the woods with a note attached saying, "This traitor was executed by the League for Independence of Vietnam for actions against the people."

My mother used a piece of cloth to wipe her silent tears without uttering a word. My father quietly left the room to go to his bed. He lay down, his right arm on his forehead, thinking deeply about the incident.

I followed my father, sitting next to his bed, and under the dim light of the oil lamp it seemed as if the wrinkles on his face were getting deeper. My father usually didn't talk about politics or the danger we might be in, hoping to protect us from fear. He kept all the pain and stress inside, but now he told me in a monotone voice, "Your brother had just finished helping me nail a few pieces of pinewood planks from the pine tree at the back of our yard to the front wall of the house. Then he left. We have no clue what happened to him or where he is now. We don't know if he is safe or even alive." My father had been looking for the empty burlap rice bag to insulate the house after he finished nailing the wood planks, but he had not been able to get what he needed. The wall still had many gaps between the planks. The cold air and fog entered the house through these holes, making it colder.

He was remembering the help that my brother had rendered to him for this task, and now his son had disappeared under strange circumstances with not a clue about his safety. "Do, his friend, told me that Tan left the game alone around nine o'clock, but I do not quite believe his statement," I said.

"What makes you think that way?" my dad asked.

"Something about his behavior made me think he is not honest," I said.

"They have been good friends for many years," Dad said.

As a lumberjack and farmer, my dad didn't have a formal education and he basically believed that man was born with a good heart;

he always believed that people were genuinely good. As an eight-year-old child, I didn't dare to challenge my dad's belief because he was very conservative and I was taught to respect my parents. I quietly left his room to sit with my mother in the kitchen. I hadn't eaten much since this afternoon, and I was very hungry. The cold weather at this time of the year made me shiver ceaselessly. It seemed to start from inside out. My hunger became unbearable so I walked over to get a slice of the rice cake. I wanted to share with my mom, but she refused to eat. Although I tried to eat it, my fear and worry only allowed me to finish half. I huddled closely to my mother, hoping to get some warmth from her, but it didn't seem that she had any heat of her own. She was so thin, just skin and bone. Now she wept constantly, so I took an old blanket and put it over Mom's shoulders. Still she sat motionless.

The night was quiet. I was able to hear the monotonous ticking sound of the old table clock, the sobbing of my mom and sister, and the humming of insects, especially the chirping of crickets. The hooting and howling of the night owls was so close that it made the night even more frightening. I looked at the clock, which showed three in the morning. This was the second night I had kept a vigil besides the night I spent with my brother when we cooked rice cake.

The night seemed endless, especially since I was waiting for my beloved brother, who I was not sure would come home. Dogs barking from a distance, owls and other night sounds made the waiting even longer. Then I heard some noise, as if someone might be knocking on the door. But after listening closely, I realized it was the breeze scraping the branches of a plum tree against the wooden planks of the house.

The monkey chatter from close by, and the roosters started to crow, letting us know that the dawn was coming; however, we were still in the dark about my brother's whereabouts and safety. After a long, sleepless night spent waiting in desperate fearfulness for my brother's fate, the faces of my father, mother, and sister were tired and haggard, their eyes red and puffy.

However, we didn't know how deeply Do was involved in the disappearance of my brother. About nine in the morning of the next day, my father reported to the police that my brother was missing. They asked a lot of questions, but he could only tell them what he knew, that my brother had gone out with a friend for a game of dice-rolling and never came home after that. My father also informed the police the name of the friend my brother went out with. Then he reported to Tan's supervisor at the National Geographical Directorate that Tan had disappeared.

Early in the morning before going to the police, my parents contacted Do to learn more about what had happened to my brother and whether my brother had gone out with someone else besides Do during that night. He was not home. His parents told my parents that their son hadn't said anything about my brother and had packed enough food for two weeks of work. He was a lumberjack, and he had left earlier for work in the morning. My family also contacted all the members of the soccer team to find out if they had any news about Tan, but they all were taken aback by the news of my brother's disappearance. Since my father was also a lumberjack, he knew where Do and his partner set up the operation in the woods, and he decided to go there immediately. Do's partner and a helper were working, but Do had not showed up for work yet. My father now awakened to the realization that there was something fishy about the behavior of Do.

My family lived in sorrow with the absence of my brother. We didn't know what to do besides pray to God and Buddha for his safe return. Word passed around; neighbors became aware of my family's tragedy. They stopped by our house to share their sympathy and give words of encouragement. People in the village knew that in the past a person who mysteriously disappeared or was quietly kidnapped in the middle of the night by the League for Independence of Vietnam had no chance to survive. He either had been kidnapped or taken to a prison, or his decapitated corpse had been dumped along the edge of the woods. It was a very difficult time for us. We did realize the reality of the situation, but we couldn't just dwell on the negative. We couldn't cry all the time. We had contacted other government agencies besides the police for help and we also did our own investigation, but all to no avail.

The third night after Tan's disappearance was dark and cold. It was around nine, and we had just finished our supper and were sitting around a shallow bucket of heated charcoal, trying to get warm, still waiting hopefully for my brother's return. We heard from far away a sudden burst of *pop...pop...*pop. At first we thought it was firecrackers, but following it came all kinds of loud explosions, including the rattle of machine guns that continued for almost forty-five minutes. Then everything went silent. This was the first time in many years we had heard gunfire, so we had no idea what was going on. My dad, mom, and sister were all shaking violently because they were extremely frightened for us and for my brother's life. My father locked all the doors and secured them with strong bamboo rods. It meant another sleepless night for us.

CHAPTER
3

Game of Dice Rolling

Three nights before, Do and my brother quickly left home around four in the afternoon. They joined other people in the hamlet for a game of craps as soon as they arrived and stayed in the game until around five thirty, by which time they had made a good amount of money. Do gave all their winnings to my brother to entice him to play more games; Do wanted to win a bigger prize by going to another game with people who had more money playing at a different location.

"This game is small. We want to win big. Let's go to another location," Do insisted.

"I need to get home before ten to have dinner with my family," Tan said earnestly.

"Don't be worry, you will get home before then, but we want to win big."

They walked for about fifteen minutes then they started to descend a slippery mud trail toward a cottage located on the left side of the trail. The cottage was sitting at the bottom of a hill on a piece of land dug into the leg of the hill just big enough to fit the cottage of twenty meters by ten meters.

Do was very anxious; he walked behind my brother and kept pushing his back to urge him to walk faster. My brother was annoyed with the way he acted, so he turned his head and yelled, "What is wrong with you? Why do you keep pushing me? Do you know that the trail is narrow, treacherous and steep?"

"I don't want us to miss a game."

After struggling down the slippery muddy trail, they got close to the cottage. My brother didn't see anyone, and the house didn't look like a place setting up for a game of dice, so he turned around to ask where the other players were, but didn't get a chance.

Do had already disappeared, and my brother immediately felt an acute pain in the left side of his back. The barrel of a gun was pushing hard against it. He realized that he was being kidnapped at gunpoint. He was shocked and afraid. A cold, stern male voice ordered him walk into the house. As he walked into the dark cottage, he smelled mildew and dampness. The wavering dim light coming from the oil lamp on the wooden table at the center of the room didn't provide enough light for him to see much of anything, except some old white T-shirts at the a corner of the table.

"Face the wall, don't turn around, and put both hands against the wall now," the stern voice ordered.

"I didn't do anything," my brother implored.

"Shut up. You are to be punished if you open your mouth again," the assailant again ordered while pushing the barrel of the gun harder against his left side.

He kicked Tan's legs apart and far away from the wall. Another man searched Tan's body thoroughly and took away all of his money and personal identification papers. He also took Tan's jacket and ordered him to take off the pair of shoes. The gun barrel was constantly pushed hard against the left side of Tan's back while he was being searched.

They then yanked both of his arms backward and tied his upper arms tightly with electrical telephone wire. Tan was frightened and nervous, and now with the pain created by the wire he almost fainted. They then ripped the T-shirt on the table to blindfold and gag him.

The men then led him to a different room in the house and threw him on the dirt floor.

Tan felt like there was no blood going to either of his arms and hands. He felt a tingling in both of his hands as numbness gradually took over.

Sitting in the dark, Tan now tried to remember all the events that had led to his current predicament. He didn't have any clues as to why they had abducted him or who was behind this plot. While thinking about all of his loved ones at home, Tan heard a man screaming loudly and a sound as if the man was struck by a hard object, followed by an order from a leader.

"Shoot the bastard on the spot if he runs again."

Tan then heard a constant groan from the unknown person. It sounded as if he was in a lot of pain from the recent blow. Fear consumed Tan, and he wondered helplessly what these men were planning for him and the other captive. About fifteen minutes later, he heard a big thumping sound as if someone had thrown a sack of rice on the floor. He then heard the groan right next to him; he now knew that the person who had been beaten earlier was now in the same place where he was sitting. Being blindfolded and gagged, Tan was absolutely in a panic for not knowing what would happen to him next. He just couldn't believe that his good friend of many years had betrayed him. He understood that his life was now hanging by a thread.

He hated himself for trusting his friend blindly and for causing so much pain and grief for his parents, siblings, and fiancée at home. He started to wonder and he understood the peril of his life under the current situation. He left his fate in the hands of God and Buddha. Upon further reflection, he concluded his captors must belong to the one group responsible for all of the killing and kidnapping in the hamlet, none other than the Communist organization called the League for the Independence of Vietnam or Viet Minh. Its policy was rather to kill by mistake than to forgive by mistake.

Tan didn't know how long he had been sitting at the house, but he was finally yanked by the right arm and lifted up and tied together with the other prisoner. Together, they were led out of the house. He didn't know where they would take him, but in his mind he would try to count his steps from here to wherever they were going. Tan wasn't used to walking barefoot on rough terrain, so his feet started to bleed as he stepped on sharp objects like rocks, tree roots, wild ferns, and thorny bushes. He was led downhill in the woods for more than an hour. It was sloping, slippery with dead leaves, and wet. Since he couldn't see, he continually walked right into thorny bushes, and he was cut in many places. He fell down many times, dragging with him the other person, and the other person fell down even more times, dragging Tan down with him as well. Any time the guards pulled him up from the falling, he felt like someone was cutting into his flesh using a sharp knife because they had tied the telephone wire too tightly around his upper arms.

He heard the guards talking, so he was aware that there was more than one guard watching them.

Tan heard a rush of water, and it grew louder as they approached. Then the guards ordered them to stand still for a long time. Tan guessed that they were standing on the bank of a large stream or creek while the guards looked for a shallow area to cross. They then forced him and the other captive to jump into the stream. The water was up to his chin. It had rained heavily the last few days, so the current was quite strong. He didn't know how to swim, and his arms were tied behind his back, so he took on a good amount of water. They finally got to the other side of the stream with quite a bit of struggle. One guard pulled and the other guard pushed them out of the water. The pain he suffered at his upper arms was unbearable. Besides the pain from being cut by thorny bushes, Tan also felt like leeches were attacking him at many spots from the neck down, and he was afraid that they would get into his nose or ears.

They now had to fight another battle climbing uphill after crossing the creek; there was a thick layer of dead leaves and the sharp incline of this area made the effort of climbing the hill nearly futile. One guard pulled the prisoners in front, and another guard pushed them from behind. The dense trees and undergrowth made the journey thousands of times harder. It was difficult for the guards to climb, let alone for the prisoners who were blindfolded and tied together.

After many hours of intense struggle, they finally reached the destination. This time of the year, the temperature of this region was much colder than the rest of the country, but my brother was still perspiring profusely because he had expended great effort climbing the hill following the guards and because of the pain he had to endure.

Upon reaching the destination, the guards tied both prisoners to posts in an awkward position such that they couldn't stand or sit down but were always in the kneeling position.

After securely tying Tan and his fellow prisoner, the guards pulled the piece of T-shirt from Tan's mouth and gave him a ball of cooked rice the size of small fist plus some sea salt. He couldn't hold the rice, so the guards had to break it and feed it to him and the other prisoners. Listening to the conversation between the prisoners and the guards, my brother believed that there were three prisoners at this location all together, one to Tan's right and the other to his left. He didn't know how far apart they were from each other, but he was able to hear their voices clearly. According to their accents, he recognized that a Southerner was on his left and a Northerner was on his right.

They let the prisoners drink some water, and then they gagged them again. It was either late at night or early in the morning because my brother heard the chirping of crickets and other insects. He was exhausted, but he couldn't sleep because of the kneeling position he was in, the acute pain in his arms, and the itchiness created by the blood-sucking leeches and mosquitoes.

He couldn't see, but he could hear the chattering of monkeys, so he knew that the dawn had just arrived. He had now been in custody for almost twelve hours. Before leaving the cottage, he had planned to count his steps, but he was not able to do so because they had slipped down and climbed up so many times, making counting impossible.

Tan heard the birds' chirping, so he guessed another day had just arrived. One of the guards introduced their high-ranking leader to talk to the prisoners.

"This is comrade Hoai Nam [simply translated as Southern Nostalgia]. He wanted to talk to you guys," the guard said.

"I wanted to clearly announce that you are arrested by the League for the Independence of Vietnam for activities against the Vietnamese people," Hoai Nam said.

"This is a serious crime, punishable by execution. However, I am not in the position to make a decision. A committee will meet to decide on your fate within the next few days," he added.

My brother believed that he hadn't done anything to harm the Vietnamese people. All he did was work for the Printing Department of the National Geographical Directorate. He also mentally searched deeply to see what other reasons they could have to kidnap him. It could be the soccer team, but it had nothing to do with politics; they just wanted to have some fun. Besides, he had to make a living, but if the Communists accused him of having activities against the people, then he had no way to defend himself. He knew the consequence and he had no choice but to accept whatever decision they wanted to impose on him, though he knew in his heart that the accusations against him were wrong.

Suddenly, he remembered everyone in the family. He thought of the good times he had with me cooking the rice cakes, and of the time he helped me haul firewood home to cook rice and to heat up our house. He thought of a good, simple dinner with the whole family. Tan thought of the love that my mother had for him, of the assistance that he had offered my father to install the wood planks, and of the time he spent with his fiancée at her home. He remembered every little thing, and he cried quietly for the first time since he became an adult.

He asked himself why the Communists always chose the most sacred time to inflict pain on innocent people like him, but then he thought the Communists might see things differently.

My brother had been in custody for almost three days now. The constant kneeling position caused considerable pain. He could not sleep and had very little food to eat. The injury to his upper arms became infected, and the pain intensified. My brother's health condition was deteriorating quickly, and he didn't expect to see any of us again. Even though the guards didn't impose any additional torture on him, he thought what he had to suffer now was enough to kill him in a few days. All kinds of bugs competed to attack his exposed skin, and the worst was the mosquitoes. Many spots on his body were unbearably itchy. He knew those were the places where the leeches bit into his skin. He wished he could scratch, but his both arms were tied behind his back. It had been three days now, so they had probably dropped off after having filled their bellies with his blood, leaving behind patches of skin that were oozing and itchy.

When he heard the insects, he knew that it was getting dark and he would soon be fed. The guards ungagged him and fed him stale-cooked rice, salt, and water. The piece of cloth was then pushed back into his mouth again.

He thought it would be wonderful to have a piece of rice cake with carrot pickles and a cup of mouthwatering rice wine, but he knew that this might be his last wish. He felt bad for thinking about those small things in this critical situation, but no one could stop him from dreaming, and that might help him strive harder to live on.

He focused on how to make his injuries less painful by shifting a little bit to the right so that the pressure wouldn't be placed too much on the wire that cut into his flesh.

While focusing on shifting, he heard a burst of gunfire and then all kind of weapons, from machine guns to hand grenades, not too far away. He heard a big commotion among the guards; they didn't exchange fire with the attackers, instead scrambling to disperse. The skirmish lasted for about forty-five minutes, and then the whole area returned to the normal tranquility that he had experienced for the last three nights.

He felt cold, and his whole body was soaked with some kind of sticky liquid that smelled like blood. He wondered if he was injured. All he heard was the whirring insects, and he knew that the guards had already abandoned this post, so he used all his might to strain against the post. He endured excruciating pain in his upper arms as he straightened and bent his knees, using this sawing motion in an attempt to break the wire. He knew this was his only chance to get out of this horrible place.

He sweated profusely, his perspiration soaking his wounds and causing unbearable pain, but he realized that this was a life-and-death situation, so he kept working hard on breaking the wire that tied him to the post. He was exhausted, but after an hour of struggle, he fell forward flat on his face. Finally, he was disconnected from the post, though his arms were still tied. He believed that one of the bullets must have partially severed the telephone cord binding him to the post; otherwise, he would never have been able to pull himself free. Elated, he determined to get home. He kneeled back up and bent his head forward as low as he could and stretched his right hand as close to his mouth as he could to remove his gag and blindfold. When these things came off, he felt like a massive weight had been lifted from his body. He tried to stand up and walk over to other prisoners to see if they were all right, but his legs didn't cooperate, so he crawled over to tap on their shoulders. Neither one responded. It was too dark to see, but he felt the blood on their clothes and bodies. He assumed that they had been hit by bullets during the skirmish, and he thanked God that he was still alive. He knew that he had to move away from this place immediately, so he crawled out as far as he could to a thick bush to hide should the guards return. While he was there, he stretched his legs and made some leg movements to get the blood circulating normally again. It didn't take long for him to stand up and take few steps; he thought that he was able to recover relatively quickly probably due to fact that he played soccer, which might help build strong leg muscles.

He had to get home, ultimately, but had no idea how. He didn't even know which direction to go, and in the darkness he couldn't see a thing. Thick trees surrounded him, and there was no moonlight. He faced with an insurmountable challenge to find his way, but he couldn't just sit there and pray. He knew from his heart that God and Buddha would help him, but he had to take the first step. Needing to see the electrical lights to find his way out of the wilderness, but he knew his hamlet didn't have electricity, plus this time of the night people always turned their lights off. He decided to look for any electrical lights with a hope just to get out of this area. Deciding to climb to the highest point on this mountain, he knew from this vantage point he would probably be able to see the lights. He carefully walked uphill, and even though he was hungry and exhausted, he didn't stop until he saw the lights. They didn't seem too far away, maybe seven to eight kilometers as the bird flies. He was so happy that his heart was throbbing out of rhythm. Trying to recover his breath for a few minutes, he started to run in the direction of the lights.

He hurriedly descended the mountain and ran toward the light. The mountain was too steep and full of dead leaves that made it treacherous, and his arms were still tied behind his back. He lost his balance and fell and rolled down the hill until he hit a tree and lost consciousness. Upon regaining his consciousness, he found his face was covered in blood, his entire body was in pain, and it was still very dark.

He sat up, leaning against a tree trunk for a while, trying to regain his strength. Completely disoriented, he didn't know which direction to go. He decided it didn't matter; he had to get out of this place. It was difficult for him to stand up with his arms bound behind him, and his whole body was in pain as if he had been beaten with a rice-pounding pestle. Finally managing to take a few steps forward, he started to run. He then heard a small bird chirping above his head, so he kept following the bird wherever he heard the chirping until he was too tired. He sat down on a piece of rock to rest, and the bird still circled around above his head, still chirping.

After several hours of walking and running up and down the hills, he still hadn't crossed a creek he had crossed three days ago. That made him very nervous about the possibility that he was going in the wrong direction. In spite of this concern, his gut feeling didn't allow him to change course, and he continued to run for another hour following the mysterious chirping of the bird until he saw lights from a few houses. He quickly ran toward them, and as soon as he got close to the houses, dogs started to bark loudly. They were two-story brick houses surrounded by fence or block wall and they had electricity, so he knew they belonged to either French people or high-ranking Vietnamese officials. Therefore, he tried to stay as far away from them as he could.

When he got to the road, he was able to recognize exactly where he was. He had no doubt that he would be able to get home in about an hour on this paved asphalt road. While running home, he thought about the insidiousness, conniving, and vindictiveness of the Communists. They could set up an ambush around the house to abduct him again since it was still very dark. He was in dilemma because he didn't want people in the hamlet to know that he had escaped from the kidnappers and he also didn't want them to see him bound and in tattered clothes covered in blood.

In order to avoid being seen, he needed to get home while it was still dark. He decided to run home, and instead of taking the main road, he took the alleyway to get home through our backyard. When he got close to our backyard, our neighbor's dogs barked loudly. He didn't enter the house immediately but hid himself in the banana bushes next to our pigpen for at least fifteen minutes to listen for any strange noise or the sound of footsteps.

Our parents and sisters were very tired after several sleepless nights, but they still didn't go to bed; instead, they each sat at a corner of the house quietly looking into the dark distance. My mother was still sitting at the same place on the wooden board, chewing her petal and leaning her back against the wall. She also held a piece of cloth in her right hand she used to constantly wipe her eyes to absorb tears continuously coming out. She didn't utter a word. It was only three days, but my mom seemed grayer, her eyelids drooped, her cheeks and eyes were sunken in, and her face showed sign of extreme desperation. Even though I was only eight, I felt very sad to see the emaciated body of my mother after only three days of waiting for her son in sorrow.

When the dogs in the neighborhood barked in unison, my parents were gravely nervous because they didn't want to face with an unexpected visit from the Communist agents, but on the other hand they prayed that that would be my brother. To my family, the prospect of my brother's return was extremely remote. My parents and members of my family didn't have any idea that my brother was close by, but our beloved dog, Lulu, did.

Lulu suddenly stood up, sniffing around and making small whining and yelping noises. He then ran toward the back, scratching on the rear door. He started barking and yelping vigorously as if he greeted a family member coming home after a long time of absence.

My father saw his abnormal behavior and said, "Lulu, calm down." Then he heard a slight knock on the back door.

My father hesitated to open the door right away until he heard a whisper from the door. "Mom, it's me, Tan. Open the door."

Upon hearing this familiar voice, my dad was absolutely astounded. When my dad opened the door, my brother immediately slipped in. When she saw that Tan's body was covered in blood, my mom broke down crying, but Tan put his hand on her mouth and softly said, "Shh...shh...Mom...don't cry...don't cry...they may be around." Things were happening so quickly and everyone was so happy they didn't even know what to do.

Tan told my father, "Dad, get a pair of pliers to cut the telephone wire around my upper arms."

He then whispered into the ears of my mother and sisters "No sobbing...absolutely quiet...boil some water to clean my wounds." My dad then pulled my brother into his room and let him sit on a chair next to his bed while he searched for a pair of pliers; his room was also storage where he kept all his tools. My mom used a safety pin to pull the wick of the kerosene lamp to make it brighter so my dad could see the wire to cut.

My mom used a pair of scissors to cut my brother's shirt off, and then my dad used a pair of pliers first to cut the wire that held my brother's arms together. He moved from one wire to another, meticulously removing the rest of them.

"Dad...easy, Dad, it is very painful." The wire was wrapped around my brother's upper arms so tightly that it carved into his flesh and blood oozed out from the cut, and his lower arms and hands had turned dark blue.

"Your hands don't seem to have any blood," Mom said, weeping.

"I don't have any feeling in my hands, must be poor blood circulation," my brother said.

My sisters then soaked a piece of cotton in warm water to clean the wounds and rubbed them with some kind of alcohol. The expression on my brother's face indicated that he was in pain when his wound was tendered.

"The cuts are so deep, they may be infected. You should go to the hospital," my sister said worriedly.

"Let's clean the wounds. I have to get out of here quickly," my brother said. After cleaning the wounds with alcohol, my sisters applied some medication called teinture d'iode, and since we didn't have bandages, they didn't wrap anything around the wounds. They then used warm water for him to clean all the blood on his body and got him some clean clothes to wear. He then immediately moved away from my house through the back door to his fiancée's house, where he stayed until the morning.

He reported to the police in the city, and they kept him at the police station for three days for investigation while treating his wounds. They then sent him to Dalat General Hospital, and he remained in the hospital for three days under police guard. He moved to his friend's house in the city to stay and he enlisted in the army a few months later. He only came home during the day when the road was not too bad.

I had been taught to believe that the Communists fought on behalf of the people to free Vietnam from foreign occupation, but after this, I could never again see them as a force for good. How could they claim to work for the good of the people and then inflict so much suffering on Tan and my family? We were a part of the people of Vietnam, too, and I knew with certainty that Tan was no danger to the country. I now wondered about the other disappearances I had heard of that was carried out by the Viet Minh. How many of those people had been innocent, and not conspiring against the people like the Viet Minh claimed? I was only eight, but I realized now that the Communists wanted to control the people, not free them, and I would never again believe their lies or trust their promises. I would never be truly safe as long as the Communists held any power. It was a lesson that would serve me well and, in the years to come, would prompt my decision to flee the country or die trying.

CHAPTER

4

The Collapse of the
South Vietnamese Government

In 1975, I lived in Saigon with my wife, Huong, and our four children. I was working for the American International Underwriters, Inc. At the time, the city was besieged. All of the other provinces of South Vietnam were lost to the Communist troops except Saigon, its adjacent areas, and Tactical region 4. The Communist troops had already positioned tanks and heavy artillery pieces and missiles around Saigon, and they were ready to destroy the city if the Saigon regime didn't surrender.

On the night of April 29, 1975 they shelled Tan Son Nhat airbase and the ARVN General Staff headquarters. My house was located just a kilometer from the perimeter of the airbase and the ARVN headquarters. The Communist mortars and missiles were notorious for not accurately hitting the right targets; they always missed the targets by a few hundred meters. We clearly heard the sound of the incoming missiles cutting through the air, and when it hit the ground, the entire sky was filled with the extreme, bright blue light that turned night into day to the accompaniment of ear-piercing thunder. Our hearts leapt in our chests any time a missile hit the ground around us, and we all gathered on the first floor of our house to pray. Whenever a missile hit, we felt like the entire sky was collapsing.

The Communist troops launched the missiles all night, continuing until late in the morning. When the morning arrived, we ran carrying our children into the church that was about two hundred meters behind our house. My wife was so afraid that while running she almost dropped our youngest son, who was a few months old. Along the way, we saw the beheaded body of a priest at the gate of the Catholic seminary. His soutane was soaked with blood, and the gate was knocked off the ground. I was too frightened to look at it closely, but it seemed like a missile had hit the gate when he was trying to close it. We didn't know how long he had been there, but it could have been since last night when we first heard the loud explosions.

Now people of all religions poured into the church like water running into a valley in the monsoon season. People were sitting everywhere in the church, around the altar, in the aisle, and in the pews, and we were packed like fish in a can. We all prayed to God for our safety, and at this moment we all looked up to Jesus. If just one missile hit the church at this time, the death toll would be very high. The pastor had a tough time getting to the altar because people were sitting everywhere. He had to worm slowly through the crowd. When he got to the altar, he looked up and prayed to God to give full forgiveness to every single one of us in present at the church. I felt so much at peace with myself, and I felt like we were under the protection of God even though we still heard the ear-splitting roar of incoming missiles. We kept our ears to a battery-operated radio to hear the news about the fighting and the result of the negotiations between two sides. We knew that the Communists would definitely massacre the denizens should the leaders of the regime in Saigon refuse to surrender. We prayed to God that the president of the South Vietnamese government would soon offer surrender to the Communists to avoid a bloodbath.

To our relief, the Communist troops stopped launching missiles later during the day on April 30, 1975 after the surrender was announced on the national radio by our last president, General Duong Van Minh.

I was relieved to know that at this time there would be no more shelling but I was very fearful of the Communist troops because I hadn't seen or had contact with them before. I didn't even know what they looked like. I ventured out to the streets of my area in Phu Nhuan district, and the scene was unbearably painful and horrible to see. Many corpses of young soldiers were strewn everywhere on the streets. Their uniforms, combat shoes, guns, ammunition, and military backpacks were littered everywhere.

The war that had ravaged the country for the last twenty years had now finally ended. There were a lot of people happy about this, but many were sad as well.

I had to report for work at the American International Underwriters, Inc. the next day per instruction from the Saigon Military Management Committee, and while riding my bike to work, I saw a crowd at the corner of Hai Ba Trung and Hien Vuong Streets looking at something. Out of curiosity, I stopped to look, and I saw an awful image that still bothers me to this day. I saw a young man lying on his back on the sidewalk. Both of his eyeballs seemed to have been removed recently because blood still coming out of the sockets. His intestine and stomach were spilled on the cement sidewalk and covered with dirt and sand, and his wounds were swarming with all kinds of flies. Incredibly, he was alive. He said that he was an officer of the Army of the Republic of Vietnam; he was wounded in the battlefield and was brought to Cong Hoa Hospital for treatment about two weeks ago. When the Communist troops took over the hospital on April 30, 1975, they pushed all the wounded soldiers of the Saigon regime out on the street. I offered him a small amount of money, but he refused to accept it. He just wished to be taken to his home in the Mekong Delta region. I just couldn't imagine how cruel and inhuman the Communists were in the way they treated another human being, and now this picture vividly demonstrated to me the ruthlessness of the Communists who now had full control of the country.

The Communist propaganda radio system worked to its full capacity to tell people that the provisional government of the Republic of South Vietnam Liberation Front would do everything to keep people happy and free. They said they wouldn't touch a thread or needle of the people, and most of the South Vietnamese people didn't have any experience living with the Communists, so they were exhilarated by these promises and accepted the Communists eagerly and glad to know that the country would now be free of war.

There was nothing to do at work, but I had to report for work every day. After three months helping them liquidate all the accounts under my responsibility, they let me go. When I was with the company, I was in charge of the Group Health Insurance Department, and all of our customers were Vietnamese employees of the American Embassy and US military agencies. My job required me to travel extensively to the customers' workplaces, and I had a good relationship with my customers. I didn't know whether this was the reason, but I was constantly approached for questioning by a Communist individual who was assigned to take charge of this company. Honestly, I didn't know anything else besides the group health insurance business and I always provided consistent answers to this person while I was still with the company under the control of new management.

After completely consolidating their power, the Communists imposed very strict rules and took away all the basic freedom from people. The Communist leaders implemented a very insidious retaliation program toward the high-ranking public officials, police officers, and ARVN officers of the former regime. The Communists rounded them up and put them into the "Reeducation Camp," which was basically a hard labor prison. Many of them died from starvation, extremely hard living conditions, and inhumane treatment of the Communist cadres assigned to the camp. Wives and children of the former officials and ARVN officers living in the cities were forced to move to the new economic zone, their houses taken over by the Communist cadres or officials.

One of the most famous slogans of the Communists was that "people can turn rock into rice by their hard work," and they therefore forced all people dwelling in the cities to move to the new economic zone without any support from the government. Living in the jungle, without medication, sufficient food, or proper clothing, they contracted malaria, got sick, and often returned to Saigon and other cities en masse, trying to survive. They had already lost their houses, so people had to live on the streets, doing anything to survive. They couldn't get a job working for the government, and their children couldn't go to school because they didn't have the required family census book or proper identification, and they were also discriminated against because they had connection with the former regime.

My family faced the same predicament as other ordinary people living in the city; our family was visited daily at all hours by unwelcomed visitors who were members of non-governmental organizations affiliated with the Communist regime, such as the Vietnam Women's Union, Vietnam Youth Union, and Fatherland Front. They spent hours at our house indoctrinating us about the political and agricultural policies of the revolutionary government and encouraging us to move to the New Economic Zone. They also mentioned that we would eventually lose our monthly food ration should we continue to stay in Saigon, and they also wanted to borrow our house for a unit of the people's army to stay temporarily.

The visits became more frequent with each passing day, the harassment became more intense, and with the prospect of losing our monthly ration, we finally decided to leave Saigon.

We knew how hard it was to live in the New Economic Zone, so we decided instead to go back to my wife's hometown in the Central Highlands where her father had a tea plantation.

My father-in-law and his family had moved to the South from North Vietnam in 1954 without a penny after the country was divided into two parts at the seventeenth parallel. With hard work, the support of Ngo Dinh Diem's government, and the guidance of his parish's Catholic priests, he was able to acquire a vast amount of land to grow tea and to set up a green tea refinery factory for domestic and foreign consumption.

After conquering South Vietnam, the local Communist leaders amicably recommended my father-in-law. They told him that "the country is now united and we are all needed to work hard to rebuild the country. You are a national bourgeoisie who produces goods for the society. The government would not take away anything from you and you should be praised for your hard work and dedication." My father-in-law had a big warehouse full of fertilizer for his own use and also for retail sale to smaller tea farmers. Believing the Communist propaganda, he hired workers to spread all the fertilizer on his tea fields, prune the trees, water them, and he focused on doing his best to increase the production.

Though we had to endure some hardship at my father-in-law's plantation, the first two years were not too bad. I had to drive a truck to take workers to the field to pick up tea leaves and to bring tea leaves to the cooperative factory for processing, where they paid for the product.

The Communist cadres from the district smelled money. They came to visit my in-law quite often and they said that the policy of the government was to turn all private land into agricultural cooperative and that he would lose all the property. However, they said they knew a very high-ranking Communist official who could help to delay for a few years the transfer of his land, and if my in-laws wanted they would deliver a bribe to this person. He lost so much money to this scam. I asked him to be careful with his money because if this was the agricultural policy of the Communist regime then no cadres, regardless of rank, could change it.

At the end of the second year, they invited my father-in-law and other people owning land or tea plantations to a meeting to talk about the land policy. They brought them to a luxury hotel and treated them very well during their three weeks' stay.

While they were at this meeting, the Communist cadres got all of the villagers together and forced them to revolt against my father-in-law and all the landowners. One of the Communist leaders from the district asked villagers, "Do you know why the landowners and plantation owners are so rich?" There was no answer. He continued, "They have been sucking your blood for so long, when without you they couldn't manage a hundred hectares of tea.

"The Revolutionary Forces must take their land and give it back to you. You are the legitimate owner of the land, and you deserve it.

You didn't have land or you had a small piece of land before the revolution, and now, you know what? All the land belongs to you. You are the owner of thousands of hectares of land. Yes, I am saying you. Therefore, you must work harder to increase the production to make the country richer and the people stronger."

"Do you agree?" he asked.

There was an infiltrator among the people. He raised his fist in the air and said, "I agree!" The villagers followed him to raise their hands and agree. The Communist leader then asked, "Whoever doesn't agree, raise your hand." Then his eyes started to sweep across the room to see if any hand was raised. The room had more than a hundred people, but no one said a word, and it was as quiet as a desert plain. Living with the Communists just for a short period of time but with the experience they had before moving to the South, people quickly learned that in order to live in peace without being harassed by the police of this totalitarian regime, people had to "close their eyes, shut their mouth, and cover their ears."

Most of the people in the village were Catholic immigrants from the North in 1954. The Communist party leaders wanted a tight grip on this village, so they moved all the Communist cadres from the North into the management positions such as village party chief, police chief, chairman of the tea cooperative, chairman of goods distribution store, and all the positions they deemed important for their control.

The villagers were divided into teams of ten to fifteen families, and each team was called a production unit and was led by a team leader chosen among the people of the team. Land was then divided into many small pieces, and each production unit took care of one piece of land. Members of the team had to turn in all of their production tools and all of the equipment in their possession to the cooperative, which had full disposal of these tools and equipment. We were now members of the tea cooperative.

People were very careful when they talked, especially about things that they didn't like about this regime, because the Communist leaders had planted informants among the people. At home, we were also cautious talking about things we didn't like about this government in the presence of our children because they would tell their teachers. The Communist leaders had fired all the remaining former regime teachers and replaced them with North Vietnamese teachers, many of whom were members of the Communist party.

As soon as they had consolidated their power, the Communist Party immediately implemented a very thorough police system that aimed at watching over the domestic movements of the population. Every ten houses were controlled by one area police officer, and the head of each household had to report to this police officer when there was a visitor coming to the house and again when this person departed. Police had the right to enter the houses of the villagers anytime they felt the need to do so.

We had an experience of this uncivilized behavior of the police when we were eating supper. The area police officer, without knocking on our door, walked in and pulled a chair up to our supper table then said, "It is kind of late to eat supper."

"We got home late from the field today," I said.

My in-laws had given us some pork bone soup the day before, so we had a bowl of chayote soup with meat bone on our table. He walked in so suddenly that my wife didn't have time to hide it.

"Well, your family still has meat to eat. That's a luxury," he said mockingly.

"We haven't eaten meat for months, and that was actually not meat, it was bones," I said defensively.

"I understand, but we all need to work hard and save in order to rebuild the country," he said. "I just stopped by to visit and to see how your family is doing," he added before leaving.

"Thank you," I said, wishing I could kick him out of my house quickly.

A month later, I caught a cold. I didn't feel good, so I took a day off from work. While I was at home reading a book in English about the foundation of group health and life insurance, this police officer again came into my house without even knocking on the door. He then asked me, "What are you reading?"

"A book about life insurance," I said.

"Let me see, what language is this?"

"English."

"Who gave you permission to read a book in a foreign language?"

"It's just an insurance book."

"I am telling you, don't try to fool me! I know what this book is all about. You are trying to communicate with the defeated imperialist America, but that is in vain. Don't dream—that will never happen. Do you understand?" he said with a sneer. "First of all you are lazy—you don't go to work—and secondly you try to talk to the enemy." He stopped for a second to think then said, "I forgive you this time, but if you get caught doing this again the price you will pay will be very stiff. I am taking this book away."

I was furious that this police officer had entered my home uninvited and confiscated my property. I knew that by controlling my reading material and the languages I used, he wanted to limit my very thoughts. However, my outrage was outweighed by my fear of being arrested. After this incident, I was totally disappointed in this regime, and I had doubts about the future development of this country when the government was using narrow-minded people like this police officer.

When my simple, basic freedom was taken away, my freedom to read what I wanted, eat what I wanted, to have privacy in my own home, I felt as if I were being suffocated, as if I didn't have air to breathe anymore. I hadn't experienced anything like this under the former regime, though we didn't have as advanced a system of democracy as Western countries. I had learned about the different political systems in the world when I was studying law in college and theoretically understood what Communism was all about. Fortunately, I hadn't had a practical understanding because I hadn't lived under the totalitarian regime until today. I now was experiencing life behind the iron curtain. I had taken freedom for granted under the former regime. I didn't see how precious it was until I lost it.

We were forced to be members of the cooperative. We had to work in the field all day to turn the tea leaves over to the cooperative for ten kilograms of rotten rice, and sometimes some sliced dried cassava per person each month and two pairs of clothes a year. Cassava plants are hardy shrubs that yield starchy roots as well as edible leaves. I used to work in the office and was not good at doing the field work. I couldn't produce at the level other team members did, and therefore I couldn't get enough foodstuffs for my family. As a father, it was very painful for me to see my children eating cassava, corn, and sweet potatoes every day without a piece of meat or fish. The young cassava leaves now became a delicacy for our family. They were soft and tender after being boiled to a certain degree, and they were easy to swallow when dipped in a little bit of fish sauce or salt-water. My children loved them and suggested mixing fish sauce with a little bit of sugar, garlic, and lemon. I knew that was not too much to ask for, but the problem was that we couldn't find any sugar to make them happy since sugar was a luxury item. I didn't know how well-nourished they were, but it seemed that the more they ate, the thinner they got. Their weight loss became too much to ignore, so I told my wife about my observation. We agreed to sell many of the things in our possession, such as a small black-and-white TV that we'd had for a number of years, a small National refrigerator, and all the furniture to get money to buy food for our children. The people who had money now were the ones who came from the North or the high-ranking officials because they had power and they also knew how to circumvent the system to make money. These people paid high prices for the items we had to offer.

My wife felt bad that we were selling the things that had been with our family for so long, but we also agreed that our children were much more important to us than anything else.

A few days later, at about one in the morning, we were awakened by a male voice amplified by a megaphone. An official was making an announcement in the street.

"The curfew is being enforced. Nobody is to go out into the street. Violators will be shot on the spot." This terrified us because we thought they were going to arrest someone, but usually when they wanted to arrest someone they just did it at night quietly without letting anyone know. We didn't know what was going on and were too worried to go back to sleep. When the morning came, we checked with our neighbors to see if they knew anything, but they were also in the dark. At eight o'clock, they announced that the Provisional

Government of Revolutionary South Vietnam had decided to change the national currency, and each family was allowed to change one hundred thousand dong (piaster). That amount was equal to one half of the price of my TV, which was sold a few days ago. Nearly all of the money we had accumulated after selling our belongings had now evaporated into smoke. They didn't need to steal people's money directly; they had a much better way to make my people much poorer overnight. We had lost all our money in 1975 when the former regime collapsed because we couldn't take our savings out from the Vietnam Savings Bank, and now we lost our money again to this dictatorial regime.

The economy of the country was faltering, and there was now a serious shortage of food throughout the nation, especially in the cities. People now had reasons to illegally carry goods from the rural areas to the cities to make a little extra money. Checkpoints were therefore set up on all the major highways and main roads to stop the illegal transportation of so-called contraband. The people who illegally carried goods for resale were often wives or children of the former regime officials or military officers wanting to make a few bucks to feed their children and to support their imprisoned husbands. The personnel working at these checkpoints were young farmers or teenagers who had dropped out of high school. They did exactly what their Communist checkpoint leaders told them to do and they confiscated everything they found. It was despicable to see many old and young women crying, begging at the checkpoint for leniency from the police officers or market protection agents.

These checkpoints were also used to check the identification of the passengers on the buses and their permits for travel. It was not easy to get travel permission because we had to submit an application with a compelling reason for travel to the area police officer for approval. The application would then go to zone chief for approval, after which it would go to the village police chief for approval, then to the district police chief for approval before one could travel. It took a few days before we could get permission and then it was very difficult to get a bus ticket, since most tickets were sold to government employees. We had to get tickets through the black market if we needed to go somewhere badly, and it was much costlier this way.

In many cases, we couldn't go anywhere because our permits had already expired before we could get a ticket. It was impossible to know what was in their minds, but it appeared that the Communist leaders didn't want people to have freedom to move around, so they put all kinds of restrictions to discourage the people from traveling.

Under the former regime, I was able to support my family with my salary and we had a comfortable life, but now my wife needed to learn a skill to make some money to help me. We looked into hair cutting, hair permanent waving, and makeup for women because we thought that all women wanted to be beautiful regardless of which political regime they lived in. My wife was just twenty-four years old and had a high school education and a willingness to learn a skill, so we took a risk and invested a big portion of our savings for this purpose. Our village was a rural area, so my wife needed to go to Saigon to find an instructor from whom she could learn the skill. That was our plan, and now we needed permission from village leadership, especially the village police chief, who was also a Party member and came from the north of Vietnam. My wife went to his village office for his signature, and while she was there, he asked her to kiss him. My wife tried to avoid it nicely by saying, "Too many people are here. I can't do it."

"Let's get into my office and close the door."

My wife said, "That is not in Vietnamese culture for a married woman." He kept on insisting that my wife kiss him before he signed, but my wife told him that she would leave the application with him and pick it up later. He then signed. He was about fifty years old and he always wanted to flirt with wives of the imprisoned ARVN officers. These women also needed permission to visit their husbands in the "education camp" twice a year, and he used the same trick with them as he used with my wife.

We knew that this man was essentially God in this village and we didn't want to upset him. Because he signed the travel permission for my wife to go to Saigon for training, we invited him to our house for supper. We killed one of the two ducks we were raising to make soup and duck salad for him to eat with rice wine, but I wanted to limit the amount of wine for him because I didn't want him to get out of control. While sitting at the table, he winked at my wife and used his foot to flirt with her. Despite her contempt, my wife kept her cool in dealing with him and only told me about this afterward. His unethical behavior made my blood boil, but I had to control my anger to avoid a confrontation, which I knew would have severe consequences.

A few months later, in order to suppress any rebelliousness from taking seed, the local Communist party leaders announced that there was a rebellious reactionary group opposing the management style of the party leadership, and that therefore the party and people were hunting them down and arresting them. My name was somehow on the list of people who were sympathizers of this group. So one Saturday morning, the chief of information service department from the district came to my house.

He knocked on my front door. When I opened the door, he walked right in, sat in a chair in my living room, and demanded something to drink. I was flabbergasted since I didn't know who he was and yet he behaved as if he were my close friend. Looking at my face, he probably knew that I was astonished, so he said, "Buddy, it could be that you haven't met me, but your father knew me very well. I am the chief of the information services department in the district."

"Yes…can I get you some tea?" I politely asked.

"Buddy, that is fine, but I want to tell you something very important," he said.

"Please tell me," I said.

"I want to help get you out of a serious problem. In our last meeting, my colleagues at the district mentioned your name as a member of the rebellious group opposing the government, and they are going to arrest you," he said.

"Well, I have no idea what you are talking about," I said, gravely fearful for my safety.

"Let me tell you in very simple terms so you can understand. You are a reactionary and rebellious agent, and the government is going to arrest you and put you in jail. However, I can get you out of this trouble if you give me one million piaster," he bluntly insisted.

I gritted my teeth at the thought of this man blatantly trying to make money off of me despite my innocence. The amount he asked for was several months' worth of my hard-earned money.

"Well, I don't have that kind of money, and I need money to feed my children. I just can't help it if they want to arrest me, and I know that I am innocent," I said.

"Go to your father-in-law, he is a landlord and I am sure he has money," he countered.

"There is no justification for borrowing money from him, and I don't think he would loan it to me for this silly reason," I said.

They didn't arrest me because they had no proof or evidence of anything and they couldn't substantiate any relationship with this group or this guy just merely tried to extort money from me.

They did, however, pass words around that they would eventually isolate me from the population because I was an educated person and the son-in-law of the landlord. They said that I was not allowed to and did not deserve to mingle with the local people.

The economic policy of the Communists in Vietnam was to eliminate the ownership of private property, and it accordingly required all of the villagers to bring the products they produced to the Tea Cooperative. As long as they met their quota, they took home the same ration as everyone else, which was barely enough to live on. People had no incentive to work hard, and since they could only resist passively by not putting all of their effort into taking care of the tea plants, they took the fertilizer home for their own use and didn't spray the insecticide when needed. After a year or two, the tea production drastically declined.

In the same manner, under the former regime Vietnam was the second-largest rice producer in the world after Thailand, but now people had no rice to eat and the country's economy was in very bad shape. The Communist Party prohibited private business, and everything had to be done through the government cooperative. The cooperative, however, was a failed enterprise and had nothing in the store to sell to people; there was nothing on the shelves: no sugar, no rice, no bread, and no meat, nothing except a few pieces of dried fish hanging in front of the store for flies to visit. People in the village had to use the barter system to survive.

I didn't know whether it was their policy or not, but the local cadres came to my house taking inventory of all the livestock we had, which included five chickens with one egg-laying hen, two ducks, and one pig. Our pig ate whatever we ate, except for rare occasions when we had a piece of meat or a few pieces of dried fish. However, it still grew to almost twenty kilos after one year. We didn't want them to force us to sell the pig to the cooperative at a lower price, so we decided to circumvent the system by slaughtering the pig to get meat. The problem was that I had never, ever killed an animal, let alone slaughter one. Also, I was fearful of blood. My wife had to ask for help from a friend, who suggested using an electrical current to kill it at night so no one would know. We reported to the area police officer that our pig died because of sickness and gave him some of the meat so he would turn a blind eye.

The Communist party leaders firmly believed that the command economy system was much better than a market economy. They had implemented this policy in North Vietnam throughout the entire time they were in control of this region, and it had failed to provide enough foodstuffs for their people. Now, regardless of this obvious failure, they still wanted to implement the same system in the South, and unfortunately, the South Vietnamese people now suffered the same fate as their brethren in the North.

The party leaders determined to lead the country to a Communist state, so they forced everyone to work hard under the control of the cooperative to move quickly, forcefully, and surely to this "heaven on earth" as propagandized by the Communists: "From each, according to his ability; to each, according to his need." I didn't know when we would get to that utopian state, but at this moment they used all kinds of tricks to take away everything we had.

When communicating with people, all cadres of this regime repeated the same slogan, which was sometimes placed in a conspicuous location in government buildings for people to see: "The people are the owner of the country; the government is a manager." They were very deceptive with this slogan, aiming at fooling the peasants and workers. However, the people of Vietnam were not stupid. They knew well that the Communists were nothing more than crooks, but no one dared to say anything because they were fearful of being retaliated against or imprisoned.

Living in this society, I just couldn't swim against the current, and though I didn't want to associate with the Communists, we also had certain needs for survival. I needed extra money and firewood to cook with for my family, so I was willing to do lumberjack work over the weekends in addition to my regular work at the tea field. A friend told me that a high-ranking official of the district wanted to cut a deal with us: he would give us permission to cut trees down for firewood, provided that we divided it equally with him, so he got half and we got half. In addition, we had to haul his portion of wood to his house. He said that he would stand up for us in case we were stopped by police officers or forest rangers.

I didn't think this was a fair deal because we had to spend money to buy chainsaws and gas and rent a truck to carry the wood, in addition to providing the labor to cut down the trees and haul the wood to his house. For all this work, we only got half of the wood, while he would get another half of the wood for just signing the paper. However, we realized that without his permission we wouldn't be allowed to cut wood at all. In spite of their everyday slogan, proclaiming the people owned everything, this manager had a lot of power and privileges while the owner had none because of a simple reason: the officials were not voted into office by the people. Therefore, the officials had no accountability to the people; no matter how much they abused their power, the people could not vote them out of office.

Honestly, I took a risk in getting involved with this project because I had never done this type of work, but I badly needed firewood for my family and some extra money.

We hired an experienced logger whose job was to select a tree and cut it down with a chain saw. My job was to trim all the branches and clear a path with a machete for the logs to be rolled downhill. We had to get all the logs to a flat spot where a truck could get to for loading.

We lost money on this deal, but something good came out of it that changed my life and my family forever. At the end of the working day, we were dirty and tired, and we needed some water to wash off before going home. We were not aware of the creek nearby when we came to work, but when we were walking down the hill to go home, we saw a wide creek with a sandy bed. The water came down from the top of the mountain and was clear and fresh. It was not too deep, and we were soon blissfully enjoying ourselves in this wonderful, cool stream. While bathing, I saw a single yellow leaf floating along the current and I said to my coworker, "This leaf will eventually go to the sea."

"It will probably be rotten before it gets there, but, then, so what?" he said.

"I wish I was this leaf, so…" I stopped there for a second to let my imagination run wild.

"Are you nuts, buddy?" he jokingly said. I kept silent to brood over a thought that had just flared in my mind.

"Oh! I know what you meant now, you want to go overseas, right?" he added with a smile.

"You just said it," I answered, a little sad, for I knew from my heart how wistful that wish was.

"Well, my brother lives on an island called Phu Quoc, and he has a boat for carrying fish sauce to the mainland of Kien Giang province every week," he said.

"Let's keep this idea in mind, but I don't think it's practical," I said sadly. I knew the harsh punishment for trying to leave the country. With the chances of success so slight and the price for failure so high, it seemed insane to even contemplate trying to flee.

However, insane or not, this idea captivated me and percolated in me for the ten-kilometer walk home. I didn't say a word to anyone.

Even though we faced much hardship in our daily lives, I tried to convince myself that the country was now independent, that we all needed to chip in our small part to build the country. But more and more, I saw the injustice, the oppression of freedom, the corruption, the mismanagement of the economy, the deceptiveness of the officials, the vengefulness of the Communists against the people with connections to the former regime, against the religious leaders and, most importantly, I didn't see any future for my children in this society. Those were the things that constantly pushed me to the decision to find way to get out of this country. Did I love Vietnam, and did I want to stay to live with my brothers and sisters and to take care of my parents' graves? Yes, I did love this country with all my heart and I did want to stay, but not under the current circumstances. I had to get out. My family had to get out of this country at any price.

We were under constant stress due to a chronic lack of foodstuffs and medicine for our children, as well as constant threats from local officials that I would be arrested. Given the situation, my wife occasionally complained that I hadn't focused on taking the family out of the country during or before the collapse of the Saigon regime. While working for AIU, Inc. as a manager, I had had an opportunity to leave the country with my company two weeks before the May 30, 1975 event. I should have left with the other personnel of the company, but I loved this country. I didn't think America would drop an ally who had been working with them for so long, and I wanted my children to grow up in the country where they were born. Then I was so naïve, and I didn't know much about Communism. I had a very shallow vision, and therefore my wife and my children had to pay a heavy price for my stupidity. As a father, I felt strongly that I was responsible for supporting and bringing happiness to my family. My children did not choose to be born and be with me in the world. Since for some heavenly, mysterious reasons my children were with me, I had to make sure they each had a decent life as a human being.

I thought about this matter for a long time and wanted to talk to my wife about it, but the words kept sticking in my throat. One day after the Sunday church service, I asked my wife to stay back for few minutes so I could talk to her about one of the most important issues relating to our family.

"What is the matter? Can we talk when we get home?" she said.

"Yes, but our children are around and it is not safe to talk about this issue at home because our house is not soundproof. People can hear us from a kilometer away when we talk inside the house," I said. I then continued in a soft voice, "I know that you are not happy with our current living conditions, and I know that I am part of the problem. You have complained a few times about the consequences of my negligence in not taking the family out of the country when we had a chance, and I am very sorry for this. However, I want to put a stop to this, and we need to talk about a possible solution that both of us can accept. Whatever the outcome, we will live through it without any more complaint."

"Can you spell it out clearer?" Huong asked eagerly.

"We believe in God and that everything that happened in our lives must have a reason, but having said that, I still regret my unwise decision to stay back in Vietnam. I honestly tell you that I just can't live here under the current regime. We should try to find a way to get out of this country. How we would do it, I don't know yet, but we must try. If we have to die together, we should accept it, and if we can't make it we should also accept whatever fate God gives us. And please, no more complaining or else I'll go batty," I added with a smile.

I didn't stop there. "Please pray to Jesus Christ and the Virgin Mary to let us know whether we should go or stay. We need to have an agreement that we will accept the outcome, which we believe God will give to us," I said with earnestness.

We prayed for fifteen minutes in the church after mass then we walked out in front of the Virgin Mary's cave. Then I pulled out a small piece of paper from my shirt pocket, folded it symmetrically, and ripped it in two halves. I wrote yes on one and no on the other and then rolled them up into small balls and put them into my right palm, shook them up, and presented them to Huong. I prayed to the Virgin Mary for a few minutes then I asked my wife to pick one.

"You do it, I am too nervous," she said, a little puzzled.

"You saw it, there was no trick. This is a privilege! Please pick one, and we will act according to the outcome of today's vote," I said with a smile.

She moved her hand over the paper balls and used her thumb and index finger to pick one up, but upon touching it, she pulled her hand back and looked at me.

"Go ahead, it won't bite you," I said, and she closed her eyes and picked one up with her right hand.

"You open it. I am still too apprehensive," she said, turning the tiny paper ball over to me.

"Well, if you insist," I said then slowly opened it up. I showed it to her. It was a "Yes."

Tears began rolling down her cheeks. "But how?" she asked with an inquisitive expression on her face.

"As I said, I don't yet know, but we will work together to figure it out," I said confidently.

We thanked God for giving us the direction to follow in this very perplexing situation. What we did was almost like a test of God's love, but there was no one else we could turn to for help, except Him.

I was planning on the way home from church to talk to my wife about the exchange with my friend at the creek, but she was too emotional from earlier so I decided to refrain from telling her.

My wife had a plan to go to Saigon to learn how to cut hair, but in the meantime we both had to work in the tea field to get points for our family ration at the end of the month. We used an empty can of Guigoz powdered milk as a lunch box because they never rusted and could be used for many other purposes as well. Before preparing our lunch, she asked me, "Do you want both sliced cassava and sweet potatoes?"

"Just put sweet potatoes underneath and cassava on top," I said, putting on my military boots, which I had picked up on the streets of Saigon after April 30, 1975 and saved.

"I put three pieces of dried fish on top. I just grilled them on charcoal this morning, and they are good," she added.

Lowering her voice, she said, "I will put a small piece of meat at the bottom so be watchful when you eat."

"What about you?"

"One piece of fish is enough for me," she said.

"Honey, at lunch break, meet me at the same place we used to have lunch," I said.

Since we left the house early, my wife left a note on the kitchen telling our kids where their lunch portions were and then we took off.

We went to work on the same bike, and at lunchtime we got together, sitting down underneath the jackfruit tree. It was really cool out, and I felt fantastic. The weather in this region of Vietnam was the best. It was always seventy to seventy-five degrees Fahrenheit all year round. It did, however, have quite a bit of rain in the summer.

I stretched the piece of plastic I used as a raincoat on the ground in the shade of a tree, and we sat against the tree trunk. I pulled out the Guigoz lunch box from my bag and dug deep to the bottom of the can to get the piece of meat to share with my wife. She refused to eat and said, "You worked hard cutting those old tea tree branches all day. They are very big, probably the size of your wrist or bigger. Right? You need to eat. I only pick up tea leaves. Don't worry about me."

Oh how generous my wife is! She has sacrificed for me and my children all her life! I suddenly realized that tears coming out of my eyes.

"Just take a small bite to make me happy, please," I said.

Then I quickly put a piece of cassava and a piece of dried fish in my mouth and started to chew. It was tasty and satisfying, but mostly because I was so hungry. After swallowing the food, I asked her to look around to see if anybody was near. After making sure there was no one around, I told her about the story of the single floating leaf when I was at the creek.

"I think the sea route appears to be safer. It is very risky to take the land route because you have to go through Cambodia before you get to Thailand, and I heard many people get raped and killed by the Khmer Rouge," she said.

"No, no absolutely not. We will never take the land route," I agreed.

"It wouldn't hurt to do some investigation to find out. Do you agree?" she asked.

"It will cost money and I am not sure we have enough money to support this ambitious endeavor. I think we need to sell our house. We can get two or three taels of gold for the house," I suggested.

"Where are we going to stay?" she asked.

"You and the kids can live temporarily at your parents' house while I am looking into the possibility," I said.

"The Communists already confiscated their tea factory and kicked them out of the house. They only have a little corner of the house to live in," she said sadly. "Well, let me tell you something that I haven't talked about before, though it's not such a big thing. As you already know, my parents always taught me about saving for the rainy days. Yes, that is what I did for all those years we were together. When you were working, your salary was deposited to the bank so we could draw interest, though unfortunately we lost it all. We had some money reserved for our food. You also put aside some money for me and the kids to have breakfast. I didn't use all the money, so any time I had a surplus amount, I bought a small piece of gold in the form of a ring, a bracelet, or an earring, and I saved them for the rainy days. If we add them together, we have now about three taels' worth of gold. You know I don't want to spend lavishly with this jewelry because I thought we would need them someday, but I think this is the most critical time to use them," she ruefully said.

I couldn't hold back my tears. I said, "You are wonderful and you are our family's savior."

"That is enough of that. I will talk to that jerk, the village chief of police, to get you permission for travel, and I will put together the money for the trip. You need to contact your friend to let him know of our decision," she said.

"I have a concern. That guy will try to confront you again," I said.

"That's nothing. That beast won't have a chance," she said.

CHAPTER
5

My First Journey

I met with the younger brother of the friend I had discussed leaving with me to the city of Rach Gia, where we rented a small room in a motel. After staying there one night, I accompanied him to the harbor, where he would take a boat to the island. I was very nervous to see his papers checked by the police when he stepped on the boat because they weren't authentic. I was unsettled until the boat took off.

The harbor police had very strict rules to control civilians who came from the mainland to all of the islands because they suspected that people would use the islands as a point of departure for escaping the country.

My companion for the journey used counterfeit travel papers to go to the island so he could talk to one of his brothers, who presumably lived on the island and had a boat. I waited impatiently at the motel for a few days for his return. While I was in town alone, I contacted some of my wife's relatives who lived in the suburbs or nearby rural areas. They said that people throughout the country couldn't stand the harsh treatment and the economic collapse of the new regime, that hundreds of thousands of people risked their lives to find way to get out of the country.

Since this area was on the coast and had many waterways leading to the sea, it seemed like more people came here to find ways to flee the country. They said it was impossible for people coming here from Saigon or other provinces to know whether the organizer of the trip was genuine or bogus. Many people lost everything down to their shirt putting their trust in someone who had no experience organizing the trip or to swindlers, and more often than not they ended up in a hard labor camp for a couple of years for the crime of illegally leaving the country. The more I learned, the more I was in distress. I was so depressed that I went back to the motel and stayed there without eating anything for two days.

Finally, I was introduced to my friend's oldest brother. He seemed to be a very nice man; he looked more like a fisherman than a businessman, had dark skin, and was a man of few words but was very polite. I wanted to find out more about him than what his brother had told me, so I invited him to a place to eat where we could exchange some information. I learned during this meeting that he had actually been living on the island for more than five years. The boat he operated was not his but belonged to a businessman living on the island, and was used to carry fish sauce from the island to Rach Gia twice a month. He also wanted to leave the country but didn't have the means to get out unless he stole the boat from the owner. Right off the bat, I didn't like that idea. I didn't want to discuss more than what I needed to know on this deal. I told them that I would like very much to work with them but I was sorry that things didn't work out. After finishing the meal, they left and I went back to the motel for one more day, resting and thinking about what to do next while I was here. The money my wife had given me for the trip after she sold her ring was almost depleted, and I hadn't been able to do anything worthwhile.

I was under a lot of pressure thinking about the futility of this trip, thinking about my wife working hard and saving every penny for this trip. Had I not wasted money for this trip, my children would have had many better meals.

Walking out of my motel, I headed directly toward the harbor to escape my deep emotional distress. I stopped by a small vendor's stand on the sidewalk to buy a cheap pack of cigarettes and a box of matches, though I hadn't touched a cigarette since high school, when a friend gave me one. I opened the pack, lit a cigarette, had a long puff and inhaled all the smoke into my lungs. The cigarette smoke made me cough incessantly. I stopped walking, put my hand on my chest, and continued to cough for almost two minutes. My nose was running and my eyes were watery.

I chose a bench at the harbor to sit where I could have a clear view of the ocean. It was beautiful. It made me think of a day when we could walk onto a boat heading toward the open sea. Would it be possible? Given the tight control of the police and our humble financial resources, the chances that we would be able to leave the country by boat were very remote.

Watching the boats going in and out piqued my curiosity as to how the police controlled the passage of the boats from the river to the port. In actuality, they only checked the identification and other related documents of passengers or civilians on the passenger boats as they passed through the checkpoint. They didn't physically go into a boat unless they suspected it of carrying contraband or illegal persons.

I smoked more than fifteen cigarettes in less than an hour, one after another. My lips were burned and my mouth had a strong smell of nicotine, and I didn't feel hungry though I hadn't eaten much. I felt as if I were a balloon filled with hydrogen, until I fell asleep on the bench.

Waking up, I found that it was almost four and I realized that I was here on a mission to find out more information on a "single floating leaf." I was disappointed because the bare truth had been revealed, and it was a failure. I was very distraught.

I couldn't escape the reality any longer and I had to return home tomorrow to tell my wife the truth—the failure of my trip because of my vulnerability to trust others so quickly. I wanted to stop by the house of my wife's relatives to say good-bye. They asked me to stay for dinner. I felt bitterness in my mouth, maybe from too much smoke. I didn't feel hungry and I wasn't in the mood to eat or drink. I just wanted to go back to the motel to pack up my clothes for my departure the next day.

While we were sitting at the table in the living room drinking tea, my wife's cousin asked me why I didn't stay at their home but instead was staying in the motel. I told him that I had come with another man for the purpose of finding out whether or not a relative of this person had a boat.

"You wanted to sell tea to people living on the island?" he asked sincerely.

"Well, no, that wasn't the purpose. I wanted to find out if he had a boat and if he wanted to get out of the country so we could tag along," I said.

"You think it is that easy? How much did he ask you for?" he asked uneasily.

"Actually, he didn't have a boat, and I didn't pay him anything yet," I said.

"There are many scammers in this area waiting to make money off people who desperately want to leave the country," he warned.

"Your mom told me about this the other day," I said.

"Unless you have relatives living here and know for certain that the trip is organized by people you can trust, you need to be very careful. Otherwise, you lose everything, or even spend time in jail."

"I understand," I said.

"You know, when I talked about people you can trust, I meant those who have a boat and also want to leave the country. People who just want enough money to reinforce the boat, to buy gas and food for the trip, and some extra money to use when they reach the refugee camp," he added.

"I see," I said.

"A few greedy fishermen whose houses are not too far from ours became rich overnight because they used their boats as bait to bring people down from Saigon, and after stripping people of all their gold, they ruthlessly left those people stranded. Some went back to their homes empty-handed, but some unlucky ones were arrested and sent to jail," he indignantly said. "I know a trip in the making, and the organizer can be trusted. You know Tuan, my younger brother, he is in his first year of college, and my parents are thinking about sending him on this trip. He needs a good school," he continued.

"How much do they want for an adult?" I asked.

"I don't know. My parents talked to them, let me call my mom," he said, then cupped his hands at his mouth and called. "Mom, would you mind coming here for a second?"

"Just a moment, my hands are dirty from frying all these fish. Let me wash first," his mom said from the kitchen.

"It will just be a few seconds, you don't need to," he said.

She pulled a cloth from her shoulder to wipe off her hands as she hurriedly walked into the living room.

"Mom, how much did they want for a person on the trip you planned to send Tuan?" he asked her.

"They told your father and me that it cost two taels of gold per person. I did ask them to bring it down, but they didn't budge," she said.

"Thanks, Mom," he said. She then went back to the kitchen to cook.

He turned to me and said, "Now, you know, you can talk to your wife about this. How many kids do you have? I forgot."

"Four," I said.

"You can talk to them about the price for your kids when my parents introduce you to them," he said.

"Thanks," I said and I immediately thought about the amount of gold my wife had saved over the years. It didn't amount to anything. It would take four taels of gold for me and my wife, and eight altogether for my four kids for a total of twelve. (Each tael, at that time, was worth approximately $1, 220). We could get three taels of gold if we sold our house, and that didn't even come close. I just didn't want to think about it anymore because the more I thought about it, the more frustrated and sick I felt.

Most of the people living in this area were rice farmers, so they had rice to eat. It was so wonderful to see a rice bowl with full of white rice, the fresh fried fish and big bowls of squash, and shrimp soup. I had craved for cooked white rice and fried fish for long time, but I just couldn't eat much because my mind was totally occupied with all of the other things. After having a few cups of rice wine, I said that I needed to leave and get some sleep.

My wife's cousin took me back to the motel on his old Honda motorcycle, and he reminded me to contact him in case I wanted to get on this trip.

While I was sitting on the bus on the way home, I felt torn apart between impossible choices, and I didn't know what I should do to get this complicated matter resolved. I didn't have much money left, so I only bought five kilograms of rice and a piece of dried rice pancake to chew along the way, which, when I drank some water, would hopefully expand to fill up my stomach. I left early in the morning, around six o'clock, and I didn't get home until almost eight o'clock in the evening on the same day. My kids surrounded me, hoping for something to eat, but I hadn't bought anything because I didn't have money, and they were sad. My youngest son held on to my arm asking all kind of questions: "Where have you been? Why did it take you so long to get home? Do you have anything to eat?" He was almost five years old but he was so small and skinny he looked as if he were three years old. I asked them where their mom was, and they said Mom hadn't gotten home from work as yet. It was almost eight o'clock in the evening, so she was probably very busy at work.

I then heard the door open. Huong appeared at the door with her bike. She was soaked with perspiration from head to toes, her pant legs were both rolled up above her knees, and she was panting. I asked her what was happening. She irritably said, "The goddamn truck didn't come to pick up the tea today. They said it had broken down. We had to carry the tea leaves via bike to the cooperative. Do you remember my father's truck, the one you operated for almost two years? The cooperative used it, but they didn't take care of it properly and this was the result. The other equipment could break down soon too. Thank God, the tea leaves weren't burned; otherwise I would have lost all the credit for today."

We helped each other to cook dinner, since the kids had to study. "Go study...I will let you know when supper is done," she told them. She then turned to me to ask, "Did you bring some rice home?"

"Yes, but only five kilograms. I ran out of money, and I didn't want them to confiscate the rice either," I admitted.

"I have some chayote squash in the cupboard. You can help me wash and cut them into vertical slices," she said. "Let me mix some rice with the cassava today. We have been eating cassava for so long now and we've worked so hard. We can treat ourselves a little bit better today. Are you okay with that?" she asked, setting up a fire to cook the rice.

"Sure," I said with a laugh.

"I will use the charcoal to grill a few pieces dried fish, then we are all set for tonight," she said with a smile.

"You are all covered in sweat and you smell, too. Don't you want to take a shower first?" I teased.

"Let me put the rice pot on the fire cooking pit. Then I will take a shower," she said.

While I was cutting squash, my wife took a shower and changed her clothes. She walked in while I was finishing the last squash. She had changed into a clean, light polo shirt and pulled her hair back into a ponytail. Huong was twenty-six, and she was thinner than she had been a couple of years ago. Nevertheless, she was still very beautiful though she was underfed and working in hard labor conditions. I remembered the first time I met her; I had to compete with so many guys to win her heart. Her parents wouldn't let her marry me because I was so poor. I didn't have a stable job then; I was only a first-year student studying law in college.

To make matters worse, I was a Buddhist Southerner and she was a Catholic Northerner. But I loved her. She was so beautiful and in comparison, I was mediocre. It was difficult to iron out the differences between our two families, and it even proved unsolvable. Despite the hardship, it was enough that we loved each other, and we decided to marry in a Catholic church regardless of our families' disapproval. We didn't accept the old-fashioned Vietnamese culture in which the parents chose the spouse for their children. We broke the rules.

However, that was all the past, and I reminded myself to focus on getting supper ready for the kids to eat so they could go to sleep. I used some lard we had put aside when we slaughtered our pig to stir fry the chayote, and my wife put a few pieces of dried fish on the wood charcoal. She flipped the fish back and forth a few times, and our dinner was ready for the whole family. My children enjoyed a simple meal and they loved the stir-fried chayote. They also recognized that the rice was tastier than usual. In order to improve our diet, we had planted a few chayote plants, and they gave us a lot of fruit. We couldn't eat them all, so we traded what we didn't use with our neighbors for other goods.

It was already ten o'clock in the evening. My kids had all gone to bed, and while sitting in the kitchen, my wife asked me about my trip. I whispered everything in her ears. She let out a long sigh and didn't say a word. We went to bed, but my wife kept tossing and turning; she couldn't sleep, and neither did I.

The next morning, our haggardness clearly showed on our faces from the lack of sleep and too much stress. Although we were very tired, we couldn't stay home. When we met again at the same place for our lunch break, Huong said, "As you already know, we now have close to three taels of gold in the form of jewelry, and we would be able to get about two more for our house, but then I don't know where we would live. We can't go back to live with my parents." She stopped to think for a few minutes then continued.

"We still, however, have to make a decision. We can't sit here lamenting over it. They said that they would isolate you from the population. I don't know when, but it is coming. If we wait until the last minute, then you won't be able to go and neither of us will leave. We need to do something with what we have, and I know it is a tough decision to make, but we have no other choices. I thought about this all night last night. I didn't have a moment to close my eyes. I trust my uncle. He has made many good choices in the past. He has four boys, two of whom are now in Europe, and he is now sending his youngest one out," she said with conviction.

I knew what she was getting at. I said, "I agree with you that a decision has to be made, but I don't feel right leaving you and our children struggling to survive without a father. Our house is in very bad shape, with all the wood planks falling apart because of termites and weather, and you have to use buckets to catch water when it rains. It is a ramshackle structure waiting to collapse. It looms above you like you're surrounded by a bunch of beasts waiting to eat you alive. As a husband, do you think I would just take off given the living conditions and environment my wife and my children are now in?"

"So you think I should be the one to go, or that the kids should be the ones to go? Think logically and don't let your emotions get involved. We have to find a way out and we are looking into the most practical way to do it," she said. "Secondly, they don't let you roam freely here, anyway. I don't want them to put you in a concentration camp." She was becoming emotional. "Let's hope that you will be able to get to a free country. I know it is a very slim chance, but we have to hope. You will then sponsor me and the kids. I promise you that I will do my best to take care of the kids while you are gone."

"This is a big sacrifice on your part. It is difficult to know when we will be reunited," I said emotionally. "Our children have no idea what we are planning to do, and we probably will have to keep it that way, but I can't just quietly disappear. That would create a lot of questions among the police and village authority. If it were to fail, I would be in big trouble when I came back."

"You are right! We will create a lot of family problems. Let the neighbors know, let them know that we no longer can get along, let the kids know. They mostly ask our children about our family anyway. This will damage our children's self-esteem, but this is the only tactic we have to employ at this moment," she said.

My wife then sewed a pocket inside of the front part of my underwear and put all the gold jewelry in a small bag, which she put into this pocket for me.

I contacted my wife's uncle to let him know that I wanted to be a part of this trip and that I would come down in a month. I wanted to know when they were sailing. I also started to set the stage for the theatrical play that my wife and I would have to carry out: the more dramatic, the better.

I then set out to play without any script. I invited some of the young workers from the tea production unit to my house. We bought rice whiskey to drink, and I killed the only duck we had left to eat at home while my wife was at work and my kids were in school. We left everything on the table, and I took off to another place to drink again. My wife came home and reacted to this angrily, culminating in a big argument when I came home that night. I broke several plates, threw tables and chairs around, and screamed and yelled. I woke all the neighbors up. They had to call the area police to restrain me and order me to go to sleep. I didn't go to work the next few days because I was hangover. We pretended to argue again about the problems of my being lazy, making no money, drinking too much, and also having an affair.

We knew this would hurt our children's feelings, but the play had to be carried out as flawlessly as possible to show the children and the neighbors that we didn't get along.

After several weeks, the word got to the village police chief and he was very happy to know about our family problem. He told my wife to get rid of me and kick me out of the house. I was drunk all the time, and they called me up and warned me that if I kept waking the neighbors up they would put me in custody for a few days.

One night when I came home drunk, I woke all the neighbors up and threw things around the house during a tantrum. The area police put me in handcuffs and threw me into the village temporary holding cell. They handcuffed me to the door of the cell, so I was not able to stand up or go to the restroom; I had no other option but to urinate where I sat. I was screaming and yelling all night about the problems we had at home, demanding to know why they didn't arrest my wife but instead arrested me. They took the handcuffs off me in the morning and asked me to sign a paper to promise that this wouldn't happen again. I signed the paper but I did it again.

To the Communists, domestic problems were not serious crimes, but rather a petty case. They did, however, pay very close attention to those who were involved with organized political groups opposing their control; the people who were involved in these activities were dealt with very harshly and were even sent to a hard labor camp for many years.

My children were very scared and saddened by the way I behaved, and it tore my heart into pieces, but both my personal safety and my ability to eventually free my family depended upon evading the suspicion of the village officials.

This went on for three weeks before I took off without letting anybody know.

They questioned my wife about me, asking about my whereabouts and when I left the house. She told them that she went to work in the tea field and when she came home from work, I had left without telling anyone. She said she didn't know and she didn't care because I was a burden to the family, and that she was happy that I was gone.

They recorded everything, and things were quiet after that. It indicated that I had been able to fool them at least this time, but I had a long and difficult road ahead of me that during which I would need to deal with the deception and maliciousness of the Communists.

The happiest person in this drama was probably the village chief of police, since he knew now that the thorn in his side had been removed and he could come and go to my house any time as he pleased. Huong was friendly and nice to him, but she also very firm that the relationship between them couldn't grow because she was a married woman with children, and he was a married man and also a village chief of police. She didn't want any bad rumors because her husband was not home, and it was also in contempt of the Vietnamese culture.

My children kept asking her about me, especially my youngest one, and he cried all the time missing me. One time my kids came home and told my wife that their friends told them that I was now in New York, and they wanted to know where New York was and to go there to visit me because they missed me so much.

When I arrived in the Rach Gia province, the organizer put me in a house located next to the river bank with my wife's cousin, Tuan, where we would stay to wait for the taxi boat to pick us up and bring us to the big boat for the open sea. There were three of us temporarily living here to wait for the taxi boat, and we all had to pay them one tael of gold as a deposit, the rest to be paid at the time they pick us up for the big boat. We stayed there for almost two months, during which time the police raided the area several times. Luckily, people in this area didn't like the Communists so they always informed us before the police crossed the river to check on the houses lying along the river. In order to avoid being arrested, we went underneath the balcony, submerging ourselves under the water and using a plastic straw to breathe until the raid was over. Thankfully, the weather of this region was very warm, since otherwise we would have died of hypothermia.

One day when we were on the balcony, we saw a group of police stopping a little boat to check the papers of a young man. We didn't hear the exchange between them, but we saw the police shoot the man in the forehead with an AK-47 when he was trying walk back inside the boat. The man fell into the river, and his corpse was afloat about three hours later. A few young people tried to pull it to the bank, but these kids were then arrested by police for the crime of propaganda.

The police began carrying out these raids more often, and in order to avoid an incident like this, the owner sent me to another house about two kilometers from his house to stay for a few days, while my wife's cousin was sent to a different house until things quieted down. The oldest boy of this new family was now in Australia; he had left about six months before on a trip organized by his friend who was still in town.

While I was at this house, I found a novel in English and read it to pass time. While I was flipping through the pages of this book, I heard a greeting from a young man. It turned out to be the man who had organized the trip that had included the oldest boy of the family. He introduced himself and said that his name was Manh. He asked me if I knew English well, and I told him that I could use English for daily conversation. After we talked for a while, he asked me if I wanted to go with him on a trip that he would organize soon. I said that I would love to do so, but I had already paid the trip organizer and I would lose my deposit if I got out of the deal. He wished me luck and said that if for some reason I couldn't go, then I should contact him. He frankly said that he needed someone who could speak English to help him. "In case we meet a foreign ship at sea," he told me. I gave him my address.

My wife and children missed me a lot, and Huong also wanted to know what was going on with my trip. She took my youngest son with her to visit me where I was staying temporarily; however, we couldn't stay there overnight, so we rented the corner of an attic in a house located next to the bus station to stay for two days. My wife told me that she wanted me to go back to live with her and the kids, saying they missed me so much and they asked for me every day when they came home from school. She said that regardless of how hard our life was going to be, how horrible what we had to face, she just wanted me to go home with the family and she just wanted family to be together. My son didn't leave me for a second; always holding on to my arm everywhere I went. He appeared to have lost some weight and hadn't grown any taller. I knew very well that our children were extremely malnourished, though we fed them the best that we could.

I had to explain to Huong the situation I was in and that if I decided to get out of the deal, then I would lose the tael of gold I had already paid the organizer. We also had tried very hard to get to this point in this endeavor, and it would be wasteful if we didn't pursue it further.

It was very sad that I had to say good-bye to my wife and son, but any good time always comes to an end. When I took my wife and son to the bus station, they both got on the bus, and my son didn't let my hand go. Holding onto the small and bony hand of my son, my heart was wrecked because I couldn't do any better to assist my children given the condition I was now in. My son wanted me to get on the bus, unable to understand that I had to stay back for the trip to go overseas. When the bus started to take off, he screamed loudly, asking the driver to stop so I could get on and begging me to jump on the bus to go home with him. He said, "Daddy go home with me, I love you. Don't live with that woman."

I realized that my wife had made up a story to tell him about my affair with another woman, so that in his mind the reason for me to leave the family was my infidelity. Huong also cried aloud, so much that the other passengers thought she had been robbed. On the way back to my temporary living quarters, my tears fell constantly, though I tried not to sob aloud to avoid the attention of passersby.

While waiting for the boat, I was not only fearful of being arrested by the police, but I also worried a lot about the prospect of being cheated because the organizer kept procrastinating on picking us up for the trip.

Finally, one night about two months later, a member of the organizer's team stopped by to tell us that they would pick us up at three o'clock the next morning. Each of us had to have an additional tael of gold ready for them when we stepped into their boat tomorrow. We waited anxiously for the boat to come, and no one in the house, including the owner, could get any sleep.

At three o'clock, we heard the boat engine. Then, it was turned off, and we heard the noise of the paddle hitting the water. A man with a tough gangster's face walked into the house through the back door and collected the last pieces of gold from two of us. My wife's cousin wasn't at this location at the time since the organizer said they had to spread people out to different locations so it would be easier for them to pick up. I didn't have a piece of gold, so I gave him all the jewelry I had to him. He counted each one and sternly asked me, "Are you sure adding all these up will equal one tael? You know, they will count again, and if you don't have the right amount, they will kick you out."

"I am sure," I said.

"You guys can't talk until you get to the big boat, understand?" he ordered.

He quietly led us into the boat in the dark night. Though the boat had a tiny cabin, it didn't have stairs to go down. He asked us to jump into the cabin one by one, then he closed the lid, and it became dark, crowded, and steamy hot. It was a horrible place, worse than a jail cell. We didn't want to get into trouble so we just whispered into each other's ears, and in my mind I was very happy that we finally were going out to sea. But I also thought about my wife and children left behind. I didn't know when I would be able see them again. I tried to console myself with the thought of working hard to make money when I got to a different country and sending all the money to my wife and my kids.

The gangster-faced man murmured through the trapdoor above that he had to pick up more people and bring us all to the big boat for the open sea voyage. We didn't know what was going outside of the cabin; all we heard was the noise of the dull old engine and the growl of the propeller when it hit the water. After navigating in the canals for about three hours, the operator opened the lid and told us to get out and keep quiet. I was so excited to look up, hoping I would see the big boat, but the morning sunlight dazzled my eyes.

I was completely astonished to see that our boat was stopped next to the bank of a small canal covered in a thick layer of mud and shaded with a thicket of coconut trees. We asked him, "Where is the big boat? Why are you dropping us here?"

"It was chased by the police patrol boat, so it had already taken off. If you don't want to be arrested by the police or the guerrilla forces, you need to keep quiet and get out of here immediately," he said with a threatening tone.

I was lost, confused, and absolutely panicked because I didn't know where I was and had no money left in my pocket. However, I had no other choices but to run away because everyone had jumped off the boat and was scattering. I was completely terrified; it felt like a waking nightmare.

I walked for almost an hour in the muddy rice field before I saw a group of farmers; I asked one of them to show me the way to get back to the city. He told me that it was about twenty kilometers, and he showed me how to get to the bus station. My clothes and feet were covered in mud, so I stopped by a creek to clean myself up before I walked toward the city. I didn't return to the house where I stayed, but instead went back to my wife's uncle's house. They all had an astonished look on their faces to see me, and I explained to them in detail the reasons why I had showed up at their house. They told me that Tuan had already gone last night with the big boat, and

I explained that we hadn't stayed at the same house and I didn't know what was going on, since we were all kept in the dark until the last minute. They said they would talk to the organizer, but I didn't think that it would do any good because the organizer had already gone with the boat. They let me stay at their house for the night and gave me some money to buy a ticket to go back to my hometown.

All night I writhed in mental anguish; there were no words to describe my pain and my utmost desperation. I just couldn't imagine the prospect of facing the village police chief and how I could explain to my wife about the failed trip and all the money down the drain. I was overwhelmed with so many awful things, but the worst of all was the thought that my family had to live in the most miserable condition under the Communist regime for the rest of our lives.

My wife was at work and my children were in school when I walked into the house, and my neighbors were not too friendly. It was about four o'clock in the afternoon when, sitting at the table in the kitchen, I saw my oldest son walk in the door. He pulled back a step when he realized there was someone in the house, but a moment later he recognized that it was me, so he yelled loudly to his brothers and sister, "Dad is home, Dad is home, guys!" They all ran quickly into the door, surrounding me and asking me all kinds of questions. They held onto my arms as if they were afraid that I would disappear again. Seeing the bony bodies of my children in the raggedy clothes broke my heart. If they had enough food to eat at this age, my children should have grown very quickly. The country had a shortage of everything, especially medication, and many people died from very simple illnesses because they didn't have proper treatment. I would probably go crazy to see my children if they were in this situation. My oldest son interrupted my thoughts.

"Dad, my friend said that you were in Wa-hin-ton or Nu Yok."

"No, that's not true, I was just not happy living at home, so I tried to stay away for a while," I sadly said.

My wife came home quite late that evening because she had to carry tea leaves to the cooperative, and she was very happy to see me at home. She also wanted to know what was going on with the trip. When the kids went to bed I was very sad to explain to her the situation I was in. She sobbed for a while, and after regaining her composure, she asked me if I had any gold left.

"As you already know, I gave all the jewelry you had given me to the organizer, and I also had to pay for my meals. I had to get some money from your uncle to buy the ticket," I admitted grudgingly.

"All day sitting on the bus, you are probably tired now. You need to have a restful night, and we will talk about this tomorrow," she said.

To see the village police chief was the last thing in my mind, but I knew for sure that someone would report to him of my return. In order to avoid being summoned, I went to the village office to report to him that I was back home. He was not in the office, so I asked the clerk to inform him for me.

The next morning, I received a summons requesting me to report to the village office at two o'clock in the afternoon on the same day.

I reported to the village office on time as requested. He invited me into his office, asked me sit down, and offered me tea and a domestic manufactured cigarette. He had a very heavy accent of the central province of Vietnam like Chairman Ho Chi Minh, and I guessed they both were from the same province of Nghe An or somewhere in the region. I didn't take the proffered cigarette because I didn't want to smoke.

He asked me to write a report telling him exactly when I left home, where I went, who I contacted, what I did, why I left home, where I lived, and all kinds of questions. At one point he threatened to put me in the concentration camp if I didn't tell the truth and slammed his pistol on the table in front of me. In the report, I consistently answered all the questions he had asked without saying anything about trying to get out of the country. I had to report to the village office for several days, but I always provided the same written report. He warned me that a heavy punishment would be imposed on me if I did it again.

A few days later when things had quieted down a bit, Huong brought up the issue that we had not finished discussing when I had just gotten home.

Huong told me that it was very unfortunate that we had lost almost all of our savings, but the important thing was that I was still alive to be home with the family.

"Nowadays, it is difficult to trust anyone. The entire society is in moral decay and the mistrust is so prevalent throughout the country, especially in the business of fleeing the country," she ruefully said.

"I am in sync with you on this. However, sometimes we have to take risks to get things done. We have lived together for many years and you know I'm not the man to be suspicious of everything. But, you also know that throughout Vietnam the trust is no longer there. The social structure has collapsed, and this regime has been teaching people how to lie, how to cheat, how to deceive others. The honest people have a tough time living in this society. In this case, my mind was constantly disturbed from the beginning because I was not able to verify all the facts and the progress, and I was totally kept in the dark. I didn't know whether it was a scam or genuine until the last minute and at that time, it was already too late," I said vehemently.

"No, no, I don't blame you for the lack of verification on your part, as a matter of fact this trip was introduced by my uncle," she said apologetically.

"I don't blame your uncle either. I did trust him, but I also had to take some risks, and his son actually did leave with the big boat on that day, though we don't know whether or not he has landed in a free country. Maybe my luck has just run out," I said with regret.

"Well, it doesn't do any good sitting here lamenting. It is history, and now our most pressing need is to work hard and raise our children. I know it is very tough, but we have to work together and live within our means. We have been living on the cassava, cassava leaves, sweet potatoes, and dried hard corn for several years and we are still alive, so I think we should be able to survive," she said impassively.

"Is your travel paper still valid?" I asked.

"Yes, it is good for up to six months," she said.

"That's good. You should go to Saigon to learn a trade, and I think you are dexterous and good with your hands, so you could be a good beautician," I suggested.

"It will take at least three months. Can you take care of the children while I am away?" she asked, sounding skeptical.

"I will try my best. You should focus on what you need to do," I said.

"All we have now is less than one tael's worth of gold, and I have to bring that with me to pay for tuition and to buy the hair equipment and beauty supplies. In addition, I have to rent a place to stay and pay for my meals. The money we have will not cover all the expenses, but I will figure it out when I get there. You and the kids will have no money at home," she said ruefully.

"I still have two suits and a few good shirts that I haven't worn since we got here, and you also have some beautiful traditional long dresses. We can sell them so you have extra money to use when you need it."

"Let me use what I have on hand, and if I do need to, I will come home to sell them, but they were our wedding gifts. They are so close to me, and I don't want to sell them yet, not until we really need the money."

I knew it would be difficult for me to work and take care of my children alone. My wife's sacrifice for me and the family was invaluable. I wanted Huong to have a skill so she wouldn't have to work in the tea field or tea factory for the rest of her life. It was a big investment, but I believed it would yield a good return because women always wanted to look beautiful regardless, and we also believed in working smarter, not harder.

While my wife was in Saigon to learn a trade, I was still doing the field work to earn credit for my family ration. Each able male member of the production team was assigned a quarter hectare of tea trees. After a few years, these trees grew taller and all the branches had to be cut down to the same height so the young buds could grow for female workers to conveniently pick them. Tea trees are hardwood and most of the branches were as big as my wrist, so we needed to use a very sharp machete to cut them. I gauged by eye where a cut should be, then I used my left hand to hold onto the top part of the branch to keep it stable, while with all my might I swung the machete with my right hand from the bottom up to cut the branch with one move.

I got tired quicker than my coworkers because I was not used to this kind of work, and honestly I didn't have enough food to eat. I had to stay late frequently to work overtime when everyone else had already left for home. My right shoulder was in unbelievable pain after a long workday, but I didn't have any medication to help relieve the pain, so I used some of the herbal medication we found in the woods. The skin of my right palm was covered in blisters and was peeling off in layers, and it was terribly painful.

One Friday, I stayed late as usual to finish the work when everyone had already gone home. Though I was tired, I didn't want to take a full rest because I wanted to finish the work before it was dark, so I leaned against the tea tree to catch my breath and have a sip of water. When I resumed working, I suddenly heard a slight rustling in the tea leaves. I turned around and saw a big snake, about one meter long and the same color as the tea leaves, crawling toward me. I didn't know whether it was venomous or not. With the sharp machete in my hand, I gave it a whack. I didn't see its head, but its body was still on the top of the tea trees crawling. I used a branch from the tea tree to pick it up, and I brought it to a clearing. I immediately thought it would make a good supper for my children this evening and a good source of protein.

I stopped working, rolled the snake up, and put it in my bag to take it home. I didn't forget to collect some dried tea branches for cooking. Riding home, I was so exhilarated to think about what dish I should make with this fresh meat, but decided I wouldn't let my children know that it was snake. The exhilaration brought back memories of the past when I was still working in the office, when I always took my wife and children to a nice restaurant for dinner on Fridays.

My children were home now, and no adult was at home with them. I knew for sure they were sitting around in the kitchen to get warm under the dim oil lamp waiting for me. I tried to pedal harder so I could get home with my kids, but I was exhausted after a long workday, and at times I had to push my bike on the steep road.

They were joyous to see me home, and they helped me to unload the tea branches and stack them neatly in the right place.

I quickly washed my hands and started to prepare for our supper. I asked my oldest son and daughter to pick up some young cassava leaves from the backyard, clean them, and boil them until they were tender and tasty. Meanwhile, I peeled the skin off the snake, cut it into chunks of five centimeters, and then used some of the hog lard to fry it in the pan. The smell of fried meat was so appealing, and my kids just couldn't wait to enjoy the good dish of eel, which I had told them the meat was. After frying it, I put it in a porcelain pot with some minced lemon leaves and chopped lemon grass to enhance the fragrance, then put in some water to cook under a low heat for about a half an hour. I also put in some salt, just enough for taste. I wished we had some sugar, since it would have better taste, but I thought we could enjoy it without sugar.

Today was Friday, and I wanted to give my kids the royal treatment, so I increased the amount of rice to forty percent instead of ten percent as my wife instructed. Voila, we had a wonderful meal of simmering fresh snake meat, snake sauce to dip the boiled cassava leaves in, and a mix of freshly cooked rice and sliced cassava root.

They devoured the food and they told me, "Dad, you are a good cook, and you could open a restaurant."

"I don't need other customers, I already have four here," I teased them.

I had to give my wife a lot of credit because I was not able to take care of my children as well as she had done. I couldn't wash their clothes as clean as she did because we didn't have soap. All I could do was to soak their clothes in a bucket, take them out, and put them on the cement floor next to my well. I then stepped on them, turned them over a few times, rinsed them, and hung them up until they were dried. Most of our clothes had a dark color, black or brown, so I could not tell whether or not they were clean.

We didn't have a phone, and if we wanted to communicate we had to send a letter or wait until we saw each other in person. About two months from the date my wife left for training, she came home to sell some of the clothes we had so she would have extra money to pay for her tuition and the hair equipment. She saw our noses and faces full of smoke, so she knew right away that we were refining black tea illegally at home because we needed extra money to buy food. Everyone in the village was doing it; they couldn't depend on the rations provided by the tea cooperative. It was impossible to hide this work from the area police officer, but he would turn a blind eye if we gave him some of the money we made.

By now, Huong was in training for almost four months and she should have finished by this time, but she had to come back to the village before the course was complete to vote for the legislative. We all had to vote, and each of us had to carry a certificate with the signature of the local authority and a stamp to certify that we had participated in this process. The Communists wanted to show people that their political system was very democratic because people had the right to vote for their representative in Congress like any other developed country in the world. It was easy for them to convince the uneducated farmers who didn't know anything about politics that their elections were democratic and just like those in the West, but others saw this process as a bad joke because it just wasted the people's time and money.

Just a few weeks before the election date, the local Communist leaders called people to the village auditorium where they announced names of a couple of handpicked candidates who were also members of the Communist Party. Even though all candidates were members of the Communist Party, people were specifically instructed to vote for a designated person nevertheless. The funniest thing was that we didn't even know who the candidates were and we didn't see their faces before or after the election dates. With this insidious approach, the Congress of Vietnam under the Communist regime only had party members as our representatives and therefore they only supported and protected the interests of the Party, not of the people.

Politics weren't our concern, but the nice thing was that the election allowed my wife to be home with us for a few days. Our children seemed to be happier; we heard laughter throughout the house, and the atmosphere was more vibrant. I knew that my wife would complete the training in a couple of weeks, so we needed to set up a place for her to do business. We had to remove a few chairs and a table from the living room, but we didn't know where to store them because our bedroom, which was adjacent to the living room, was too small and only had room for a bunk bed for our kids and a bed for us, with no room for anything else. We kept our clothes in cardboard boxes placed underneath our beds. We wished the furniture were in better shape so we could sell it.

We worked like bees. I carried a bucket of water, and my wife used a rag to clean the floor and scrub out all the dirt around the corners. Our children helped clean the chairs and table, and since we needed to keep two chairs in the living room for our customers to sit, the table was then moved to our in-laws for storage.

Huong had to go back to Saigon for training, and we waited for two weeks, but she didn't come home at the end of the second week. I received a letter from her saying that the instructor wanted more money, and so she had to stay back and work for him for two weeks without pay to make up for the shortage. She also needed money to buy additional hair equipment. My bike was old, but it had a strong frame, and it was good for hauling bags of tea leaves and other heavy things. I could get some money for the bike and send it to her. I had to make a tough choice because this was the only bike I had, but my wife also needed money for her business. If I sold it, then I would have to walk to work, and I would also have to carry the firewood home on my head and shoulder at the end of the working day. It was a tough decision to make, but I realized that my wife had sacrificed so much for our family, and now I had a chance to do my small part in return.

Finally, Huong came home with a few things she needed to do her business, and I helped her to set them up. We collected pictures of European women with different hairstyles from old magazines to hang on the walls. We now had the first hair shop in the village. The problem we ran into was that all the girls and women were working in the field during the day; they could only come to the shop at night. We only had electricity for a few hours at night, and many times, while our customers were in the dryers, the electricity was shut off. We needed to have our own electricity at night or whenever we needed in order to effectively serve our customers, and for that we needed to have an old generator, but we had run out of money. We wanted to borrow money to buy a generator, but no one was willing to loan.

We were deeply concerned with our financial situation, and we tried to think about whether we had anything that we could sell. Our TV, refrigerator, clothes, and bike were already gone, and we thought about bringing the deeds of our house to a pawnshop to get a loan for one tael of gold. We would pay interest monthly and pay it back when we had saved enough money. Having discussed the pros and cons of this option, I told Huong that if we couldn't pay back the loan on time, then they would take our house, and that was much too risky.

Unable to come up with a workable solution, we had to make do with what we had. Despite the difficulties with electricity, she was able to bring in more money than what she had earned picking tea leaves for the cooperative, but the most important thing to me was that she didn't have to work in the rain and under the hot sun any longer. As usual, the area police officer quickly smelled money. He visited our house more often and he always sat at the shop for hours, observing without saying a word. No girl or woman would come to get her hair done when he was sitting in the shop because they didn't want to see his face. We knew the limitations of our rights, so we had to be flexible with him and give him some money or a gift for him to leave us alone.

I still worked in the fields for the cooperative to earn credit for our family ration. In addition, I now had a new job sweeping the floor, cleaning up the shop, and greeting our customers. Our children also helped us with small chores after school. We all had work to do, and we worked as industriously as bees. Things went relatively well, and we were pleased with the progress.

We wanted to work hard to better ourselves, and if everything went well, then we didn't want to leave the country even though the country was facing economic calamity because of the policies of the Communist Party leaders. We didn't pay attention to politics, and we just wanted to have a peaceful and simple life with enough food to eat for our children.

Having to work in the field today, as usual I packed my Guigoz container full of mixed cassava and rice, a few pieces of cooked pork, and a full canteen of boiled water. I had a military shirt that I had picked up on the streets of Saigon when an ARVN soldier dumped it in 1975. I wore it to work in the field every day, and through time and hard use, it was ripped in several places. Huong used discarded pieces of material she got from a tailor shop to mend the shirt. She wasn't concerned with the color of the throwaway pieces as long as they were still good for mending our old clothes. Sometimes, she had to put many layers of material at one spot, and that spot might have multiple colors. As my wife was cleaning the shop, I put on my shirt, and with a lunch box in my left hand and a sharp machete on my right shoulder, I took off for work.

As I was walking past the village office on my way to the field, two guerrillas stopped me and dragged me into the office as if I were a criminal or would try to escape. They yanked both of my arms so hard that my lunch box clattered to the street and food was scattered everywhere. My machete also fell on the street, but thankfully it didn't hit anyone. I was absolutely shocked and couldn't guess at the reason for this sudden confrontation. They put me into the office and locked the door until their boss arrived for work.

"What did I do for you to apprehend me?" I demanded. They only told me somewhat ominously that I would know soon.

About a half an hour later, four people entered the room, including the police chief. They all had very mean faces, and they asked me where I had gotten my shirt and why I put so many different colors on it. They weren't happy with my answer, and one man made a face that looked like he wanted to eat me alive. He held his right fist in front of my nose and screamed into my face.

"You are degrading and insulting the revolutionary government! You are a son of the landlord and you are pretending to be poor. You portray the people's government as the one who made everyone suffer, turned them all to poverty and impoverish the country!"

"We know who you are, you are educated under the puppet regime, and you are not even worthy to be fertilizer," he snarled with the heavy accent of the central provinces of Vietnam.

He then added, "We were very lenient with you. We allowed you to live among the people, but you don't behave. You have to pay for this."

"You are not poor! If you are poor, then why do you have meat to eat?" another, younger guy mocked me.

They called my wife and asked her to come to get me out. The village official didn't want to accept that the material sold by the cooperative was very poor in quality, and a shirt made with this material would be ripped after a couple of washes. They complained when I wore the multicolor, mended shirt, and they also harassed me when I wore a ripped, unmended shirt; they probably just wanted to find a reason to get rid of me. My life here made me think of a tree that didn't want to shake but couldn't stop the wind from coming. I explained to my wife my speculation on their intentions, and she was also very sad to agree with me.

The police and other government agencies usually arrested people whom they suspected or accused of engaging in subversive activities at night, and once they were arrested, that person would disappear. The family wouldn't get any information about their loved ones. My days were numbered, and as I didn't know when they would decide to bring me in, all I could do now was continue my daily routine of work, helping my wife, and raising my children; beyond that, I put my life in God's hands.

It was seven o'clock in the evening on Wednesday, and after unloading a bundle of dried tea branches I had carried home from the field, I was soaked with perspiration. While I was drawing a couple of buckets of water from the well in my backyard and splashing myself with cold water, my wife yelled from the shop, "You have a letter from someone named M…nh"

"From whom?" I asked.

"Manh," she said brusquely.

Neglecting to put on my soiled shirt, I ran immediately to the shop to pick up the letter, and I had to apologize to the women sitting in the chairs to wait for their turn to get their hair done.

I devoured the letter in which Manh told me to contact him immediately if I still wanted to go the New Economic Zone, writing that he had a car to help carry my belongings. Since the government usually censored people's mail, Manh had to use a secret code to let me know that if I still wanted to get out of the country, then I had to contact him immediately. I explained to Huong that the letter had arrived a few days late and I was fearful that Manh had already left the country. Huong, however, still wanted to meet Manh, so we planned to leave home the next day. The problem we had was that if Manh was ready and wanted to leave immediately, we wouldn't be able to go even if he invited us because our children were still at home and we couldn't leave the country without them. My wife had a different view on this. She thought that I should be the one to go first so then I could save the whole family later. I didn't agree with her because my children were very young; my oldest one was only eight and my youngest one was almost five, and at these ages they needed me the most.

She quietly asked me, "Are you sure that they would even let you stay home with the kids?"

"I don't know," I had to admit.

"If we knew for sure that they wouldn't create any trouble for you, then I would very much want you to be home with us. However, you saw with your very own eyes that they are trying to remove you from the population. I think it will be too late to wait until then to do something, don't you think so?" she said with conviction.

I was very sad to think about the prospect of leaving alone, but I couldn't ignore her persuasion and the indisputable fact that my life was at their mercy.

We didn't mind spending extra money to buy the bus tickets, but I knew it would be almost impossible to get the travel permit the next day. Huong quietly told me, "This guy loves money. Let me use it for our needs." I was just sadly amused at what she said. Huong collected all the money she had made that day plus money she had from the last few days. She counted it and then put it all in an envelope and headed toward the house of the chief of police. She didn't forget to assure me that she would be all right because his wife was at home, and even he wouldn't dare to act out in a way that caught his wife's attention.

Leaving our children at home with my wife's aunt was our last resort; however, we needed to arrive tomorrow to see Manh. Finally, we got the travel permission. Our children wanted to go with us because they had never been left alone without one of us in the past. We admonished them to stay home with Auntie and behave while we were gone and told them we would be gone just a few days to buy some rice and good things to eat for them.

We left early in the morning while our children were asleep. I kissed each one of them on the cheek a good-bye, for I didn't know whether I would be back. It was difficult to hold back my tears.

Determining to get to Rach Gia the same day, we took the earliest bus and paid a very stiff price for two tickets. We had to change buses in Saigon, where the bus station was bustling, noisy, dirty, and terribly hot. We couldn't fight with other passengers to buy tickets, so we had to spend an exorbitant amount of money to get two tickets from the black market from here to our destination. When we had to cross Hau Giang River on a ferry, all the passengers got off the bus. My wife naïvely left her baggage on the bus, and by the time we reached the other bank, our baggage had disappeared and there was no one to turn to for help retrieving it. Thankfully, we only had a few pairs of old clothes and a few bags of green tea to give as a gift, nothing of value. However, we learned a lesson that when people were poor, they would do anything to survive.

It took us more than twelve hours on the bus. We were trying to save as much money as we could, so we only bought a few pieces of dried rice pancake to munch on and some coconut water to drink.

At nine that evening, we got to the house where I had stayed temporarily to avoid the police raid on my previous and failed attempt to leave the country. I explained to the homeowner, whom we called Uncle Bay, and his daughter that we had received a letter from Manh asking us to contact him immediately. They said they were aware of the letter and said that it had been sent out more than two weeks ago, since Manh wanted us to have ample time to contact him. Somehow, thanks to the ineffective operation of the post office, we had received the letter too late.

Hien, the owner's daughter, sadly told us that Manh had already gone with his family on a trip just seven this evening. His brothers and other relatives, about forty people, were on the boat. She told us that since they needed additional fuel, she had helped Manh to carry a twenty-liter can of diesel to the departing location at six today, and the boat was scheduled to leave at seven. If everything had gone smoothly, they would have reached the river mouth by now.

My heart froze in my chest, my head was spinning, and I was totally devastated. Hien and my wife had to help me to a chair for me to sit down. They got me a glass of cold water, rubbed eucalyptus oil on my temples and my forehead, and laid me down on a bed. At this time of the year, this area was particularly hot, and the temperature in this airtight room was hovering at forty degrees Celsius, but I still felt cold. My clothes, however, were all wet with perspiration. It seemed as though the blood wasn't getting to my brain. I didn't have any feeling, and my skull felt numb.

It took almost ten minutes for me to regain my senses, and I asked my wife to hang the mosquito net because I had already been bitten all over; this region was famous in Vietnam for mosquitoes. It was hot inside, but I didn't want to go outside of this room because I wanted to minimize contact with anyone as much as possible. Lying in bed, I was thinking about how unlucky my fate was. Manh was the only one who could help us to find a better life, and he was now gone. Thinking about the prospect of continuing to live with the injustice, with the cruel and inhuman group of officials in my village, was really dreadful to me, and I dreaded seeing them again. As a father, however, I couldn't abandon our children regardless of how difficult it was for me. I had to get back to our children, who, I knew, were waiting for us at every moment.

We didn't see any light at the end of the tunnel, and we had no one except Manh who was willing to assist us on this almost impossible endeavor. There were so many scams in this business that we couldn't trust just anyone, or even if we trusted them, we still didn't have the financial means to pay for the trip, which required normally two to three taels of gold per person. Despite Huong's attempts to console me, I still had a deep sense of desperation, and it vividly showed on my face while I was lying in bed. We still had some small amount of money left, so we planned to buy a few kilos of rice and some dried fish, and then head back home the next morning.

Hien, one of Uncle Bay's daughters, was nineteen, beautiful and sweet. She timidly walked into the room to talk to my wife and me. She wanted to find out whether I was okay and also wanted to tell us that before leaving, Manh had insisted on meeting me and had asked her to drop the letter addressed to me at the post office two weeks earlier. I thanked her and I told her that I was fine.

At about ten thirty, while talking, we heard the sound of urgent knocking at the front door. I thought it was a police raid to check on the family census book or check on the strangers, so we stopped for a second to listen carefully to the knock again. Hien said she didn't think it was the police; they would pound on the door hard. She asked Huong and me to remain calm as she went for the door. There was only one wall separating the room we were in from the front door, so Huong and I were able to hear everything that was said. First, I heard the slide of the door latch and Hien's voice, pitched with surprise.

"What happened? Is everything okay?"

The reply came in a soft male voice: "Get inside. I will tell you, long story." The man's voice was familiar. I knew I had heard it somewhere before. Could it be Manh? My heart started pounding. I felt like a tightly coiled and compressed spring, impatient to find out who this person was. They were whispering now, so I was not able to recognize the man's voice any longer, which only made me even more anxious to find out who this person was. Then, the house returned to silence. It must have been only five minutes since this man had appeared, but it seemed like I had been waiting forever. I could hardly bear not knowing where they had gone.

While Huong and I were still sitting in silent anticipation, Hien gently pushed the cloth curtain serving as a door to one side and walked into the room. Following her was a man whom I couldn't recognize because of the dim light and the obscuring effect of the mosquito net I was sitting inside.

Hien said quietly, "This is Uncle Hai and his wife, they just got here this evening," meaning my wife and me. She didn't introduce the man to me, so I stood and lifted the net with the intention of shaking his hand.

The man said, "Hi, Brother Hai, how are you?"

I was speechless with amazement for a few seconds, and then, in tears I said, "Oh my god! Is that you, Manh? I thought that I would never have a chance to see you again." Frozen in the handshake, I added, "I thought you were gone with your family on a trip this evening."

Manh put his finger over his lips, urgently saying, "Shh!" then pensively whispered into my ear. "While I went back to get some more gas for the boat, it was detected and chased by a police patrol boat, so it had to take off without me."

"I am sorry that you couldn't go with your family, but on the other hand, to be selfish, I am happy that you are still here. You can imagine how sad I felt when Hien told us that you had already gone," I said appreciatively.

"I think God wants to give us an opportunity to work together," Manh said with a smile. "We will talk more tomorrow, and I hope you both have a good night's sleep." He shook my hand and left the room.

"You, too," I said after him.

There seemed to have a close relationship between Hien and Manh; they treated each other like brother and sister. Actually, Manh was a classmate and close friend of Hien's brother, who had left on a boat with Manh's family a few months ago and now lived in Australia. Most of Manh's family had now left the country, so he didn't have any close relatives living in town, and he temporarily lived at Hien's house. This inconspicuous home served essentially as the headquarters for all his organizing activities. Manh was very sharp and quite a handsome young man, but he always dressed nondescriptly to avoid attention from the vulture eyes of the informants or detectives. He was born and raised in this province and had graduated from the local high school. He had lived in Rach Gia all his life, so he knew the area like he knew his own name.

I had met Manh when I was in this town about six months ago trying to get out of the country on a failed trip. I had been temporarily sent to stay at Hien's house for a few nights to escape a police raid, and we had been friends ever since. Manh had promised to contact me when the trip he was organizing was ready, but I didn't take his words seriously until I actually received a letter from him.

Sleep eluded me, and I kept tossing not only because of the heat, but also because my mind was occupied with so many things. I couldn't sort out my emotions. I was overjoyed and relieved knowing that Manh was still around, yet simultaneously guilty and anxious about my children, who were at home without either one of us, and consumed with uncertainty about our family's future. I looked over at my wife and saw her right arm draped over forehead as she laid quietly, eyes closed. I wasn't sure whether she was asleep, but I was too exhausted to start a conversation in any event. Finally, sleep overcame me and brought a nightmare in which my family was in a boat in a deep, open ocean. My young son accidentally fell off the boat and started to struggle in the water. I screamed for help, and my wife shook me awake. It was already seven in the morning. I was shaken but relieved it was only a dream.

After we finished brushing our teeth with salt and washing our faces, Hien came into the room to inform us that the room we were now in had an outside wall next to a small alley, and it was very easy for the passerby to hear our conversation. She quietly warned us not to discuss anything related to fleeing the country and reiterated that we needed to keep all information strictly confidential.

We followed her out into the main room, where Hien busied herself preparing rice cakes and tea for breakfast. There was no sign of Manh. Part of me wondered whether his arrival the night before had been only a dream. It had seemed so real. I rubbed my face sleepily and opened my eyes to see Manh pushing aside a curtain to enter the room, causing a new wave of gratitude and excitement to rush over me.

"Good morning, Brother Hai, Huong, Hien," Manh said with a smile.

"Good morning," I said, trying to curb my excitement. We all sat down together around a low table, and Hien served our breakfast and joined us. "How are you feeling today? You must have had quite a shock being separated from your family last night. I know that you said we would discuss details today, but that can wait until later if you need time."

Manh nodded. "Thank you, Brother Hai, but there is no need to put anything off. I can sit here feeling sorry for myself and wondering how things might have gone differently, or I can do something about it. The sooner we get to work, the sooner I can be reunited with my family. And there is a lot to discuss before we can start."

I paused, wanting to ask how he had the strength to move forward after losing so much. The time, effort, and money he had put into making the last trip a reality had amounted to nothing for him, and now he might never see his family again. However, I stopped. I remembered that Huong and I had sacrificed the last of our savings, had put our children through the stress of seeing their parents fight, had even been willing split up the family to send me out of the country alone, and all for nothing. However, like Manh, we were willing to try again and again until we reached a place where we could live out our lives and raise our children in freedom.

While I was considering these things, Huong asked Manh about the trip he had sent his family out on the day before, and Manh began to tell his story.

"Like most of the people in Rach Gia, my family works in the fishing industry, or at least they did up until they left. Many of my relatives had already made it out of the country on previous trips, and those of us who were left here were determined to follow. As of six months ago, we owned a good-sized fishing boat, and we planned to use this boat to get the rest of the family and some friends out. Somehow, our plan was leaked and the authorities found out. They confiscated the boat, and we were lucky not to be arrested. After that, I scraped together enough money from relatives and friends to build a small boat, which is what we used last night. I'm now completely out of money, don't even have a house, and I guess I have to start again from scratch. Since you two have the same aspiration as I do, I'm thinking we should work together to make it happen."

I said, "Thank you for your trust, and for being willing to work with us. I think we have a real chance to make this happen." Huong nodded in agreement. "I guess we should get right into it. You know the area well. Do you think you could take me around today in your sampan to show me the town? If you have a site in mind for building the boat, we could look at that, too."

"I'd be happy to show you the town, but I actually don't have any idea for a site just yet. We can discuss that later, along with other important details. There are many variables to take into consideration before choosing a location," Manh said.

"Good point. I think I'll explore on foot for now." I looked over at Huong. "We should talk everything over together before we make a decision," I said.

Huong added, "We will let you know as soon as we decide, but I think it's likely that Hai will come to live here in town to work with you."

After breakfast, Huong and I stepped out of the house to buy some rice and dried fish. I had been here before, but I hadn't had a chance to see the entire town until today. I was totally overwhelmed by the many waterways leading to the sea, by all of the fishing villages lying along the coast, and by the many communities of people living in tiny shantytowns without electricity, running water or wells and houses made of coconut leaves. Before leaving for home, we returned to Hien's house to say good-bye to Uncle Bay, Hien, and Manh.

We arrived home at about midnight. All our children were in bed, and we went to bed without waking them. We didn't forget to give our friends and neighbors some dried squids, which was a delicacy that went very well with rice wine.

Over the next few days, my wife and I talked extensively about the pros and cons of the different options facing us and the risks that we would run into if we couldn't leave the country. The first option was to stay put and accept the status quo since we already had established a relatively good hair business, which enabled us to make some money, and we did have a house even if it was very shabby. The downsides were that I didn't know whether I would be free to be home with our family; our family would be living in a society where there was no basic freedom; our children wouldn't have the education they needed; and our lives would be in peril because of the lack of medication, poor medical technology, and dangerous living environment.

We also could choose to move the entire family to Rach Gia to live while I was working with Manh to build the boat. If I chose this option, then we would have to sell the house, my wife would discontinue her work in the hair business, and there was no guarantee that we would reach a country of the free world. The decision we made would have a big impact on our family, especially our children. They were the focus of our decision. We didn't want the Communist education system to influence them; we wanted instead for them to live in a country where they would have the freedom to live their lives to the fullest, where they would be able to live as human beings. We knew it was risky to choose this route, but we decided that we would rather all die in the sea than live in Vietnam under the Communist regime if there was any chance that we could escape.

The risks, however, were many. We heard stories daily about girls and young women being repeatedly raped by Thai pirates, and we knew that men were killed for defending their daughters or wives. We had also heard stories about a flimsy boat full of refugees that was struck and sunk by a boat manned by Thai pirates; all the members of the family were drowned except the husband, who washed ashore on a piece of wood from their broken boat.

I fully understood that the road ahead of us would be difficult and fraught with danger. We needed to see that reality and face it head on. Our success depended upon secrecy, so my wife didn't even mention our plans to her parents. We told our children about our plan to move to another province where we would have rice to eat daily and would no longer have to mix cassava and sweet potatoes, and they were very happy with that news. We didn't, however, tell them anything about our plan for leaving the country, for they were too young to know.

My wife then contacted the village chief of police to ask him what we needed to do to get the paperwork together for moving to another province legally. The police chief explained to my wife that the government policy was to limit moving from rural areas to the city such as Saigon or Hanoi, and there was no limitation on people moving from one province to another. After she got home from the village office, she said the police chief issued a warning, thinly veiled as a joke, about our moving to Rach Gia. He admonished that we shouldn't even think about escaping the country because the government had watchful eyes on the entire coast and had naval forces mounted throughout Vietnam's coastal territory. If we were caught leaving the country, we would lose everything. He said that they had such tight control that even a mosquito couldn't get through. My wife told him that we knew all of this and that it was not our intention to leave the country. He didn't demand outright a bribe to process the paperwork, but we knew with certainty that there would be a cost associated with the work and any effort he put into this task, so my wife promised that she wouldn't forget his help.

After we got the approval for moving, we put our house up for sale. I had initially thought that the house was worth about three taels of gold, but its wooden planks had been eaten by termites and the tin roofing sheets were rusty and damaged at many places, so buyers only offered two taels of gold. We spent one fourth of a tael of gold for the cost of paperwork, and then we were ready to pack up our belongings.

Unfortunately, amidst preparations for the move that we hoped would be the family's first step towards freedom, a sudden danger loomed. About two weeks before the planned departure date, I contracted dysentery from eating contaminated green vegetables. Since we didn't have any medication, I used some of the herbs collected from our backyard. However, the remedy didn't work, and I suffered constant acute stomach pain and was forced to sit in the restroom for hours. We wanted to leave the village as planned, so I decided to contact a local male nurse, who used to treat people with colds or minor cuts, to get a shot, hoping it would help alleviate the pain. Instead, a few hours after getting the shot, the pain intensified. Now, not only could I not defecate, I couldn't urinate either. This problem persisted for at least a week, during which time I couldn't eat anything, my skin turned an unhealthy yellow, and I lost weight becoming very weak. However, we had to leave because our house had already been sold. We had only a few bags of clothes, which at least were not hard to carry. We put them all on the bus, and on the bumpy road to Saigon, my wife and daughter got very motion sick. They started to throw up and couldn't even sit up straight, so they both leaned on me. My other kids were too small to offer any help. I had not eaten for more than a week, so I was very weak, and I thought I would be dead by the time we got to Saigon.

When we finally arrived at the bus station in Saigon, I was completely exhausted. I couldn't walk anymore and my wife had to call a cyclos to take me to my friend's house while she followed with the kids, since we would not all fit. Upon seeing me, my friend was fearful that I would die. He immediately took me to a medical doctor who had practiced under the former regime and who still had an office. After the examination, he gave me a shot. He told my friend to take me to the hospital right away if I didn't feel any better or urinate within the next few hours. My friend's house was small, so he put me on a military cot next to the restroom. Like a miracle, two hours after the injection I was able to urinate for the first time in so many days. At that moment, I knew that I would not die.

My friend had to report to the area police of our temporary presence, and I had to stay there a few days while I recovered, but the area police officer kept appearing at the house to demand we leave as soon as possible.

We wanted to stay a few more days, but we just couldn't stand the persistency of the area police officer, so we left for Rach Gia after three days in Saigon. It was impossible to predict how long we were going to stay in Rach Gia province since we didn't know when our boat would be finished or whether or not we would be able to successfully get to Thailand, where we planned to land.

With this in mind, we wanted to stretch our money, spending as little as possible, so we rented a relatively cheap place to stay where we all had to sleep on the floor on plastic mattresses. Compensating for the lack of a place to sleep, we didn't have to eat manioc, cassava, or corn every day. Instead, our daily meal had now been upgraded to a slightly larger quantity of rice supplemented with small, local fish and tiny shrimp, and in order to supplement the vegetables, my wife and kids picked some of the edible greens in nearby fields. Our children were happy with the amount of rice we had for them to eat, and our youngest son even asked me, "Dad, why didn't we move to this place a long time ago?" I just laughed with him and said that we had obviously made a mistake back then. I wanted my children to go to school, but they weren't allowed to attend until we became residents of the area, a process that would take some time.

After getting my family resettled, I contacted Manh and his friends to talk about the upcoming project. This project would have to start from the ground up, and Manh had spent all of his financial resources to build the last boat, so his funds were depleted. All of his relatives had been local residents who did work related to the fishing industry, so for them to build a boat had not been too difficult and didn't attract the attention of the authorities. However, his family was gone, and it would be impossible for him to start anything remotely resembling the work that his family had done at the same location. Anyone who built a boat without permission in this coastal province would be in trouble, and the boat would immediately be confiscated. Besides the shortage of money, determining the best location for building a boat was important, as it needed to avoid the attention of the authorities but still offer a route to the sea. The location of the building site alone could make or break our attempt. We realized that it wouldn't be possible to have it built in this province or near the coast, where the government was on the lookout for such escape attempts. We also realized that there would be a great deal of obstacles and challenges to consider in this seemingly impossible decision.

I had a chance to meet all the members of this team, and we brainstormed the selection criteria for the building site. I then asked Manh to use a sampan to take me to different locations that he thought were good candidates. I had nearly drowned once when I was a student and that left me terrified of deep water, but now I had no other choice but to live with it daily from now until the day we would reach our destination.

While we were in a sampan, Manh asked me, "Brother Hai, are you comfortable traveling through these canals and waterways?"

"Not really," I admitted.

This was my first time on the sampan, which had an outboard motor, cruising along the river, sitting in the open air while the wind whipped into my face, and the immensity of the surroundings gave me a sense of freedom. Despite my fear, it was fun to see the scenery along the canals and deep rivers. Farmers each had a little, simple shed built along the riverbank used for watching over their ducks, which ate the freshwater shellfish and insects in the rice fields. There were farmers manually harvesting their ripened rice crops, and the entire surroundings were filled with waves of lustrous gold rice fields all the way to the horizon. Boys were sitting idly on the backs of the buffaloes, singing. It was a beautiful and idyllic picture of the countryside of Vietnam. Wistfully and longing to stay in Vietnam, my beloved country, I reminded myself of the time I had spent working hard in the tea fields. How much could I enjoy the fruit of my labor? I received next to nothing for it, and it was probably the same for all of these farmers.

Manh suddenly interrupted my reverie, commenting with a smile, "You are in deep thought."

"They're beautiful," I said.

"You mean the young girls harvesting the rice?" he teased.

"No, I am talking about the yellow rice paddy field, the buffaloes, the shed, the ducks," I responded, gesturing to encompass it all.

"They are," he agreed.

"I wish I hadn't tasted the goodness of freedom and didn't know anything about democracy. Then I wouldn't yearn for anything higher than what those farmers in the field have here in Vietnam now," I said with sadness.

"Well, I don't know how we came to this pass, but hopefully by working together we can achieve our wishes," he said.

"I do hope so, too."

We took all day to visit different areas that Manh thought were good candidates. I marked all of these areas on a map so that I could afterwards ask him a few questions about their demographic information. We presented all of the relevant information to the group at our meeting, and after a long debate, we decided to choose a small hamlet located in the Can Tho province. Even though it was far away from the coast, it is connected to the sea through a series of canals and rivers. The canal leading to the hamlet was not big enough for a large boat, but it was big enough for us.

The main reason we chose this location was because Manh had distant relatives living in the area, and he could contact them and used them as the connection with the local officials. We learned afterwards that all of the local residents were pineapple farmers, and they were all South Vietnamese, which was a benefit for us because the culture in the South made for people who were simple, mindful of their own business, and didn't pay much attention to other people's business.

Our building site chosen, we turned to the many other tasks we needed to accomplish in order to reach our goal of building a small but seaworthy boat. The first step was to raise money. The base of Manh's relatives and friends had dwindled to the point that he wasn't able to raise any money at all. The other team members were young and inexperienced in this field, so they agreed to assign the task of raising money to me.

Manh was responsible for contacting his relatives to make connections with the local officials and arranging to have the boat built. I had a very lengthy discussion with Manh and other members about a critical danger we would face, the risk of being attacked by Thai pirates when we were at sea. If the pirates who so often preyed on refugees boarded our boat, we would be defenseless, and the women and young girls would be raped. We were also aware that on many occasions, small boats of refugees were struck and sunk by the Thai pirate fishing boats, and I couldn't stand to see that happen. We needed to carry at least a rifle with small amount of ammunition to protect ourselves from pirates and also to fight back in case of being attacked by the Communist forces. They all agreed with me on this issue, but they all said that at this stage of the project it wasn't on our high-priority list.

I was new to this province and town; the majority of my relatives and friends lived in Saigon and Huong's hometown, so I had to travel to these two places to raise money. For a small fee, I was able to obtain travel permission from the authorities in my new residence.

I tried to persuade friends and relatives to participate in this trip because it was genuine, and I also explained to them that I was one of the people organizing the trip and that we would try our best to get everyone out, including my family. I didn't guarantee them that this trip would absolutely be successful because there were other factors beyond our control, but one thing I knew for sure was that it was real and I stood behind it.

We needed about twenty taels of gold just to cover the cost of building the boat, so we calculated that for overall expenses we needed fifteen people, each contributing two taels of gold. With this amount of gold we would be able to start the project right away. However, convincing people to contribute was extremely difficult. Paranoia ruled. People trusted no one, and they only put down their money when they personally saw the boat. There were a few friends who had worked with me when I was in Saigon before its fall, still trusting me, and they gave me some money to start the project. The trip wasn't a total success. I was only able to get four taels of gold, but I believed it was worth the effort.

I brought the money back, and I told Manh that I would contribute one tael of gold I currently had from selling my house, and that we should be able to start the building process soon.

We had to find out whether Manh's relatives were willing to help us with this project and how close the relationship was that they had with the local officials. We learned that as this was a small hamlet. They had a limit on the number of staff paid to manage the local government, so that the most active person in this hamlet was the police officer. Through Manh's relatives we learned that this Officer Den was a twenty-eight-year-old man with a wife and two kids, and that he was a farmer, born and raised in this area. He was a draft-dodger under the former regime, so when the Communists took over the hamlet after 1975, they sent him to training and made him a police officer. He was an uncomplicated individual who should be quite easy to please. Manh introduced me to his relatives as an official from the transportation department of the Kien Giang province. Under the Communist regime, anyone could be an informant. We couldn't trust anyone, not even Manh's more distant relatives. I had to play this concocted role the best I could, and I told them that, like any other agency of the government, we prided ourselves on our self-sufficiency and therefore wanted to increase the living standard of our employees by providing them with food and other commodities that were bought directly from the local producing unit.

Few roads existed in this area, and the chief means of travel in the region was by waterway. In order to go into the hamlet to buy goods from farmers, we needed to have a good-sized boat. We claimed that our agency didn't have a lot of money, so we were looking for the most economical way to build it. This region had a lot of good wood at reasonable price plus good carpenters who could help to do the work, and we told them that those were the reasons we had chosen this area.

We hadn't met Officer Den as yet, but in order to impress Manh's relatives, I had to dress like an official. I wore wrinkled khaki pants, an olive shirt, a khaki jacket, and, of course, a pair of sandals made from discarded rubber tire, and I didn't forget to carry a bag with strap hanging across my shoulder made from khaki material. I supposedly carried all the important papers in this bag for the agency. Even though I didn't smoke, to make myself look more like a Communist cadre I had to carry with me some domestic tobacco made by the tobacco cooperative from Hanoi and a stack of thin paper for rolling a cigarette. I had to practice how to roll a cigarette smoothly before I met Manh's distant uncle.

While sitting in a chair and talking to him, I rolled up a cigarette using the tobacco and paper I carried into a beautiful cigarette, and I sealed it with my saliva. I invited him to have one, but he refused because he was not a smoker. I lighted up my cigarette and used my right thumb and index finger to hold it. I had a puff and spat on the floor like any other Communist cadre. Despite my age of twenty-nine, I looked forty because I was very thin and dark, and I tried to heighten this effect by behaving in a very mature manner.

Manh laughed so hard when I asked him afterward about my acting, declaring, "You could be an actor! Your accent was just like them!" My past run-ins with the authorities were paying off.

We prepared a letter from the fictitious head of our agency to introduce us to the local government and request their support so we could accomplish our task accordingly. One of our friends had a good hand, and he used a sweet potato to carve a stamp like the agency used, and amazingly it looked exactly like the real one when we stamped it on the letter. Once we forged the signature of the appropriate authority, the letter was ready for delivery. We were saved by the fact that they didn't have a sophisticated system of communication; had they possessed one, we would have been arrested at the onset.

We didn't have a chance to meet Officer Den right away, so Manh gave money to his uncle and asked him to give some money to the police officer as a gift along with a copy of the letter from our agency. We didn't forget to tell the uncle to relay a message of appreciation from our boss.

We also asked the uncle to look for the best carpenter for us, one who had good experience in building boats. We met this carpenter and discussed with him our intention to build a riverboat to carry goods for our agency, but claimed that we occasionally went to the sea, so the hull had to be tall and a little sharp. We also wanted him to choose the best woods for the structure and frame of the boat, and we wanted to inspect the wood before it was delivered to the building site. We provided the schema and clear specifications for the boat; we also discussed the timeframe for completion and the costs. Manh's uncle would hold all the funds; he would provide the necessary financial support to the carpenter as needed and would also let us know when the police officer wanted to talk to us or if he wanted extra money.

The boat building was started on the fifth of April, 1980, and we planned to complete it in six months. I traveled back and forth to this site twice a month to check on the progress and also to find out if there were any signs of malicious behavior on the part of the local government. I had to take a bus to go from Rach Gia to Can Tho, and from here it took me almost four hours by sampan, manually operated, to navigate the waterway to the worksite. We hadn't yet faced with major obstacles or problems while the boat was being built, except a request for additional money from the police officer.

I also traveled to Saigon frequently to look for additional funding and also to buy binoculars, a sea compass, and a few pairs of military uniforms with full ensign and ranking which would be used later in our plans.

When completed, the boat would be fourteen meters long and three meters wide, and with a boat of that size we needed to install a relatively big engine. We had put in a request for a machine shop in Saigon to order for us a marine engine that was big and strong enough for our boat. Besides spending money for all the materials for the boat, we also needed to spend money to lubricate the system to get the proper papers to move the engine and other peripherals to the building site.

By the time the boat's wood structure was completed, our engine was also ready for installation. We had to hire four mechanics to move the engine from Saigon down to the worksite, and it was an overwhelming task. The mechanics had to stay on the worksite for two weeks to install and test to make sure the engine worked as expected, and I had to be there to verify that all the work had been done as specified. While the mechanics were installing the engine, the carpenter filled all the gaps between the wood planks with some kind of special caulking materials to seal the cracks off.

After seven months, all of the work had been finished, the engine installation had been completed, all of the cracks had been sealed, and the fuel tank had been put in place. We informed Officer Den that the project was complete and the boat was ready to be moved to a canal. The police officer hadn't said a word while the boat was being built; all he wanted was to get some money from us. Now that the boat was ready for launching, he gave Manh's uncle an order to keep the boat out of the water. He ordered that it remain on dry dock, and according to him, this was an order from his boss who was head of the District Communist Party.

We asked Manh's uncle to set up a meeting for us to discuss this critical issue with him, and during this meeting, we explained to him that we needed to have the boat back to our agency as soon as possible. We argued that it wouldn't be beneficial to any of the government agencies if the boat were to stay on dry dock because its planks would be cracked by the heat, and no one wanted to damage the people's property. We also informed Manh's uncle that we would offer Officer Den more money if he agreed to have the boat moved to a little canal next to the house. We finally were able to successfully persuade him to give us permission to move the boat to the canal, and he said that he would accompany the boat with us to report to his boss before we took the boat back to our agency.

We wouldn't have the opportunity to fill the gas tank and we also didn't want to heighten his suspicions, so we had the oil dumped into the tank at night. We needed to have the tank at least two thirds full; we estimated that with that much diesel we would have enough to get to international waters. We had a female team member who quietly dumped two gallons of diesel into the tank every night. It took her almost two weeks to get the tank half full, and we planned to carry with us four additional twenty-liter containers of diesel. Once we received notification from her that the oil tank had enough diesel, we contacted Manh's uncle and asked him to report to the officer the date that we would like to bring the boat to see his boss.

We pretended to be happy with his suggestion that he would go with us to meet his boss on our way out. Obviously, we absolutely didn't plan to meet his boss, and we all knew very well that we would definitely be arrested if we brought our boat to the office of the district chief.

Our relatives, friends, and foodstuffs were placed in two sampans, which were positioned along the river where we would pick them up on our way to the sea, provided we got all of these obstacles cleared up.

All six members of our group dressed up in the uniforms of the Communist troops, and I always wore my khaki uniform as a Communist cadre. One of our members had the job of securing weapons, but he was not able to acquire any, and at the last moment, he gave us an old M-16 rifle without the heat shield. We thought it was not wise to bring it onto the boat because Officer Den would suspect that we weren't from a legitimate government agency.

Upon our arrival, the police chief greeted us at Manh's uncle's house and we presented to him a letter with the appropriate signature and seal from our agency asking for assistance from all the local authorities to expedite the boat retrieval process.

Manh's relatives had a small party to celebrate the completion of the project and to bid farewell to the boat. Since I had a lot of work ahead of me, I only drank moderately as a courtesy, and I used the opportunity to talk to Officer Den about the policies of the Communist Party and the dictatorship of the proletariat. I didn't know whether he understood all that I said, but then again I myself didn't know what I had talked about; all I did was to repeat what I had read in the state-run newspaper. I just fooled him because I knew he hadn't graduated even from the elementary school.

While we were eating, Manh's aunt pulled him aside to ask whether our group was from a legitimate government agency. He told me about this before we stepped into the boat, and this raised a grave concern in me. Though she was a naïve farmer, she was able to detect us. How could we fool an experienced police officer? My mind was constantly occupied with her suspicion, and I wondered whether Officer Den had already set into place a plan to catch us and was merely biding his time.

We took the boat out on Friday, November 14, 1980, and our group consisted of one former Navy SEAL, three former ARVN soldiers, Manh, and me. We all stepped into the boat at six o'clock in the evening with Officer Den.

Den had a .45-caliber pistol tucked in his belt, which I pretended not to notice. Manh's uncle also wanted to tag along, and we couldn't refuse him without appearing suspicious. Officer Den chose a seat at the best position on the boat's stern, where he had a broad view of the boat. He casually pulled out his pistol to load a bullet into the chamber and then tucked the gun back inside his belt. He didn't say a word, but his face looked very serious.

Manh made a final check to make sure that everyone was on board, and then he asked the operator to move the boat along the small canal to the Cai Lon River. It was so narrow that we had to move the boat very carefully at a snail's pace. At this speed, it would take us at least an hour before we reached the river, which in comparison to the canal was very large and deep. Our plan was to stop the boat in the middle of the river, pretending that the engine had a problem and needed to be fixed. We would then hit the officer with a hard piece of wood in the back of his head, take his gun, tie him up, and put him in the boat's cramped cabin until we got to the river mouth. Once we reached the sea safely, we planned to give him an inner tube from a tire. We didn't want blood spilled on our boat, and we didn't intend to kill him because we knew he also had a wife, children, and parents waiting for him at home. Manh's uncle wouldn't be a big problem because he was old and would probably be very scared when we beat up the police officer.

When we were about a half a kilometer from the Manh's uncle's house and were slowly cruising along the canal, I heard the distinct, unmistakable sound of gunshots.

"Stop. Stop right away," Officer Den ordered firmly.

I went cold. After a few interminable moments of numbness, I managed to regain my composure enough to respond naturally.

"What's happening, comrade?"

"Stop," he demanded again.

From a thick bush of water coconut on the right bank of the canal, a man dressed in black suddenly jumped on the boat carrying an M-16 rifle. He immediately moved to the bow of the boat and sat down as if he already had prior instructions. His position mirrored the police officer's perfect watching seat at the stern. With these two advantageous positions and their combined firepower, the men had the ability to control the entire boat. The man said nothing, and Officer Den acted as if nothing were out of the ordinary. He said casually that the man who had just jumped on the boat was the leader of the guerilla squad working for the hamlet.

We were caught by total surprise and knew we needed to change our tactics quickly to deal with the new situation. However, we also needed to avoid any discussion that attracted their attention and suspicion. Based on the way he had arranged for the two of them to take the most advantageous positions on the boat, we had no doubt that Officer Den had a plan to capture us or to thwart our intentions to bring the boat to sea, so we needed to act quickly and prudently before they rounded us up.

While the boat was slowly moving along the canal, I watched the shores with trepidation, fervently hoping no more guerillas with weapons would jump aboard.

We reached the river at about seven o'clock. We saw lights from houses on both banks, which was concerning because we didn't want anyone to hear in case a protracted fight broke out. When the boat reached the center of the river, the engine suddenly burped a couple of times then stopped. Manh pretended to be upset, asking the mechanic, "What the hell is going on?"

"I think the oil pump has a problem. Let me check it out," the mechanic replied loudly.

I went down to the engine room and whispered the new plan to Manh, which we had communicated above deck with subtle gestures. The SEAL and I would handle the guerilla; Manh and other guys would handle the police officer. The mechanic lowered the anchor and pretended to work on the engine problem as the SEAL and I struck up conversation with the guerilla at the bow. We waited for about fifteen minutes, until in the dark the SEAL gave me a signal then elbowed the guerilla hard in the chest, throwing him off balance.

Swearing furiously, the guerilla shouted, "What is this, Den?" There was no time to lose. I threw myself on him, desperate to pull the M-16 rifle from him. He was stronger than I expected. I strained as hard as I could at the gun in his hands, but I couldn't yank it away from him. He got the gun around to point the barrel at my face, and I had to continuously move around him to keep him from getting a clear shot while I grappled for the gun. My only saving grace was that he had to dodge and block the punches from the SEAL, so he couldn't get his hand on the trigger.

Once my friends heard the yell, they struck Officer Den in the back of the head with the wooden stick we had just for this purpose. He immediately jumped into the river, and one of our team members was able to pull the gun off his belt. A member of our team then pointed the captured pistol at the guerilla's head and said, "Let the gun go or I blow your head off." The guerilla took a good look at the pistol, then let his gun go and jumped off the boat into the river. We saw them swimming to the bank, but we didn't want to kill anyone, so we let them go.

Manh turned to his uncle. "I guess you know what this is all about now. We're leaving the country, heading for open ocean and then Thailand. Do you want to swim ashore, too? We won't keep you here if you don't want to come with us."

The older man shook his head. "I'll stay."

We felt relieved that we had rid ourselves of the armed men without a gun going off once. We hurriedly retrieved the anchor and restarted the engine, then set the bow towards the sea. We were planning to pick up our friends and relatives on the sampans moored downstream on our way to the sea. As soon as we took off, a fast-moving boat approached. This new boat had floodlights so bright they made the entire section of the river behind us as bright as day. We thought that it was the river police patrol boat, so we moved as quickly as we could to escape from being caught. The boat appeared to pursue us for about four kilometers before it stopped.

When the boat following us cut its engines, I asked Manh if we were going to pick up our family and friends. Manh said, "We passed the point where we were supposed to pick them up."

"Are you serious?" I was in disbelief.

"Yes, brother Hai. I am very sad, too, but we can't return. It's too dangerous," he said with sadness.

"You mean...you mean?" That was all I could say. The words wouldn't come. My whole body turned cold, and my mind was paralyzed with shock. I sat flatly on the deck, saying nothing. My family was back there, just a few kilometers upstream, and now I might never see them again.

Catatonic, I was sitting on the deck, when Manh tapped on my shoulder, sat beside me, and said, "Brother Hai, I know that you are in shock and pain. I was separated from my family, too. I was the one left behind with my family in the boat. But I want you to know that this was absolutely beyond our control. You and I know we were planning to pick them up, but we had to focus on our current situation. If we were captured, we would have been executed."

"I understand, but I don't know when I can see my family again…my children…they are too young," I managed.

"Believe me, I understand. But for now, the only thing left is to keep moving forward," Manh said.

Regardless of my grief, the boat continued implacably towards the sea. We got close to mouth of the river at about eight thirty, but it was so dark we didn't see much of anything, and neither of us knew this area well. Somehow, the alluvium that sheltered part of the deck got wedged against something spanning the river.

Since the boat was not heavy and the water was not too deep, we were able to hop into the river and push and pull the boat until we cleared the obstruction, which was invisible in the darkness. We reached the coast without further incident by nine. As soon as we entered the sea, it began to rain heavily, and a big wave lifted the boat up at least five meters and then dropped it down forcefully. As we pitched in the rough waves, immediately four people on the boat doubled over with seasickness. They had to lie down below decks while the rest of us had to fight the waves to get out. This was the first time I had been on the sea, let alone rough seas, but I was not seasick so I worked along Manh and the SEAL, managing the boat to get out into deeper waters. However, the waves did not subside. They grew even bigger as we navigated further from the coastline; the violent waters lifted the boat up in the air ten or fifteen meters high and slammed us down to the trough between the towering waves. Water splashed all over the bow and ran toward the stern of the boat each time a wave struck. Water started to enter the engine room and cabins, and the boat was rocked up violently. It was dark and we couldn't see anything, so we had to move very slowly to avoid hitting rocks or the coral reef.

There was little we could do. We were very hungry, as we hadn't eaten anything all day. All we had were a few sausages, so we put a couple of them on the muffler to cook and shared them among the three of us who were well enough to eat. We saved the rest for the other four since we didn't have anything else to eat on the boat. Through it all, we struggled with the waves. The boat pitched violently up and down all night, and the waves were so big that we were afraid that the boat would capsize or break apart.

The four men who were seasick vomited in the cabins and on the deck, often unable to make it to the edge of the deck to throw up over the side. They couldn't eat anything, and they lay motionless, exhausted from the ongoing ordeal. The wind and rain relentlessly pushed the boat back toward the shore despite our efforts to move out to international waters. Any time the boat was hit by a big wave, it sharply veered off course, and we heard ominous creaking and grinding noises from the planks. We continued like this for days, making little or no progress.

As time went on, the rain grew heavier, the wind grew stronger, and the waves grew bigger. We were soaked from both rainwater and seawater and cold to the bone. Worse still, we were so hungry after three days of eating nothing that we debated among ourselves whether or not we should return to shore. Going out to deep sea was impossible, but coming back to shore was no less dangerous because we had to face with the tremendous risks of being arrested. We decided to put it to a vote. We roused the men who were laying in a seasick stupor and voted by a show of hands. Of our group of six, three were for continuing on, and three voted to turn back. We were no closer to making a decision. Manh, however, explained to us that with the experience he had from working with his family as fisherman, he didn't believe that we would be able to make it to international waters in our flimsy boat under these stormy conditions, so he urged us to return to shore, and we finally all agreed with him.

Once we turned the boat around, our way was unhindered. Had we made such good time on our way out, we would have already reached international waters days before.

The local governments of the coastal provinces knew that this time of the year the sea was very rough, so they had police and guerillas guarding the shore, waiting to arrest people who turned back because of bad weather. We knew that we needed a plan to avoid capture at the coast, but it was difficult for us to think straight under this intense pressure, cold and hungry as we were. Somehow, we needed to come up with a way to get out of this alive and uncaptured.

Manh's uncle was another big problem that we had to take care before the boat was docked or abandoned. We couldn't take him along with us because he would possibly reveal to the police our illegal activities, but we didn't want to kill him either. I told Manh to give him some sleeping pills for now. He would be so drowsy by the time we got to shore that we could harmlessly leave him on the boat while we disembarked. Meanwhile, we sat around and discussed our options. One of the ARVN veterans began.

"When we reach the checkpoint, we need to surprise the police and guerrillas. We have a gun. I say we use it. It's dark and rainy, so we can catch them by surprise. We wait until we get close enough to shore, then one of us will shoot at them. While they're reacting, we'll scatter and run. Some of us may be captured, but I think it's the best chance we have."

The ex-SEAL shook his head. "With one M-16 rifle and a pistol? And barely any ammunition? We wouldn't stand a chance. We don't want to get in a firefight with these guys."

Manh said, "I agree. Worse, we have no place to hide, and the local agents know the area well. They would catch up with us eventually. No, we need a more creative and flexible tactic. I don't think you're wrong to suggest using the gun, however. I just don't think we should shoot it."

"What is your take on this?" I asked.

"Well, you know that no civilians are permitted to own weapons. That makes it risky for us to let the police know that we have guns, but we can also turn it to our advantage. Brother Hai, don't forget that we are dressed as members of the transportation department," Manh said with a smile. "All we need to complete the disguise is some prisoners."

Four of our guys volunteered to take off their shirts; they only wore a pair of boxers and a T-shirt apiece to pretend that they were the suspected escapees.

By the time we got close to shore, through the fog we could see a few spots of light from houses lying at the edge of the village. At about three o'clock, we stopped the boat a few hundred meters from the shoreline and checked to make sure Manh's uncle was asleep;

then we all jumped into the water to walk to the village. The water was deep, up to my chin, and I didn't know how to swim. Others had to help me wade through the waves to shore. It was so quiet that we were able to hear the groan of insects, the noise of our wading through the water, and especially the *ribbit, ribbit* of frogs everywhere.

We then walked along the trail toward the village, and as soon as we reached the perimeter, dogs started to bark, only a few at the beginning, but gradually all the dogs along the trail were barking. My heart was beating out of rhythm, and I guessed the others were probably equally anxious. The atmosphere was quite heavy since we kept absolutely silent, focusing on how to persuade the people mounting the checkpoint to let us through. We all agreed that we would only shoot at the men and run in case we faced with a big problem or they tried to engage in a dispute.

I held the pistol; Manh held the M-16 rifle and walked behind the other four. We walked in the dark for almost an hour along the trail until we got to the checkpoint mounted by the young guerillas in the village. As we approached, we began to kick and shove the other four, hitting them with the butts of our guns and threatening to kill them if they ran.

The ramshackle bamboo hut that served as the checkpoint was now clearly visible on the right side of the pathway, and a bamboo post was mounted on a tree trunk spanning across the pathway to create a gate about five meters from checkpoint. The bamboo post would only be lifted up for people to go through after they were cleared by the guerillas guards. We knew that we would be able to fool them because they were young, naïve, and uneducated, and, more important still, they didn't have a sophisticated system of communication and worked independently of other agencies or organizations. We wanted to make sure that neither Manh nor I betrayed any sign insinuating to them that we were illegal escapees. We showed them our authority by walking directly to the gate without asking them for permission.

With a firm voice, Manh commanded one of our friends disguised as an escapee, "Quickly lift up the gate." As soon as he touched the bamboo post, we heard a loud, angered voice from one of the guerillas

"M——, stop." I also heard the clicking sound of bullets being loaded into a rifle chamber.

Manh turned around, approaching the checkpoint, and asked one of the guerrillas who appeared to be in charge, "What's the problem, comrade?"

"You get my permission?"

"What permission?" Manh asked.

"Permission to get in or out of our hamlet," the guerilla growled.

"I thought permission was for private citizens or people living in the hamlet, not for government officials like us who are on a very important mission," Manh retorted.

"Who are you and what are you doing here?" asked the guerilla.

"We are from a special unit of the department of transportation of this province, and we arrested these four civilians who are betraying the people and Party not only by leaving the country, but also by aiding others trying to leave the country," Manh said firmly.

"Any papers to show that you are officials?" asked the guerilla. The other two were still holding weapons pointed at us.

"It was an emergency. We had to jump the gun to get this done, otherwise they would have already escaped the country," Manh explained.

"Why didn't you contact the police on this?" the guerilla asked.

"Police? We couldn't even report to our agency's highest Party leader, let alone the police. Accordingly, we will report to them afterward. Would you look for your leader to ask for permission to arrest a robber committing an atrocity? No. You would have to arrest him right away and report later. Right? " Manh said.

"But cooperating with the police is the right way," the guerilla protested, sounding uncertain for the first time.

"There are many agencies that are much more powerful than the police, but I don't blame you for not knowing this. Did you read the recent ordinance by the province chairman stipulating all local and provincial units must assist any special units arresting the betrayers of the people and Party, and outlining a punishment for those who obstructed them or failed to aid them?" Manh asked, conspicuously showing the rifle he held.

"No, comrade." The guerilla's earlier blustery authority was gone, replaced by fear.

"Yes, we are comrades. And you and I, we only do this for the Party and for the people. I had to go through so much pain to get this done. These guys will be prosecuted before the people's court, and you are part of this successful operation. I will give your name to a provincial committee for an award," Manh said with a smile while writing the name of the guerilla in charge. To make the things more real, Manh asked for the name of his unit.

After our exchange, they agreed to let us go through the checkpoint, and we all felt a wave of relief. We disassembled the M-16, put it in the bag, and called a three-wheeled motorized cyclos to get home. I got to my rented shack around six o'clock in the morning. My children were still asleep, but Huong had thought I was already gone, and she started to sob when she saw me. I asked her to calm down. We both knew it was highly dangerous if people in the area knew of our failed trip.

She saw blood on my right foot and asked me what had happened. I told her that I had walked barefoot on a rough trail and might have stepped on some sharp objects, but I didn't even know when and where. The cut was on the bottom of my right foot, and it was deep. It could be that I had been so nervous and focused on the task at hand that I hadn't even known what was happening around me or even to me. She boiled some water to wash the wound and ripped up my old T-shirt, wrapping it around my foot to stop it from bleeding.

There was no doubt in our minds that the government would send informants and undercover detectives throughout the region to look for us, and I was so fearful of being arrested that I stayed in bed for the whole week without eating anything. During this time, the wound in my foot became infected, but this was the least of my worries. I was consumed with fear for how the government would punish me when I was found.

We eluded the government's notice by staying inactive for at least two months to avoid being detected or recognized by the government's watchful eyes. We didn't meet or make contact with other members of our band of would-be escapees during this period to wait for things quiet down. All of the members of our team went home or left the area except Manh and me. We were the only two people who stayed behind because we didn't have any place to go.

Our family's savings had reached an all-time low, and my wife asked me to find a cheaper place to rent, as we couldn't afford any place in the city. We decided to move to the rural side where there were small cottages, which we could stay in temporarily for a small amount of rent. I would also be able to catch fish and shrimp in this area to supplement our daily meals. This hamlet had about hundred houses, and most of the poor people had cottages located on either side of a small shallow canal. I rented one of these cottages at an affordable price. This cottage was small; it had only room for one queen-sized bed and a cooking pit. Upon arriving at the new rental shack, Huong was extremely uncomfortable looking at the surroundings and the living conditions of the people in the area since she hadn't seen anything like it in her life.

"Is there any running water or wells in this area?" she nervously asked.

"I am afraid that there is no running water. I saw a well somewhere when I visited this area earlier. People living here are very poor. They can't afford the costs of bringing running water to the area," I softly and carefully answered.

"You mean.?" she asked with a raised voice.

"Yes, they wash their clothes, shower, clean their vegetables and fish in this canal," I said. She wrinkled her nose in disgust at the thought, and she quietly stood there looking into the distance for a few seconds. I knew what had just gone through her mind, but given our current financial constraints, we both knew there was no other choice.

She raised her eyebrow and said, "I didn't see a latrine anywhere."

"Except for the well-to-do families, all the poor people in this area don't have indoor latrines. They use the canal to defecate at night, and they also use it as a dumpster. You know when tide recedes, the water pulls everything in the canal with it to sea," I said.

"Disgusting!" she exclaimed.

"I am with you, but this is the only place that offers the lowest rent, and it's all we can afford for the time being."

Putting my family through these horrible living conditions wasn't my preferred choice, but in order to extend our time waiting for the trip, we all had to sacrifice.

My children now were mingling with all the children in this poor section of the hamlet. They jumped in the canal to swim like other kids, helped me to catch fish, and also accumulated dead coconut leaves for cooking. I wanted them to go to school, and despite our change in fortunes, our children behaved well, respected their teachers, and did well in school compared with other kids.

One afternoon, when I was sitting on the bank of the canal cleaning fish, my daughter came home from school and happily yelled, "Daddy, Daddy, I want to show you something!"

I knew it must have been very important to her, but I didn't turn around because both of my hands were very busy with a live little fish I had just caught.

"What?" I asked cheerfully.

She leaned on my back, showing me a new pencil, and said, "My teacher gave me this pencil as a reward for solving a math problem that my friends couldn't do!"

"Easy, don't lean too hard or I will fall into the canal," I warned, laughing. "Wonderful, show Mom the pencil! We will have fish for supper tonight."

She started singing "Nobody Loves Uncle Ho Chi Minh More Than Children," and she cheerfully walked to the cottage. I was happy to know that my daughter was doing well, but on the other hand I was also sad that I was not able to give them better environment to grow up in.

As soon as my son came home from school, he asked my daughter, "Where is Dad?"

"He is cleaning fish at the canal," she said.

He ran up to me and said, "Dad, guess what I got today?"

"A pencil?" I guessed with a smile.

"No, not a pencil. I got a certificate for being the best reader in my class," he said, puffing out his chest and showing me a piece of paper with big letters written by hand saying, "Reading bee."

"Well done! We will have fish for dinner tonight," I said.

"Fish! Yummy, yummy! I love fish," he said happily.

My children, however, were running into a minor problem: since they had a Northern accent, they were ridiculed a lot and complained to me that they were often laughed at by their friends when they talked.

The knowledge that my children were doing well in school pushed me even harder to find a place where they had the opportunity to see, to learn, to develop to their full potential, and a place like that could only exist in a country that had freedom, respect for democracy, and human rights.

A few days later, my wife stormed into the house, a basket full of wild, edible vegetables in her hand. I was sitting on a stool, rinsing some fish for our meal.

"I just can't stand to live here any longer!" she burst out. "It is just simply abominable, filthy! I have never lived in a place like this in my life! The water in the canal is literally full of human feces."

"What happened?" I asked cautiously.

"The canal was full of human waste today, and I had to wash vegetables in it, shower in it, and wash our clothes in it, in that stink," she replied, her voice pitched to break.

"You can use some fresh water I just bought in the big jar to rinse the vegetables or for anything you need," I offered.

"Do you know that the Cambodian monks at the nearby pagoda even dumped partially cremated human remains into the canal? The other day I saw a human skull in the canal while taking a bath, and I almost fainted! I was so scared that I immediately ran into the house. How much longer? Well, I don't think I can take it anymore!" she said with consternation clearly written on her face.

"Please understand…I know you and the children are suffering too much, but please stick with me and give me one more chance,"

I entreated. My older son jumped in to defend his mom. My other children piped up, too.

"They pick on us all the time in school. We left friends behind to come here…we're going home with Mom."

"I stay with Dad; my teacher likes me and nobody picks on me in school," my daughter said calmly.

My wife then turned around, looking directly at my daughter's face and asked in a dry tone of voice. "So you would rather stay with your father. Right?"

She looked down at her feet and mumbled, "But you stay…stay with Dad, too," tears suddenly streaming.

"If you and the three boys adamantly want to go back, then I can't stop you…I hope you are happy with your decision," I said brokenly.

I was very sad to see every day that our children had to live in this kind of unsanitary condition, but we had come a long way to get to this point. Since we had already anticipated that we would have to live in poverty and shortage if we failed, this shouldn't have been a surprise to us. For now, there was only one thing I could do, appeal to them for patience. They finally relented and agreed to stay along with me.

I started to see Manh again intermittently to discuss with him whether or not we should pursue our aspirations further. We realized that we didn't have any money on hand this time, and we would face with an uphill battle to raise money for the next trip.

We knew that the road before us was full of difficulties and challenges, but that wouldn't stop us from pursuing our goal of seeking freedom. We remembered a statement from one of the famous Vietnamese writers, Nguyen Ba Hoc, which said, "The road is difficult to walk on, not because of the mountains and the rivers, but because of the fear of the people to cross these mountains and rivers."

Manh's old high school friend who was working for the police forces informed him that the local government was launching a campaign aiming at arresting a group of people who had left a boat at the seaside, and this person didn't even know that Manh was one of the persons in the group being sought. In order to elude the relentless pursuit of the police, Manh temporarily hid at a different house about two kilometers from Hien's house, and this house had a tunnel connected to a neighbor's house so Manh would have an escape route in case there was a police raid. There were very few close friends who knew his new hiding place.

Despite being sought after, we still attempted to find way to contact each other to discuss the plan for our next project since we didn't have much time.

Anytime I wanted to meet Manh at his hiding place, I had to make sure that there was no one following me before I entered the house. I dressed in normal clothes for a farmer, walking with bare feet. I also carried an old straw bag in my right hand with fruits and some betel leaves, and I behaved like a farmer, bringing gifts from my own backyard to an elderly relative living in the city. One time when I walked into the house, Manh asked intensely, "Did you see anyone standing across the street in front of the house?"

"No, I didn't," I said.

"I looked through a hole in the wall earlier, and I saw a cyclos driver peddling up and down this street several times. It was very suspicious," he added. "They were very aggressive in looking for us, so Brother Hai, you need to be extremely cautious."

"If I ever saw an individual suspiciously loitering around, then I would walk right past the house," I said agreeably.

"You are probably thirsty. You walked a long way under the burning hot sun. You want some coconut water?" Manh said.

"Yes, thanks," I said.

"I hope it will quench your thirst. You had to carry a heavy bag, walking under the hot, burning sun," Manh teased, handing me a cup.

I raised the bag in the air and said with a laugh, "This bag is not heavy. It is my charm that is a burden, and I have to carry that everywhere I go."

"Well, take a few minutes' break to enjoy the fresh drink, and we will discuss what we need to do for the next endeavor," he said dryly.

He pulled out a piece of paper and a pencil and then sat next to me at the table, saying, "Brother Hai, I don't know whether you met our mechanic's family. His wife and four children were on a sampan moored along Cai Lon river waiting for us to pick them up. They were arrested by the police and detained for almost three months at the local jail."

"Did they say anything about us to the police?" I asked.

"Despite the interrogation, they didn't say anything about us because they didn't know much of anything about our trip. All they knew was that they were waiting for us on the sampan," he said with a deep sigh. "They have just gone back to Saigon."

"My wife told me that when she and my children stepped off the sampan to walk into the town, it was raining heavily and she saw the police and troops everywhere in heavy arms. She overheard that they were looking for some soldiers who had beaten up the police and stolen a boat earlier," I said, a chill running down my back.

"We left in time, thank God, and one more thing you would probably want to know: the boat that chased us when we were in the river was not a police boat at all. It was a civilian boat carrying pineapples! It was behind us, and it turned on the floodlight to let us know of its presence and also to avoid hitting us," he said. "We were in panic and nervous, so we just took off. Well, it was all God's will," he said sadly.

"Had we picked up everyone who was supposed to be on the boat, we would have been in deep trouble when we returned to shore because of rough seas," I realized.

"Honestly, I wouldn't even know how to deal with a situation like that," he said.

"Had that been the case, we would all have been arrested and executed," I said with concern.

We were keenly aware of the severe consequences we would face if we were arrested by the government, but our yearning for freedom was so intense that we couldn't sit idly and watch any opportunity for escape go by.

Manh, two remaining members from the group, and I reassessed our current financial status and our capability to start a new project. We also relied on members of our group who had access to the local government intelligence sources to find out details about how the government controlled the coast.

Manh said he still had about one half tael of gold's worth of money, which could be used for members to travel, but was not enough for doing anything else. The four of us didn't have a penny left, and we had to struggle every day to feed our families. The situation appeared to be very grim, so we decided to stop our discussion and agreed that we would go home and come up with ideas. Then we would meet again in three days. As much as I yearned to escape, I couldn't see any way that we could move forward without money.

Manh knew that I didn't live in town, so he gave me some money to buy a bus ticket. On my way walking to the bus station, I thought about my children, who were always waiting for me to come home, hoping to have something to eat. Instead of buying the ticket, I used the money to buy two meat submarines. I asked the seller to wrap them tightly with discarded newspaper, and then I put them in my straw bag and started running home. It was almost five o'clock, and I needed to get home before dark, so I ran until I was tired. I walked, then ran, then walked, then ran.

In order to get to my rented cottage, I had to cross a bamboo bridge spanning the canal. My children were always sitting in front of the cottage facing the bridge, waiting for me when I was away. It was almost seven thirty when I got to the bridge. It had begun to get dark, but just seeing my figure, my children immediately recognized me and yelled, "Dad is home, Dad is home!" They sprang right up to run for me. One held my arm, one pulled the hem of my shirt, and the other two jogged along behind me.

"Let's get home! I have some good food for you guys," I said, smiling.

They devoured the submarines much more quickly than I would have thought possible. I sat on the bed, watching them eat, and the scene made me love them even more. The failed meeting had left me depressed to the point that I just wanted to give up on escaping the country, but when I saw the skinny bodies of my children wrapped in old, tattered clothes, it pushed me to work harder for their future.

One day living in this hell seemed to be a year for me; however, three days had passed and I was supposed to meet Manh and other team members at his house at ten o'clock in the morning. I hadn't been eating much in the last few years, and my stomach seemed to be shrinking, so just one small root of boiled cassava would be sufficient for my breakfast. Instead of one, I took two boiled roots of cassava and a lemon, and I put them in my straw bag. I would eat one when I felt hungry and save one for lunch. I told Huong that I was on my way to meet Manh and that I would be home around five. She gave me a big hug then pressed a small amount of money into my hand for a bus ticket there, reminding me to take the bus home if Manh gave me some money.

I left home around seven that morning, crossed the bridge, and then started to run until I felt tired and hungry. I chose the shade of a big tree on the side of the road then sat down, leaning my back against the tree trunk. I opened my bag and started to savor my first cassava. It was sweet and so good when I was hungry. I finished it in no time and was still hungry. I wanted to eat the second one now, but then I wouldn't have anything for lunch. It was extremely hard to resist, but I decided to save the second one so I could have some energy, even a little, to run home this afternoon. I didn't have water, so I bit a chunk of the lemon. I didn't swallow right away, but I chewed on it for a while, and the sourness made my dry mouth excrete saliva. Over time, my waist had gotten smaller, so I used burlap from a discarded rice sack as a belt to keep my now-baggy pants up.

I got to the area of Manh's house fifteen minutes early. I looked around to make sure that there was no one around, and then I entered the house. Manh asked me whether I had eaten anything as yet. I told him I had had a breakfast of cassava and lemon.

"What a combination," he said with a smile.

"Well, they filled me up," I lied.

"I have cooked rice and simmering pork meat if you want to eat," he offered.

"Save it for lunch," I said reluctantly. "Where are the other two?"

"Only three of us are here today. Khang is with his friend, a police officer, eating breakfast," he said. I knew exactly what he meant, and I had a cup of cold water while waiting for the other member to get here.

Upon walking into the house, our friend said with a frightened voice, "Brother Hai and Manh, I wanted to tell you something I saw on my way to your house."

"What happened?" I asked nervously.

"Well, I saw a group about twenty-five to thirty men and women being tied together with a rope and forced to walk toward the street from the shore. The police kicked them and hit them with their rifle butts, forcing them to walk faster toward a bus waiting for them on the street. I heard that they were teachers from a local high school. They boarded a boat to flee the country last night, but unfortunately their boat got stuck on a sand bar at the river mouth, and they were arrested." He breathed rapidly as he talked.

"Everyone wants to leave the country," I said.

"Brother Hai, do you remember a famous Vietnamese comedian who said that a light post would also leave the country if it had legs?" Manh said lightly, laughing a little.

"Yes, and the rumor was that the government put the comedian in jail," I said sadly.

"He has been in jail for a few years now," he ruefully said.

The image of people being arrested and the stories of escapees being raped by Thailand's pirates, of course, concerned us quite a bit, but that wouldn't deter us from working toward our goal of leaving the country. There were so many things that we needed to do to get the project started. Sometimes, we thought we were magicians trying to make something out of thin air. Off the top of our heads, we knew that we needed money, we needed a location, and of courses a lot of details had to be discussed before we could put a plan together.

We couldn't answer most of our questions at the moment because we didn't know a lot of things, but there was one thing we knew for sure: we needed money very badly and we had strong determination. We didn't have abundant resources to set up a lofty goal; it had to be a humble plan with a small boat capable of carrying us across the sea from Vietnam's coast to the bay of Thailand. With that in mind, we only raised enough money to buy a small riverboat and reinforce the boat's frame to make it strong and stable enough to withstand small waves. The group agreed to give me the task of raising money again, and I grudgingly accepted it because this was a very demanding job, but I didn't think anyone else could handle it. Manh was responsible for searching for the location to build a boat, as before, and Khang would focus on securing weapons. Other members had the job of collecting information on the government's method of monitoring the escapees, and also to find out where was the best location for loading our friends and relatives. Those were the outlines of our tasks, but we needed to discuss more in detail how each of us would carry out our responsibilities.

After a long discussion, we had lunch. It was a good meal, and since I hadn't had pork for a long time, it seemed to have a different taste than I was used to. In order to avoid the attention of the neighbors, we didn't leave the house all at the same time, departing instead in half-hour intervals.

Manh knew that I didn't have money, so he again gave me some money for the bus ticket and again I didn't use it for the ticket. This time, I bought a dozen oranges. I put them in my straw bag and ran home. Though I smelled the sweet fragrance of the oranges all the way home, I resisted the urge to eat one, waiting to eat with my family. As I walked in, Huong was struggling to light up a fire to cook rice using the dried coconut leaves my children had brought. She didn't see me enter, and when she turned around she saw a shadow behind her. Huong was terrified, pulling back a step.

When she recovered and recognized me, she fondly said, "You devil, why you didn't let me know when you walked in?"

"You were busy stoking the fire! I have something to share with you," I said, grinning with anticipation. I pulled out a beautiful ripe orange. I started to peel off the skin, and the smell of the peel was utterly tantalizing. I broke the orange in half and gave her the bigger half. She took the proffered food but said she would save it for the children. I said, "Go ahead and eat it, I still have a lot more for them," and I showed her the bag full of oranges.

A few minutes later, juice running down her chin, she said, "It was sweeter than I remembered. When did we last have an orange?"

"Five years ago, if I am not mistaken," I said.

I was exhausted from running back and forth from my place to Manh's house, so I lay down on the bed for a moment until my kids came home, listening to Huong cooking. Though her cooking pit was right next to me, I still fell asleep as soon as I lay down, until my children woke me up when they got home from school.

They surrounded me and tried to pull me up so I could eat with them. I sat up and pleasantly told them, "You guys have been doing well in school and behaving very well, so I decided to reward you with something good." My youngest son was very quick to talk, so he piped up first.

"Candy. Right, Dad?"

"Not really, better than candy," I said, pulling from the bag four big oranges. Their eyes widened, and I gave one to each of them. They jumped up and down with joy and asked me if they could eat it now. I suggested that they have supper first and then they could have their orange.

Huong noticed me limping, and I saw the concern in her eyes. I told her my back hurt because I slept on the uneven dirt floor with just a plastic mattress, and in the morning when I woke up the back of my shirt was soaked with water because of moisture coming from the floor, and that made my back hurt badly. My right leg was almost paralyzed, so I limped when I walked. We had only one bed, which was used for my wife and our three young kids.

Huong found the courage to ask the owner of the nearby brick house to let my eldest son and me sleep on his cement veranda every night, offering to watch the house for him when he was not home. Once in a while he gave me a piece of pork meat or a few kilos of rice, but I didn't want to take them since even though I was poor, I was not a beggar. It was embarrassing to receive them, but he kept on insisting that I accept for our children and also in payment for watching over his house.

It was very painful to think back on the days when I was a manager of Group Health Insurance making good money, living in a beautiful home, and eating good food. Now we lived like beggars, sleeping on a stranger's veranda. Many sleepless nights I thought, *Is this how the life of our family ends up?* I knew that I could never return to the way things were in the past, but I also strongly believed that with hard work and determination, we would no doubt reach our goal someday of a better future.

After a few days, Manh and I met to discuss in detail how much money we needed to raise by adding up all the estimates for purchasing a river boat, dismantling and reinforcing the boat structure, purchasing a diesel engine and an outboard motor with propeller, and some miscellaneous costs. We estimated that the costs would be in the vicinity of eight taels of gold.

I set out to travel to Saigon to meet my friends and to explain our project to them. I faced with a lot of challenges because of the previous failed trip, but most of them understood that we were genuine in our efforts to organize the trip. Many of my friends said they didn't have a lot of money and truthfully so, because after several waves of currency changes by the government, not many people had any money left. However, they were willing to contribute a couple of taels of gold for a family of four and after four days of working in Saigon. I was able to bring back only four taels of gold, which was much less than what we had planned to raise. Nevertheless, for a civilian such as me to travel freely without interference or harassment from the government was unheard of, and after my uneventful trip to Saigon, we realized that our team members' groundwork for building relationships with the local government officials had born fruit.

I didn't have a safe place to keep the gold, so I didn't want to keep a large amount of gold in my hands overnight. I contacted Manh immediately upon returning to Rach Gia to give him the taels of gold I had collected. Now that we had some money, we needed to quickly get together to work on the project because every day we ran the risk of arrest. We decided to carry out two tasks simultaneously: purchasing a riverboat and securing a location for overhauling that boat. Since Manh knew the area well, he was asked to look for the location.

Khang and I would travel to the countryside to look for a boat. We didn't have much money, so we had to limit our spending and be careful with every penny we spent. With that in mind, we wanted to buy an old riverboat, but the wood planks had to be thick and relatively intact. As always, we needed to avoid attention from locals and officials, so we placed a big bamboo basket full of pineapples at the center of the sampan and scattered some of them here and there in the sampan to show people that we were merchants here to purchase fruit from local farmers to bring to the city to make a profit. Any time we saw a boat that appeared to meet our needs, we stopped to ask the owner if they wanted to sell, and we always offered a slightly high price to entice them, but not so much as to make them suspicious. We had seen many boats during three days of navigating throughout the canals and rivers of the region, but we had not found one that really met our needs. We speculated that people living in the deeper region of the countryside had built their boats a few years back, making them more likely to sell, and since those farmers didn't have a lot of money to buy an engine, some might leave a boat docked. Most of these boats were built with thick and durable wood planks, which would probably be suitable for us.

With that in mind, we went deeper inland and after a long day of searching, we found a boat docked at a canal in front of a house that appeared to meet our needs. We contacted the owner, who was a sugar cane farmer. He told us that the sugar refinery cooperative sent its boat to the farm to load sugar so he didn't need his own boat any longer; he wanted to sell the boat. He wanted two taels of gold, but we argued that the boat was old and had been in the water too long, so it might have problems with the wood. We said that we would need to spend a lot of money to fix it and to put in an engine, which was very costly, and with that we offered him one and a half taels of gold. He hesitated at first, but after he conferred with his wife, he agreed. We gave him a small deposit and told him that we would pay him in full when we came back to take the boat the next day.

Manh had a friend named Dien who lived on a Chin Trieu island on a big river in An Giang province. Most of the people living on this island were members of the Buddhist denomination called Hoa Hao, and they didn't get along with the current government because their leader had allegedly been killed by the Communists in 1947. Manh contacted his friend Dien and asked to have a boat disassembled and reinforced in the front yard of Dien's house. In return, Manh would give him four seats on the trip to flee Vietnam. Dien was interested, but said that he had to get permission from the local officials to have the boat docked and repaired in his front yard. Since the boat was a riverboat and this location was far away from the coast of Vietnam, we didn't have to worry about too much scrutiny from the government officials. Manh, however, had promised his friend that he would spend a reasonable amount of money to lubricate the system if needed. Manh informed us once Dien obtained permission from the local authorities, and since Manh had a better knowledge of the boat structure and material than any of us, we wanted him to go with us to retrieve the boat. We rented a sampan with a strong outboard engine, and all four of us went to the boat site to retrieve it.

After a thorough inspection of the boat, Manh said, "The outside layer of the planks appears to have minor decay, and it was probably in the water for a while, but overall it doesn't affect the quality of the wood."

We decided to go ahead with the purchase of this boat, and we also got a handwritten sales agreement from the owner. The rural parts of this region didn't have roads for cars or motorbikes, instead they had a dense system of canals and rivers, and their primary means of navigation and transportation was sampan or boat. The majority of the people had their houses built close to either a canal or a river so that they could utilize the waterway for their daily travel. There was a canal running in front of the boat owner's house, and he docked his boat in the canal. That made our job of retrieving the boat much easier.

It took us all day to bring the boat from Rach Gia through a series of canals and rivers to its destination. By the time we got to An Giang province, it was already dark; and our dry dock hadn't yet been built, so we had to leave it in the river until the next day, securing the boat by tying it to a trunk of a big tree.

In the application to the government, Dien requested permission to reinforce the frame of a riverboat and install an F10 Honda diesel engine inside of the boat. He also stated in the application that when the boat was complete, it would then be used to carry produce purchased directly from the farmers to the city for resale, and it would also provide transportation services to the local government on request. It seemed to be a simple request, but though the village chief had the authority to sign the approval letter in one day, he kept procrastinating. We wanted to have the permission as quickly as possible because we wanted the boat to be ready by the middle or end of March of next year. Manh wanted to spend some money to bribe him, but we needed a serious justification for the amount since we were facing a severe shortage of money.

Manh told us when we met, "Since our boat is not equipped for the ocean, we need to get out at the time when the sea is calm and peaceful, and the ideal timeframe is April. I want to spend a reasonable amount of money to lubricate the system so we can get the permission sooner. Would that be okay with everyone?"

"How much do you think we need to spend?" I asked.

"Maybe about one tenth's worth of a tael of gold," Manh said.

"It is too much, I think. We shouldn't give him too much, that would be counterproductive because he would wonder where your friend got so much money, and once he knew that your friend had money, he would ask for more. We could buy him a bottle of foreign whiskey and a couple cartons of foreign cigarettes, then ask your friend to put them in a bag and bring them to his house. I believe that will do the job," I suggested thoughtfully.

The group supported this idea, and we decided to offer the more modest bribe. We bought a bottle of Johnny Walker and two cartons of Samit cigarettes, and we put them in a bag. Then we asked Dien, Manh's friend, to bring the gift to the village chief's house, and if he was not home then give it to his wife. It worked like magic! Dien had a permit issued the next day. We now had permission to bring the boat to Dien's front yard and were no longer afraid of being harassed by the low-level cadres in the village.

Even though we had permission to work on the boat, the Communists were very unpredictable, so we decided to set aside a small amount of money in case further bribes were required in the future. Since we didn't plan to build the boat from the ground up, we didn't need a boat building specialist or comprehensive design plan;

all we needed was one or two good carpenters who knew how to fit the boat ribs neatly and solidly into the boat body and make some minor modifications.

Since Dien was born and raised in this village, he knew this area like the back of his hand, and he also knew everyone in the village. Like most people living in the rural villages of Vietnam, these villagers lived together very harmoniously and always loaned a hand to neighbors needing help. According to Dien, there were several carpenters in the village. However, he only trusted two men to do the job, carpenters who had diligently and skillfully worked on his house last year. He said that most of the carpenters in the village were good, but they had drinking problems; once they got paid, they had a tendency to drink to the point that they couldn't even get up the next day. We wanted to work behind the scenes and to limit our explicit involvement on this project, so we asked Dien to represent us and to work directly with the carpenters. We hoped that with this approach we would be able to elude the watchful eyes of the Communist officials.

Even though we had faith in Dien's judgment, we still wanted him to conduct an interview with the carpenters in our presence so we could determine if they really had the skills and stamina needed to do the job. We wanted Dien to explain to them that the weak ribs had to be replaced with new, stronger ones, and more ribs would be added evenly throughout the body of the boat. He added that the keel and the hull had to be extended and two more planks had to be installed to make the hull about a half meter higher.

Other modifications would include adding a strong frame at the stern for mounting an F10 Honda diesel engine and the addition of a more solid and stable rudder. The boat at this stage had only a shell, so the stern and upper deck had to be built to have room for an opening and a door and a ladder for goods or people to be loaded into the cabin.

We didn't tell the carpenters, but since the boat was to be used to carry people, we needed to install a thinner layer of planks inside of the boat, laying these planks on top of the ribs and nailing them down securely. The inner layer would help to strengthen the boat body and also prevent people from stepping on the outer layer of planks, which might damage the boat.

We also asked Dien to tell the carpenters to add a transom at the stern for holding the outboard motor that would be used to support the main engine.

We wanted a realistic assessment from the workers, so we asked Dien to invite the carpenters to see the boat to give them a chance to assess its current condition and let us know their input, suggestions, and estimate of how long they thought it would take them to complete the project. The carpenters said that they would be able to finish the work within three months provided that all the materials and supplies needed, such as woods, nails, nuts, bolts, and braces were brought to the worksite on time, and they also wanted one tael of gold's worth for their labor and they wanted to get paid monthly.

We added up the costs. Our coffer was quickly diminishing, and if we didn't get additional funds soon, then the project would certainly be stalled. If we couldn't have the boat completed by the beginning of April next year, then the entire trip would have to be scrapped because this boat was too fragile to withstand the waves of rough seas after April.

We had to buy materials and supplies immediately for the carpenters to start working on the project, and this would take a bite out of our budget. By the end of this phase, we would be completely out of money, and we absolutely needed to have additional cash to keep the project moving. We still needed at least five more taels of gold to buy two engines, diesel, food, guns, and other unplanned expenses.

Future expenses were going to be problematic, but the most urgent job was getting the repair work started. We agreed that the workers' labor costs were reasonable, and we asked Dien to have them sign a paper to guarantee that they would complete the job as promised, forgoing pay if they reneged. While Dien was working on this, we went out to the timber yard to buy wood and logs for the carpenters to build a dock platform, and we arranged to have the boat loaded to the dock the next day.

Although it was only an empty shell, the boat was very heavy, and we needed more people to help us load it onto the platform.

Dien said that as soon as the platform was completed, he would ask for help from the young men in the village to push the boat to the platform using wooden logs. We would have to be here at least the next three months since we wanted to build a good relationship with the people in the village, especially with the young people. We decided to use this occasion to share with them a few pieces of chicken and a couple of glasses of rice wine. The villagers appreciated this proposition; the boat ended up situated nicely on the dock, and we won some goodwill as well.

I had to leave for Saigon again in the next few days to look for more money, but while I was at the worksite, I knew that Dien had a sister who was a couple of years older than me. She had a daughter and a son, but her husband had left her a few years ago for another woman. Her house was just a few blocks from Dien's house and was located right next to the riverbank. I hoped I could save on lodging and sleep on the porch of her house, where there was plenty of fresh air from the river for me enjoy. I asked for her permission; she had no problem, but her children didn't agree with it, so I had to buy toys and candy to bribe them. All I needed to buy now was a blanket, a plastic pillow, a straw mattress and a mosquito net. I folded them up in the morning and kept my few possessions at her house during the day. She would bring them out to the porch and leave them there for me at night. The river provided me with a source of water for all my needs, from brushing my teeth to bathing and washing my clothes.

After securing a place to sleep, I took off for Saigon using a set of self-prepared permits that helped me to find a place to stay temporarily without being harassed by the local authorities. While staying in Saigon, I contacted several of my close friends again to seek financial contributions for the trip. They all wanted to leave the country, but none had any money. I explained to them that we didn't want to make any profits or money on this trip, that we had only one ultimate goal, which was to get our family and benefactors out of the country safely on a boat, and we only needed five more taels of gold to buy two diesel engines and some miscellaneous items, and we were willing to show whoever contributed to the trip the progress of our project. My friends told me that they didn't need an explanation from me since some of them were on our last failed trip and they knew very well that we were genuine. I stayed in Saigon for two days at a friend's home, and I contacted many people, including my friends and friends of my friends, and despite my plea and the support from my friends, there was, however, no one who really wanted to participate or contribute money to the trip because they couldn't trust anyone any longer or simply didn't have money.

I had spent a lot of time and effort during the last two days to sell the people our project and solicit their participation, and I was now too exhausted to continue. Even though we were not able to raise anything, the effort and time put in by my friend whose house I was staying in were a phenomenon. I thanked him for his help, and yet we both felt that the project was doomed since I couldn't accomplish my mission here. I told my friend that I had to go back to An Giang to ask the group to raise money elsewhere since I had tried all I could, and my friend expressed his sympathy, but in his position he couldn't do anything more to help.

As I packed up my clothes for the return trip the next day, we heard knocking on the front door. My friend opened the door, and a man pushing a bike walked in and left his bike against the wall next to the door. He closed the door, looked at me and asked, "Are you planning to return tomorrow, Brother Hai?" I recognized that he was someone my friend had introduced to me on the first day of my trip to Saigon.

"Yes, maybe early in the morning," I said.

"Can I come along to visit the location where the boat is being prepared?" he asked. In my mind, I wanted to keep the location secret; I preferred to have a very limited access to the location by anyone, including the prospective contributors. But on the other hand, if he was not allowed to see the boat in person, then I knew that he wouldn't put the money down since he had once been cheated by the scammers and had lost three taels of gold. Had he not quickly jumped off the boat, swum to the riverbank, and ran he would have already been arrested by the police.

"Do you want to be a part of this trip?" I asked, hopeful.

"Yes, but I would like to see the boat before I give you guys my share," he said, also hopeful.

Despite my desperation, I needed to know the number of people he planned to send with us and how much he was willing to contribute for me to determine whether it was worth to let him visit the worksite. So I asked, "How many people do you have and how much you are willing to contribute?"

"My wife, me and my four-year-old child. I wanted to put in two taels of gold," he said.

"I do appreciate your willingness to be a part of our trip, but as you already know, most people nowadays have to pay three taels for one person. We're not trying to make money; all we want is to raise enough money to reinforce a boat and to buy two good engines for safely getting our family and friends out of the country. I would say three taels would be a fair share for three people, and if you agree with my suggestion, then we can go together tomorrow," I said.

He thought it over for a couple of seconds and then said, "Let me talk it over with my wife, and I will let you know." With that, he returned to his bike and departed. Around midnight he returned, breathing heavily, as I was preparing to go to bed.

He said he agreed with my suggestion, and I reminded him to bring the gold with him to contribute if he decided he was happy with the work. I didn't forget to advise him not to talk to the workers or mention anything about the trip with anyone while he was at the worksite. We would let him know the full plan and bring his family to the departure location when we were ready to leave.

After introducing him to Manh, I took him to the worksite as the workers were diligently working on removing the weak and old ribs of the boat. I explained to him that since we didn't plan to carry many people, we didn't have a big boat, but we wanted it to be solid and stable and we planned to have it completely overhauled in three months. We would keep him posted on the progress when it was possible. He was satisfied with what he had seen, so he turned three taels of gold over to me.

Manh and I got together to discuss the prospect of raising at least an additional two taels, and he understood that I had done my best for the assigned task. Now he needed to step in to look for other sources of financial support.

I was now working along with the workers as their helper; I cleaned everything after them so they could focus on their main task, and I also made sure they were doing quality work. When they needed wood, materials, or anything required for the job, they sent me out to buy it. This island had no roads or bridge connecting to the mainland or other islands, so I had to learn how to manually paddle a little sampan that belonged to Dien's family. It was tough at first, but after two weeks of practice I was able to overcome the difficulty to the point that I could operate the sampan better than many local people, and I even took members of Dien's family and his neighbors to the market almost every day. Dien's sister had not yet kicked me out of her porch, so I still temporarily used that spot to sleep at night. I cooked my own meals in the shack we had built for workers to take their break in at the worksite.

I wanted to mingle with the villagers to facilitate good relations, so I participated in all of the public and cultural activities of the village. There were two funerals during the time I was there, and I went with other young men to dig the grave and to carry the coffins. There were several weddings for young people, so I also went with members of Dien's family to clean the groom's house and to help cook and to arrange all the tables and chairs for the wedding. They walked barefoot, so I did, too. The government wanted villagers to clean the canal for the irrigation system and each had to put in several days of work, so I also attended and worked with everyone else. I helped Dien's sister in her daily work by taking her to the market to buy food, carrying water from the river, and cleaning around her house. People in the village thought that I was courting Dien's sister, and they started to treat me as one of them. They called me when they needed help, and they also called me when they got together for a drink. I tried hard to deflect any suspicions people or the local authority might have so I could get the boat worked on without any interruption.

After three weeks of working on the project, we had made impressive progress. All of the rotten and weak ribs had been removed and a few new ribs had been put in place. The swift work showed that these workers were very conscientious, and I was very pleased with the progress. They also took down the old rudder and started to measure the transom for a new one; they doubled the wood's thickness and used nuts and bolts to put the rudder together. I wanted to reward them for their hard work, but I had to play my role as a helper flawlessly, so I pretended to ask Dien for some money to buy a couple of liters of rice liquor and some fish. On a Saturday, I made mud fish soup with young mango leaves, taro, green onion, and cilantro, and it turned out to be very tasty. The group of young men who had helped us to move the boat to the wooden platform were also invited. We didn't have cups, so we poured the rice wine into a discarded Coke can and took turns drinking from it. After we finished the first two liters, we had nothing left, but the young men weren't ready to stop; they wanted to have at least one more liter. I didn't have enough money, so we all chipped in. To complement the wine, we picked some of the young mango fruits from a tree nearby. They were very sour, but they helped to make the wine go down smoother. Together, we consumed almost three liters of rice liquor. I was totally wiped out. They had to walk me to my sleeping quarters and hang the mosquito net for me.

Upon waking up in the morning, I noticed that I had two shirts on and a blanket was over my body. My friends probably didn't want me to catch a cold while I slept, and I remembered that we had all been shirtless while drinking because it was hot that night. Even though I knew that it was very bad to be drunk while I had a heavy responsibility on my shoulders, I wanted to show these people camaraderie.

While hanging out with these men, I met a young instructor named Lam, who was teaching at the Provincial Agricultural School in Long Xuyen City, which was close to the island. He was from the North and had been teaching at this school for about three years. Initially, I was very cautious in dealing or hanging out with him since I didn't trust any Communists. I speculated that Lam was a member of the Communist Party because he was a teacher at a very prestigious agricultural school and he came from the North. Lam said

139

that he wanted to mingle with us because he liked the straightforwardness, innocence, and simplicity of people in the South. He also said that he was young and single and he didn't get along with his colleagues, so he didn't want to hang out with them. Lam appeared to be sincere in his intention to join us, and he once told me that his grandfather was killed in 1956 during the Land Reform in the North. The government had accused his grandfather of being a traitor for allegedly working for the Vietnamese National Party and also being a landlord. He hated them, but he couldn't do anything about it, so he had to keep quiet to survive. He claimed not to be a member of the Communist Party out of his own desire.

Lam always brought a couple of kilos of rice to give us when he joined us for a drink; he apologized for not having money to share the costs with us. On a few occasions he had a few drinks more than he could handle and didn't want to ride his bike back to school, so he asked me to let him sleep at my house. I told him that I didn't have a house and that I slept on the porch of a friend's house. He said he didn't mind sleeping on the porch, so I borrowed a mosquito net and a blanket for him.

On one occasion, Lam asked me, "What are you going to do with the boat you're working on when it's finished?"

I said, "According to the owner, it will be used to carry pineapples and other fruit. The owner plans to buy the produce directly from the farmers to ship it to the cities for resale. He is also going to sign a contract to carry goods for the government."

Lam looked interested. "If you want, I can help you get a contract to carry fish sauce for the school. Do you think you could find out where we could buy it at a lower price?"

"I'll talk to the owner of the boat about it, but I don't think it would be a problem for us to find good-quality fish sauce at a lower price. Usually, the producer charges for the cost of carrying the fish sauce to the customer's location. You can negotiate with the boat's owner for the cheapest price for this service," I told him.

His suggestion brought to mind a fresh idea that I was very grateful for. We had been dwelling on the question of how to bring the boat to the coastal area, but we had so far been unable to find a solution. It was a long and dangerous waterway for us because the local authorities had set up so many checkpoints along the canal; they would stop any boat if they suspected it was carrying contraband or didn't have proper paperwork, especially for boats going toward the coast. We had thought about making a self-prepared document, but now this was a golden opportunity for us. Through Lam, we could get legitimate paperwork. First, however, I thought it would be prudent to carry goods on a few trips for the school to build his trust, to test the performance of the boat, and also to get used to navigation through the long canal.

The most important aspect of this new plan was to get some diesel for the engine since it was very difficult to buy a high amount and good quality of diesel on the black market. I knew it was unethical to betray a person I considered a friend, but I told myself that if we carried goods for him and he paid us in diesel and by getting us papers to travel back and forth from here to the coast, he would lose nothing when we took off for the open sea, since we hadn't taken anything from him. This was a fair business deal, and the school would only pay us when we delivered the fish sauce or other goods they wanted us to carry, so Lam would not be held accountable for anything.

Our group was very pleased when I brought this news to them. Our escape was beginning to seem possible.

Manh informed me that he had gotten two taels of gold from a former participant and that we now had enough money to get our project moving as planned. Manh had been searching for a F10 and a F6 Honda diesel engine; he found two brand-new engines in a local machine shop, and since they were new, the owner asked for a relatively high price. To complicate matters further, the store owner said that he couldn't sell these engines to civilians unless they had a purchasing permit from the local government.

I immediately thought about Lam. I knew that he would honor my request for an introduction letter to appeal to the local authorities for permission. However, I was reluctant to go to the school to ask him for this favor since I didn't want his colleagues to know that we had a close relationship, so I decided to wait until we had an opportunity to meet him on the island at Dien's house.

When he hadn't shown up after two weeks, I started to feel very nervous. I couldn't help but speculate that the school officials were aware that he had been hanging out with us and had transferred him to another place. We were all anxious to know where he was and why he hadn't visited us for the last couple of weeks. The Communists were very deceptive, secretive, and savage. They would do things that nobody could foresee or understand, and we prayed to God for Lam's safety. Sometimes I wondered why it always seemed that as soon as things started going well, suddenly our hopes were dashed. It would be easier for us if Lam were here, but we had no way to find out what had happened to him and whether he would come back at all, so we had to work on getting the engines without him. We asked Dien again to bring a bottle of whiskey and two cartons of cigarettes to the village chief and asked him for help giving us a permit. His wife, however, told us that he wasn't at home; he was on a business trip and he wouldn't be back at least for another month. We had to reluctantly leave our gifts there with his wife and went home empty-handed.

Meanwhile, the economy was getting worse. Food became quite scarce and desperation was visible everywhere in the country. The government's tight control of foodstuffs and people's movement made matters worse. These were factors that forced people to find ways to get out of the country, and they all wanted to have a safe trip for their boats so they all looked for a good marine diesel engine.

The demand for these engines was so high that they almost disappeared from the market. We didn't want to lose the engines we had recently found in the machine shop, so we needed to act. We decided to put down a deposit and to pay the owner even more money for the engines than the listed price. As we stepped into the shop to pitch this deal to the storeowner, we heard all kinds of noise. Metal pieces were strewn everywhere, and we spotted the storeowner using the welding machine to join pieces of metal to make part of a frame.

"Hello, boss," I said loudly.

He didn't hear my greeting and continued to work on the frame using the welding torch. He held a shield to cover his face from the extreme bursts of dazzling green light.

"Hello, boss," I said louder this time. He turned around, noticing us. He dropped his tools and walked back into the shop.

"What can I do for you?" he asked politely.

"We like the diesel engines you have and we would like to put down a deposit for them. We will pick them up when we get the permit," Manh said.

"Don't be bothered with the deposit. You can just pay me when you pick them up," he said.

"We would pay you more if you can hold them for us for about two weeks," Manh earnestly insisted.

"Well, I can hold them for two weeks, but you need to have a permit. It doesn't matter how much you pay me, I can't sell them to you unless you have a permit. Police inspect my shop monthly, and they would close me down if I violated the rule. I hope you guys understand," he said.

"We will try to secure permission as soon as we can," Manh said, but we knew there was nothing we could do here.

Sadly we left the shop. Since we had failed to persuade him to accept the deposit, we were very concerned that someone would snatch these engines from our hands before we got permission. It seemed like we were in deep water and had no way out. We still couldn't just sit still, waiting for things to happen. Since we could do nothing else, we sent all the members of our team everywhere to search for the same type of diesel engines.

According to our plan, the boat needed to be finished during the month of March or April, as this was the most peaceful time for the Pacific Ocean and the only time we would be able to get to international waters and cross the Gulf of Thailand with our poorly equipped boat. Time was against us, and we couldn't waste a minute. We knew that all the F10 diesel engines had the same size and dimensions, so we asked the machine shop owner to give us permission to get the measurement of the engine for the carpenters and the mechanic to get the frame ready.

The carpenters and the mechanics had to work together to build the frame for the main engine and the post for the outboard motor. We had heard quite often of refugee boats ending up drifting in the vast ocean or washing ashore on the Kien Giang province beach because of engine problems, and we couldn't imagine being in the same situation. We took the time to select the best engines we could and have the engine frame solidly built and securely mounted into the boat frame.

While the workers were working on the wood and steel frame for the engines, members of our team were still searching for the best possible engines out in the field. After almost three weeks, the workers had already completed their work and the frame was ready for the engine installation, but neither the engines nor permit had been secured.

Meanwhile, my job was to seal the gaps between the wood planks. It wasn't a difficult task, but it required a high level of attention and meticulousness. I had to find every gap, small or big, and then use a hammer and a flat chisel to push a string of burlap soaked in a special solution into the gap and caulk them with a special kind of glue to stop water from leaking into the boat. I worked every day from dawn to dark with the hope that I would be able to get it done before the engine installation. My task was almost complete, but the engines hadn't even been found. I was consumed with anxiety; I feared that all of our risks and sacrifices would come to nothing without an engine. I had left my family behind in poverty in Rach Gia, where they didn't even have clean drinking water, pinning everything on this desperate hope to escape with them to somewhere where we could be free. We had sold everything we owned and reached out to everyone we could trust to get this far, and if this trip failed, we would have nothing left. At that moment, everything hinged on our ability to get an engine; without one, we could never attempt the journey. My fear and anxiety were so great that I became physically sick and feverish. I didn't have a place to rest besides the porch, but Dien's sister was generous enough to give me some plain rice soup for a few days since I didn't have an appetite for anything else.

While lying on the porch, half unconscious because of my high fever, I felt a hand touching my right shoulder. I thought that it was Dien's sister bringing me rice soup, so I said, "Not hungry, I need to rest." I was exhausted and didn't want to be bothered, so I turned to my left toward the wall and ignored the soft touch on my shoulder. The touch, however, was more firm this time and accompanied by a male Northerner's voice saying, "Brother Hai, are you okay?"

I half opened my eyes and I saw Lam. I thought it was a dream. I was incredulous and didn't trust my fevered state, so I asked, "Is that you, Lam?"

"Yes, I just got back yesterday," he said. "I stopped by Dien's house. He told me that you were sick and staying at his sister's house," he added.

I sat right up, putting my back against the thatched wall, and curiously asked, "Where have you been?"

"I will tell you later. Did you take any medication?" he asked worriedly.

"I didn't take medication, but I already had an herbal steam bath, and I feel a little better now," I said. I realized that my clothes were all wet with sweat like someone had just dumped a bucket of water on me, and they had a pungent odor.

"Well, you are very sick. You need to stay inside of the house instead of lying on the veranda. It's windy here," he said.

"I will be okay. Don't worry," I assured him.

"I brought you some rice. I will give it to Dien's sister so she can make you some soup," Lam said.

"Thanks," I said.

"I will talk to Dien's sister about letting you stay inside the house," he insisted.

"I am fine. She is a widowed, single mother, and I don't want any gossiping about a man living in her house. That's why I have been staying on this porch for the last couple of months," I said.

"Did you eat anything yet, Brother Hai?" he asked.

"I had some plain rice soup she gave to me this morning. I don't feel like eating anything at this moment," I said. "I want to talk to you about an important issue. Are you going to stay here tonight?"

"I can talk to you for a while, but I need to get back to school tonight," Lam said.

I attempted to stand, but my head was spinning. I almost fell to the ground, and I knew that I was very weak because I hadn't eaten much for the last few days. At this time of the day, all of the workers had gone home, so we decided to go to the boat site since we didn't want anyone to hear our conversation. I wanted to get to crux of the matter right away since he was my friend and I had trust in him.

"We need a letter of introduction from your school to state that we would sign a contract to carry goods for the school when the boat is in operation," I said.

"That is not a problem, but why do you need it now?" he asked.

"We need a permit from either the police or village chief so we can buy the engines for the boat, and before giving us a permit they want to have a letter of introduction," I said.

"That's fine. I will have a letter prepared with the school logo and the signature of the principal for you tomorrow," he said.

"Thanks, and I am looking forward to getting it," I said.

He helped me back to the veranda and said, "You take care and I will see you tomorrow afternoon."

CHAPTER

6

Engine Installation

L am's reappearance averted our engine crisis, so I immediately went back to Rach Gia, where Manh and my family lived, to inform the others, allowing them to focus their attention on other tasks such as procuring money for the expensive engines. I was also looking forward to this opportunity to visit my family, which I had not seen for a long time. I asked Manh to go to the worksite right away to meet Lam for the letter, and I also asked him for some small amount of money to buy my children a couple of meat sandwiches and a dozen oranges. This time I had enough money to take a bus and didn't have to run home like the last few times. If I had to run, I would probably not have been able to make it home since I was still weak and recovering. My children were happy to see me. They surrounded me, asking all kinds of questions; my youngest one jumped into my lap and held on to my arm.

He asked, hardly pausing for breath, "Dad, where did you go? Why were you gone so long? I miss you."

"I had to work to make money for the family to eat. I will come home more frequently from now on," I said.

"Every day," he demanded.

"I can't. Daddy has to work in the city far away, and I can't go home every day," I said and hugged him.

When I was away, my oldest son slept on the front porch of the brick home by himself, and today my youngest son kept asking me to let him sleep with me on the front porch tonight. While our family was talking, a young local Communist cadre from the village stopped by to visit. He said that he was aware that I had been away for quite a while and he wanted to know where I went. I knew that this would happen someday, so I had asked Lam to give me a paper to show the local officials that I was working for Lam's school as a laborer. The documents said that job was to clean the classrooms, dump trash, and perform all the other janitorial work. The local official asked me to inform him if I was away from home for more than a few days. My youngest son didn't want to go to school; he wanted to stay home with me because he was afraid that I would leave the house while he was in school. I assured him that I wouldn't leave without letting him know.

"Are you sure?" he asked and then he curled his right index finger and made me to do the same with my right index finger. Then he interlocked our fingers, pulling hard, and said, "Dad, you promise?"

"Yes, I promise, now let go and do good at school," I said.

I stayed home for two days. I really wanted to stay home longer with my kids, but I had to go back to the job site right away to monitor the progress of our project. When my children were in school, I explained to Huong the problem we had run into and the progress we had made on the project. I was already thin and now I lost some more weight.

My wife was very worried about me. She wanted to know where I had my meals and slept while I was working on the boat, and she was fearful that I would get sick from sleep deprivation and malnutrition. I jokingly explained to her that my life was seemingly predestined for the porch. I told her that I slept on the porch of my friend's sister's house and I cooked my own meals. I assured her that though I didn't have abundant food, I had enough to eat and she should not be worried. All too soon, it was time to leave.

Upon my arrival at the job site, Manh showed me the letter that Lam had promised a few days ago.

"Have you presented this letter to the village police chief or the village chief to get a permit?" I asked.

"I planned to visit the village chief today, but he was away," Manh said.

"That's right, he won't be home at least for another two weeks," I remembered. "Do you want to wait until then?"

"I wanted to discuss that with you," he said.

"The question I have is whether the police chief has the power to issue a permit, and if he does, then I don't want to wait any longer," I said.

"Okay. Dien and I will contact him this afternoon to find out. We will give him a bottle of whiskey and a carton of cigarettes," Manh added.

"We lost one bottle of whiskey and two cartons of cigarette giving to the village chief's wife two weeks ago and we got nothing done. Don't take me wrong. I don't mean to be greedy, but we need to be frugal because we don't have a lot of money to spend. We need to find out first if he has the authority," I suggested.

"I agree," Manh said.

"Manh, Lam has helped us quite a bit, and we will need his help in the very near future. Even though he is our friend, he is not a member of our group and we should do something for him in return," I asked.

"What about we give him an envelope with some money?" Manh recommended.

"As a friend, I don't think he would take money from us, but let assume that he would take the money. He'd spend it and then there would be nothing for him to keep as a souvenir," I said.

"What you think we should do for him?" Manh asked.

"In our conversations he has sometimes mentioned something about a battery radio for him to listen to the news," I said. "Since taking over the South, the troops and cadres from the North have brought home all sorts of things they found in the South. They were in shortage of a lot of commodities; they didn't even have anything remotely like what we had in the South before 1975," I added.

We finally decided to buy Lam a small National battery radio, and we knew that he would be very appreciative of our gift.

This tangential business taken care of, we needed to focus on the issue at hand, which was to find out if the village police chief had the power to authorize a permit. We needed to be very diplomatic about this; we didn't want to hurt his feelings by blatantly asking insensitive questions. We knew that our probing would come to an unhappy ending if we didn't do the job right, since Party members were hungry for power and could be vindictive if their power was questioned.

At first, we thought about asking Lam to contact the police chief to discuss the issue because they were both working for the same system. However, ultimately we didn't think that this was a good idea because now that they had more opportunities to make money, the Communist officials or cadres didn't put their comrade-ship above material possessions or money. On the other hand, he would not dare to receive gifts or bribery from Lam on our behalf. We knew he wouldn't issue a permit for us and thus this approach would defeat the purpose.

We seemed to be short on options. Eventually, however, we thought about a different way of getting this issue resolved more diplomatically by finding out without contacting the chief of police, but rather by asking someone else.

"We can contact the machine shop owner to find out whether he has ever received a purchasing permit authorized by the village chief of police," I said.

The owner was kind enough to let us know that he had received numerous permits issued by the police chief in the past and that he was authorized to issue such a permit in that regard.

Armed with the knowledge that our bribe to the police chief wouldn't be wasted, we approached him to ask for the permit and gave him a bottle of whisky and a carton of domestic cigarettes to show him our appreciation. He furnished us with a permit right away.

After receiving the permit, we contacted the machine shop owner to purchase the engines, but now, so close to our goal, we encountered another problem. The owner told us that he only had the F10; the F6 had already been sold. He said that he had kept the engines for two weeks as promised to us. We paid him the listed price for the F10 engine and we immediately took the engine by a sampan to our mechanics for fitting. The mechanics had to spend many days to get all of the required components such as the propeller, the rod, and the exit water pipe ready for the installation of the internal engine.

Nothing was going smoothly. Some of the parts needed for the installation weren't available in town, and we had to go all the way to Saigon to purchase them. I didn't know much about the engine and parts, so I took the mechanic with me, and now we had to go through all kinds of trouble in getting the travel permit and bus tickets, and that this would also create a big dent into our already-crunched budget and timeframe.

I asked the mechanic to go to the shop where they used to buy their parts and insisted that we would only stay in Saigon for one night after we bought all the necessary items. We didn't stay in the motel, but we rent two mattresses to sleep on at the bus station so we could purchase tickets early in the morning for returning home on time. Otherwise, we would have to stand in line, and if we got to the bus station late we wouldn't be able to purchase the tickets at all.

On the way back, we were stopped by the police at a checkpoint where they questioned us about the parts we had bought. We showed them the permit from local police chief allowing us to buy the machine and the needed parts to fit the engine to the boat. We were held at the checkpoint for more than two hours. As a result, we missed the bus and had to spend extra money to get on a different bus, and we didn't get home until late that night. We had to constantly adjust our plan to cope with unforeseen events like this.

The boat was much heavier than when we first had brought it to the dry dock, so we decided not to install the internal engine until we moved it down to the water. With the help of all the young men

I had met for the last three months, it was much easier to move it off from the dock than when we had moved it up to the dock.

While the mechanics and carpenters were working on the installation of the internal engine, our team members were frantically searching for the F6 diesel engine that would be used as the outboard motor. The F6 engine was smaller, more popular, and easier to find in the market, so our members were able to buy a brand-new F6 at a very reasonable price. The new engine would be mounted on the post to support the main engine. The mechanics had to make a rod that connected the engine to its propeller, and this rod had to be long enough to reach water to push the boat. They estimated that it would take them at least two more days to get this done.

In order to evade police attention and that of the Communist officials, we built a high roof to put on top of the rear portion of the boat because with the height of this roof, our boat wouldn't have a chance to go underneath any bridges above the river leading to sea. This roof, however, could be easily removed and placed in water by two people within a few minutes.

After three months of hard work, our boat was now ready for a real test. It was ten meters long and two and a half meters wide, and it was very solid, as we expected. It needed to face a real test, and we wanted to find out whether the propeller was strong and efficient enough to push the boat forward, how fast it could go, and whether the water pump worked. We also wanted to find out how efficient the outboard motor was.

I managed the rudder and the mechanic operated the engine as we moved it slowly to the center of the river. We started it out slowly and then we increased the speed cautiously. It ran as fast as we expected, and we all were very happy with the result. After running for about an hour, we noticed that inside of the boat had a good volume of water, and we thought it was leaking somewhere. We stopped the boat and tried to determine the cause of the water. The mechanic said, "With this amount of water, the leak has to be very big if there is a leak, and I don't think the worker who worked on sealing the boat could have missed it."

"I actually worked on the caulking. I went through every single line where two wood planks met, and I filled them with burlap string before I caulked them with special glue. If it had a leak, then it should be a very small hole, and it shouldn't take in that much water," I said nervously.

"I think we should get a bucket to get all the water out of the boat, and keep it in the river for a few hours to see whether any more water seeps in," the mechanic said.

We checked back after a few hours, and we found that inside of the boat was totally dry and that our theory of water leaking didn't stand. We then started the engine without engaging the propeller and let the engine run for about a half an hour while we inspected the engine operation. We noticed that after about thirty minutes of running, a good amount of water had gathered inside the boat, and that made us believe that the engine was the culprit. One important component of the engine was the water pump, which pumped the cold water from outside in to cool off the engine and pumped hot water out of the engine into the river through a hose. This hose was too short, making most of the exhaust water run back into the boat. We had to replace it with a longer hose to get all the water to run out of the boat and into the river. We wanted to make sure no water collected in the boat again, so we let the engine run for another thirty minutes after replacing the hose, verifying that the problem was fixed.

Now that the boat had proven itself to be watertight, the first phase of the project was complete. I knew that once I reported to the team, they would be able to collectively heave a sigh of relief and shift their focus to the next step.

Stepping out of the boat, I saw the village chief and the chief of police walking into Dien's house. I was very nervous to see both of them at Dien's house at the same time. The experience I had with our last boat forced me to think about the unpleasant things these two men might bring to us. As they walked into the house, the village chief asked Dien's mother, who was sweeping leaves in front of the house, "Aunt Chin, where are Manh and Dien?"

"I don't know where Manh is, but Dien is in the kitchen. Let me call him," Dien's mother said.

"Dien, the village chief and police chief are here to see you," she called aloud from the front yard.

Dien walked out of the kitchen with his hand full of fish scales, saying, "Hi, Mr. Village Chief, Mr. Police Chief. Come on in, come on in please. I am sorry my hands are dirty. I am cleaning a mud fish, give me a few seconds, I will wash my hands and be right with you," Dien said.

"Take your time," the village chief said.

While drying his wet hands against his pants, Dien said, "Would you like to have lunch with my family?"

"No! No! We are just stopping by to visit. We heard that you guys have already installed the engine for the boat, how was it?" the village chief asked politely.

"Yes, we just had it installed yesterday. We had a small problem with leakage, but overall it was okay. Thanks," Dien said.

"What you guys are going to use the boat for?" the chief asked.

"We will probably sign a contract to carry goods for the government agencies, and when we don't carry goods we plan to buy fruit from the farmers to bring to our city for resale. Manh knows more on this than I do and he is here today, but I don't know exactly where he is," Dien said.

"Signing a contract to carry goods for the government agencies is a good idea, but buying fruit for resale is not encouraged. That is the job of the cooperative; you guys know that, right?" the village chief said.

"Yes, sir," Dien said.

Had our boat been built as an ocean boat, we would have been in big trouble with these two guys, and we would also have had to spend a great deal of money to bribe them before we could get the boat lowered into the water.

Although I needed to go inside the house to get some rags to clean the engine area, which was covered in oil and grease, I was loath to because of the Communist officials. I decided to remain on the boat, working, until they left the house. It was a hot day, and my work was labor-intensive. I knew I would be soaked with sweat, so I worked shirtless.

While rubbing the floor to remove the grease, I felt the boat rocking and I heard the noise of people stepping on the planks connecting the river bank and the boat. Turning around, I saw the village chief, the police chief, and Dien stepping on the bow. So much for my efforts to avoid them.

"Hi, sirs," I said, then went back to my work.

They ignored my greeting; they would probably think nothing of this skinny, miserable, and poor worker. I weighed less than ninety pounds. I had been very thin to begin with, and I had lost even more weight after I had the fever a week ago. Working outside under the sun had made my skin even darker, and they could probably see every rib in my body. They started walking back and forth on the boat and asking Dien questions.

"It's quite a big boat," the police chief said.

"Relatively, it would be used to carry goods, sir," Dien said.

"I know," the village chief said impatiently.

"Is this the engine that I gave you permission to buy?" the police chief asked.

"Yes, sir, it was quite good. Thanks, sir," Dien said with a smile.

"You should have a party to celebrate, eh!" the police chief suggested.

"Manh will probably do something, but I don't know what it is. I will ask him to contact you, sirs," Dien responded politely.

They stepped off the boat without saying a word to me. These guys always said their Party was of, for, and from the workers, farmers, and the poor people as a whole, but in reality they didn't want to talk to proletarians. They only wanted dealings with the bourgeoisie who could bring them money or gifts.

A few days later, Manh and Dien offered to take these two officials to a restaurant managed by the government cooperative, but they refused and instead insisted on having a party at Dien's place. It was a party full of delicacies such as steamed chicken, roasted duck, sour mudfish soup, and plenty of rice wine. We hadn't had a feast like this for a long time. The workers also had the same kind of food the officials had, but we were sitting on a straw mattress stretched out on the floor. The village chief, the chief of police, Manh, Dien, and Lam sat together at the table and sometimes gave the workers their leftovers. Dien's mother and sister were cooking in the kitchen, and I had to serve as a waiter, so I couldn't drink. I needed to stay sober since I had to serve food to them and also buy more wine for them when they ran out. People didn't sell rice wine on the island, so I had to go all the way over the city using Dien's sampan. I actually wanted to spend time with other workers, but I couldn't since they kept asking for more food, more wine, and more condiments. We didn't forget to pack for the village chief and police chief a bottle of whisky each to bring home since they had already asked for them a few days earlier.

CHAPTER

7

Testing the Boat's Endurance

Up to this moment our boat had only passed a minor test to prove that the engine was working properly and the propeller had enough thrust to push the boat forward. That, however, was only a preliminary test; it had to go through a series of much more vigorous tests to see how it performed so we could make any corrections before taking it to the sea. We would rather abort the trip than take a risk with a boat that had unproven capabilities.

I had once seen a group of teachers from a local high school trying to flee, but they were caught and manhandled by the police on the beach close to the city. Their boat had washed ashore because of engine problems while they were just a few kilometers from the Vietnamese shore. I didn't want our boat to be in this situation because if they arrested us, I had no doubt we would be imprisoned for life or executed.

Obviously, we couldn't take our boat to the sea or to any nearby provinces near the coast for testing. However, if we could get a contract with the school, then we might be able to have our boat carry a heavy load on a long trip, at least from An Giang to Rach Gia, to test for the engine operability and the boat durability. We had previously discussed with Lam, the instructor, about a contract to buy and carry fish sauce for his school.

Our boat was now ready for a real test, and it would be tremendously difficult for us to test it if we couldn't get the contract, so we frantically tried to contact Lam. As private citizens, we couldn't buy quality diesel, which was considered a strategic commodity to the government. The school, however, was a government agency; it had the privilege to buy diesel at a low price for its own use or to share it with its satellite units. Many doors would be opened to us if we could acquire the contract; for one, we would be able to buy oil directly from the school and save it for our future need. Additionally, the school also had the power to issue permission for its contractors or employees to travel to other provinces to buy and transport goods for the school.

After school ended on Friday, Lam hurried to Dien's house to meet us. We first presented him a small gift, the National battery radio, and we thanked him for all the help he had given us in the past. He told us that he had always wanted to have a radio so he could listen to the news, but couldn't afford one because he had to take care of himself and support his elderly parents with his humble salary. His appreciation and excitement were clearly written on his face. However, we needed to get to our business quickly since we had no time to waste, so we explained to Lam that we would like to have his help to get a contract with the school. Lam honestly told us that he was only an instructor and didn't have the power to sign a contract with anyone, but he could arrange a time for us to visit the school to talk to the headmaster.

Lam gave us some inside information. He said, "The school has at least three hundred students plus the staff, so the need for quality fish sauce and other foodstuffs is very high. They also need to have commodities transported from other locations to the school daily, so I think the chances that you guys will get a contract is high. I will also talk to the headmaster about this for you." He then added, "This man is very likable person, but he is very serious about business, and he isn't like many other Communist officials. He isn't fond of talking about kickback or favoritism and things of that nature, so you guys have to be careful when talking to him."

Equipped with this information, we wanted to have a meeting as soon as possible, and Lam said he would try to get it possibly on Monday and would let us know soon so we could prepare.

While waiting for Lam's response, we discussed who was going to attend the meeting and how we were going to approach the headmaster with our request. Our main goal was to get some extra good diesel oil, which we would use for our trip, and also to get travel permission. With that in mind, we wouldn't ask for a high return for our work. Dien and Manh would be our main representatives, and I would tag along as a worker in case there was a question about the boat. We also decided that we would bring our boat with us to show him our commitment.

Fortunately for us, the school had run out of fish sauce and rice, and they urgently needed a contractor to buy and transport these commodities for them, so the headmaster agreed to talk to us in the afternoon of the upcoming Monday.

After securing the boat to the post of the school dock, all three of us walked to the headmaster's office. He was already in the office waiting for us. It was a very simple and small office with a desk, a few chairs, and a bookshelf with a few dozen books. He asked us to sit down and offered us tea. He seemed to be in his mid-fifties and had dark skin, a thin build, and an austere demeanor. He introduced himself as Mr. Trong, Headmaster of the Agricultural School, and we introduced ourselves.

"What you guys are here for today?" he asked.

"Sir, we understand that your school has goods that need to be transported, and we have a reliable riverboat. We want to do this job for the school," Manh said.

"How big a load can you carry each trip, and do you have workers to load and unload goods?" he asked.

"The boat can carry about two to three tons of goods each trip, and Hai is responsible for loading and unloading goods," Manh said while pointing his finger at me.

Mr. Trong looked at me uneasily. "Him? You mean he carries a hundred-kilo sack of rice?"

"He plus other workers, sir," Manh added.

"What makes you think that you can do the job well? What I mean is, can you deliver goods on time and intact?" he asked, very serious.

"Our boat is strong. We just had it reinforced and installed a brand-new and reliable engine. We also have a group of dedicated workers," Manh said.

"When can you start?" he asked.

"We are ready, and if you would like we can start tomorrow," Manh said.

"Well, the school has three tons of rice we need brought to the warehouse here. Can you guys handle this?" he asked.

"Would you let us know where the rice is now? Is the location close to the school?" Manh asked.

"No, no, they are in Rach Gia province, about seven hours to travel by boat, and you provide the workers," he said.

"Are you going to pay the workers?" Manh asked.

"We'll pay by trip," he said.

"It would take us at least 100 liters of oil for a round trip, plus labor and time waiting to load the rice, so we would ask for 150 liters of diesel and 100 kilos of rice," Manh negotiated.

"If you need only 100 liters, why do you ask for 150 liters?" he questioned Manh.

"Sir, we spent all our savings and we also borrowed money to get our boat fixed and to buy the engine. We want to make a little bit of money by carrying goods for the government or whoever needs us. We know the school has good-quality diesel and we want our engine run on good diesel, so instead of asking for money, we ask for extra diesel," Manh said.

"Oil is strategic commodity. But since you'd be carrying our goods, and in order to be fair, I will give you 150 liters of oil and 50 kilos of rice. What do you think?" he asked.

We looked at each other and finally agreed with his suggestion. It wasn't a good deal, but we needed diesel very badly. If we were able to deal with the employee who distributed oil, we could ask him for more by paying him extra.

"When do you want the rice delivered to your warehouse?" Manh asked.

"As soon as you can," Mr. Trong said.

"In that case, we will leave here tomorrow, but in order to carry that amount of rice we need a letter from the school to give us permission," Manh asked.

"I will give you the letter tomorrow. What is the boat's registered number?"

"We don't have a number yet, but we will get it tomorrow and I will bring it to you in the morning," Manh said.

"How big is your boat?" he asked.

"Ten meters long, sir," Manh said.

"It is small boat. The village committee controls the small boats, and you can get the number at the village office," Mr. Trong advised.

"Thank you, sir," Manh said.

Since we had provided the village chief with food and all kinds of gifts, it was not too hard for us to get the registered number for our boat.

After getting our allotted 150 liters of oil, we were able to get an extra 20 liters from the man who was in charge of running the generator for the school when he gave us our diesel. He saved a small amount of diesel every day so he could make extra money by secretly selling it to someone who needed it. It was good for us and also good for him, so we kept this deal airtight.

We had the permission letter in our hands and took off for Rach Gia province early in the morning the next day with the entire diesel we had been able to acquire. We had to navigate through a series of canals, and the main canal ran parallel with a highway, so we were stopped and searched many times by the police officers and guerillas who manned the checkpoints along this canal. The permission letter worked like a charm; without it, they would have confiscated our diesel and our boat.

We left the canal, entering a big river, and we knew we were now in Rach Gia territory after almost eight hours of travel. We were trying to locate the warehouse, which was supposedly located on the right riverbank, about two kilometers from the river entrance. It was almost four o'clock in the afternoon now, and we didn't think any employees would be working at this hour, so we docked the boat in front of the warehouse. We checked our diesel. So far, it had taken us only twenty-five liters to go from An Giang to Rach Gia, meaning we would be able to save more than a hundred liters of diesel for our future use. We were very happy with the surplus amount of diesel, knowing we would need it very badly in the future.

After making sure the boat was securely docked, Manh said, "You guys stay back and watch over the boat. I am going to my friend's house to pick up a bike and get you something to eat. I'll be back in a half an hour." He put on a pair of slippers and disappeared quickly into the back of the building.

While waiting for Manh, we observed a number of boats traveling in this section of the river, but it was late in the day, so the traffic was not too heavy. We walked back and forth along the deck and around the perimeter of the building to see whether any police towers or checkpoints were in the vicinity of the warehouse building. We weren't afraid of running into trouble with them because we had a government permit. However, we wanted to find out whether this was a possible location for us to pick up our relatives and friends for the upcoming trip.

It was almost impossible to find a suitable location to load people since the local government had their eyes and ears almost everywhere. Informants were scattered along the coast, riverbanks, and anywhere else where they believed there were suspicious illegal activities. These informants weren't uniformed police officers who were easy for us to see—they were anyone—a girl selling ice cream, a boy selling newspapers, a woman selling cigarettes, a man hauling trash, a peasant selling firewood in an rickety old boat at the riverbank. It could be anyone. It didn't surprise me that there were so many people willing to do such a thing for the government; the Communists squeezed the people so well and kept everyone so hungry that just a few bucks would entice them to do anything.

While I was completely immersed in thoughts of finding a possible loading location, I heard the sound of bicycle tires rolling on gravels, and I thought it must be Manh coming back with some food since we hadn't eaten anything all day. I sprang up, intending to help Manh carry the food, but instead I saw two teenagers, one tall and one short, wearing black uniform and tire rubber sandals, each with an AK-47 rifle on their shoulder. They walked toward the boat, and when they got close to the hull, they yelled, "Is there anybody in the boat?"

"Yes, I am," I said, getting out of the boat to meet them. I gestured to Dien to remain behind.

"What are you doing here?" the shorter guy asked.

"We are waiting to pick up rice for our agency," I said.

"You have paperwork?" the shorter guy asked.

"Yes, I do," I said.

"Let me see," he said.

I walked back into the boat to pick up the letter, but as I turned my back toward them the hair of my nape stood up and a chill ran down my spine. The memory of a young man being shot by police when he was in his sampan made me so fearful, I immediately turned around to glance at them, but fortunately there was no gun barrel pointing at me and I felt relieved. I opened a box on top of the engine and pulled out the letter from the headmaster to show them.

The short guy took the letter and pretended to read it for a few minutes. It was upside-down. Then he turned it over to the taller guy and said, "You read it and let me know what it says." It was getting dark, so it was possible he couldn't read because the light from the lamppost was dim, so I suspected he might be illiterate as well.

The tall guy picked up the letter, and it took him a while to read it. He told the other guy, "They pick up rice for a school."

The short guy then asked me, "How long are you staying here?"

"We will take off after we load all the rice, as indicated in the letter," I said.

"This is our territory, you have to report to us when you get here," he said, getting angry.

I didn't want to have any more trouble with these two stooges, especially when they had two AK-47 rifles with them, so I politely told them, "We just got here and we didn't know where your office is. I am very sorry."

The short guy then raised his right fist in the air and warned me in a high-pitched voice, "This is the first time, so I'll let it slide, but I will have your boat towed next time."

"Yes, I completely understand. We will report to your office first when we get to your area next time," I said.

They both then walked off and vanished into the darkness, and I pondered how they knew that we were in the area when we had arrived less than an hour ago. That made me suspicious that there was someone reporting in to them. With this thought, I felt even more concerned about the insurmountable obstacles we would have to face in finding a possible location for loading our people.

A feeling of hopelessness washed over me, so I plopped down on top of the engine alone, praying to God for help. Dien was tired, so he found a corner in the boat's cabin to take a nap.

I fell asleep shortly thereafter, awakening when I suddenly heard again the noise of people walking on the gravel. In the dim light from the lamppost and through the fog of drowsiness, I saw three figures walking toward our boat, each with a bike. I wasn't able to recognize them, but I fervently hoped they weren't those two guerillas who were here earlier. I slid quietly into the engine room to watch them through a small hole to see what they were doing. When they got close to the boat, they leaned their bikes against one another and I heard a call: "Brother Hai, where are you?" I recognized Manh's voice, so I immediately responded in a soft voice, "I am here."

"We have some sandwiches for you and Dien," Manh said.

"You guys are probably hungry. You should eat them now. They are still hot," one of the other guys added.

Even though I was hungry, I didn't feel like eating at all because my mind was occupied with so many things. I told Manh about the recent incident we had with the guerillas, and he let out a long, sad sigh after listening to my conversation.

Manh and his two friends quickly brought down three twenty-liter plastic cans of diesel from the boat. Each tied a can to the back of their bike, and in a second they disappeared from my view. Manh came back about thirty minutes later to pick up another can. We left more diesel for our return trip than we had used to get here because we knew the engine would be working harder with the heavy load that the boat had to carry.

Manh told us that he would sleep at his friend's house tonight. Dien and I would be the ones who slept aboard as guards. It was utterly quiet at night in this area; all we heard was the chirping of the insects and the croaks of frogs and toads. I was tired but hardly slept these days. Anytime I fell asleep, I had a nightmare of being chased by the police. They were constantly at my heels, though I ran with superhuman speed through hills and mountain and flew over forests to avoid being arrested. I invariably jumped into a river to swim to the other side, and the cold of the water seemed to chill me to the bones. I woke up with a start and found that my clothes were soaked with perspiration and I was exhausted. I tried to compose myself, reminding myself that it was just a dream and that I didn't even know how to swim. Waking up was always a relief, though I woke up tired.

It was still dark, and I didn't have a watch so I didn't know what time it was, but when I heard distant roosters crowing I knew that another day had just started. I hadn't eaten anything since yesterday morning; my stomach was empty and started to growl loudly. I needed to eat something before we loaded three tons of rice on our boat. I hadn't attempted to carry a hundred-kilo bag of rice before and with my humble weight of forty-five kilos, I doubted that I would be able to carry this sack of rice on my shoulder.

It didn't matter what it was going to be, but I needed to eat something. I brushed my teeth with the river water with some salt since we didn't have toothpaste or soap. The leftover submarine sandwich had been left overnight in a bag, so it had become very chewy and it took me a while to finish it. Manh came back around eight o'clock, but we couldn't contact anyone in the warehouse since employees at this warehouse didn't show up for work until nine.

Manh brought Dien and me some coffee he had bought from a coffee shop on the roadside; it wasn't good but it was better than nothing. We drank the coffee and talked about the difficulties of locating a possible location for loading our people. We knew it would be very hard, but we had overcome so many seemingly impossible obstacles to get to this point. We couldn't give it up that easily. We all agreed that we couldn't abort the project regardless of how hard it was. We could deal with latest problem if we applied enough creativity and ingenuity. Realistically, there were so many unknown factors relating to this issue. We had to gather more information before we could even begin.

Meanwhile, however, it was time to load the sacks of rice. Manh brought a couple of his friends to help us so that we had five men altogether to do the work. Manh reported to the warehouse manager and asked to receive the amount of rice the school had requested. The manager had their employees load the sacks of rice into a small truck and bring them to the dock close to our boat. A specially designed wood board was used for us to walk on for loading rice to the boat; each of us had to take turns and carry six bags of rice. To my amazement, I was able to carry a sack of rice on my shoulder and managed fine on the stable ground. The plank to board the boat, however, was another matter. We all struggled to carry the rice across this board because it kept swaying. We just couldn't do this job; we had to give it up and hired the workers of this facility to assist us.

We had made the hatch just big enough for a person to slide through because we didn't anticipate a situation where we would have to load a hundred-kilo sack of rice through the opening, but luckily it just barely fit the size of the bag. With great effort, we transferred all of the bags to the ship's cabin with help from the hired labor.

The warehouse was colossal. Rice sacks were stacked all the way up to ceiling in what looked like a mountain. Rats lived between the sacks of rice and every time a worker pulled out a bag of rice, long-whiskered black rats scurried out, some small and others oversized and fat.

The rats had plenty of rice to eat so they were for the most part very fat; they chewed on the bags, so rice was spilled all over the floor of the warehouse. The workers of this facility earned a very low salary, so they collected the rice spilled on the floor for their family use or to sell on the black market. The rice was exposed to moisture and the hulls of the rice grains were broken as if the rice had been stored in the damp warehouse for many years. This was one of the biggest warehouses of this province and had belonged to one of the Chinese-Vietnamese businessmen before 1975. After the fall of South Vietnam, the owner had left the country under the Chinese repatriation program initiated by the new government, which had subsequently confiscated the warehouse.

Under the three tons of rice, our boat was almost two-thirds submerged in the water, and we were able to bend down and touch the water when sitting on the stern. We knew now that three tons was the heaviest weight that we could carry.

Manh and I decided to stroll along the bank of this river for a few kilometers to observe the surroundings and also to find out if it had a way leading to the sea. We were also looking for an area where there was no population so we could hide our people in the bushes before loading. However, we were very disappointed since we noticed that along the stretch of five kilometers on both sides of the riverbank, houses were built side-by-side almost all the way to the sea.

From a distance, we saw two high towers straddling the river, and upon approaching we noticed a white concrete bridge running across the river. The bridge was flanked by the two high towers we had just seen, and the towers were each guarded by two armed navy men. Manh knew this area very well, having been here before, but he just wanted to let me see it for myself, so he didn't say much. He asked me what my thoughts about this location were.

I said noncommittally, "Too early to say." I needed to think about whether the guards and the low bridge would make this route to the sea impassible.

We walked back to our boat, and Manh told me that it was almost one o'clock in the afternoon and we needed to get back to Long Xuyen so we could deliver the rice to the school the next day. The boat was heavier now, and we had to navigate slowly and carefully through the river or canals, so it would take us much longer to get to Long Xuyen. Nevertheless, we figured that we should be able to unload the rice the next day. We needed to keep the school officials' trust so we could sign more contracts to carry goods for the school, as that was the only way we would be able to bring our boat back to the coastal province again.

We collected for ourselves almost four kilos of rice that had been spilled on the floor in the warehouse. We then bought some anchovies from the market nearby. We had two pots and we decided to cook while the boat was in motion; Manh, Dien and I would take turns operating the boat. Manh was the first one to drive the boat, and I had the job of cooking. The rice was awful; the grains were all broken and full of small pieces of gravel and rat feces. I knew how bad it was to chew on a piece of gravel while eating, so I spent quite a bit of time removing as much as I could of the inedible stuff before I put it in the pot to cook. Well, it wasn't the best, but it was rice and it was not cassava roots or sweet potatoes. I also cleaned the fish and put them into a pot with some salt and river water to cook until they were soft. We had a good meal of rice and fish, and the fish were so soft we were able to eat all the bones.

On our way back, we weren't stopped by police as often as we had on the outbound trip. We didn't need to use the outboard motor, so we put the main engine at a consistent average speed. All we had to do was to maneuver a long handle to control the rudder. We always kept our boat in the center of the canal, and one of us always sat at the bow. Since we didn't have a horn, we hit our gong and yelled loudly to warn the slow-moving sampans to yield.

We got to An Giang around ten o'clock that evening on the same day and docked in front of Dien's house so we could clean up and eat supper. The next day, we used a two-wheeled cart to load the rice sacks. We brought all thirty bags of rice to the school warehouse, the principal paid us fifty kilos of rice, as promised.

After this trip, we had a better idea of how the engine performed and how much weight the boat could safely carry. We also knew that we were running out of time, so we had to seize every opportunity to sign a contract with government agencies so we could bring our boat back to the coastal province again. We needed more diesel, but for now we had at least enough diesel to reach international waters. We asked Dien to try his best to get additional diesel.

Meanwhile, Manh and I needed to spend more time in Rach Gia to learn more about the topography of the area and the strength and weaknesses of the local government so we could set up a place to load our people.

Through members of our team, we had some inside information on which areas the government focused their attention and when they actually launched campaigns to raid the designated areas. Unfortunately, we still didn't have a clue as to where all the informants were tactically distributed. One thing we learned was that the local villages or town governments had an inclination to totally control their area, protecting their regional sovereignty from the interference of other agencies. We planned to use this decentralization to our advantage, and with that we thought about setting up a decoy at one location for the local guerillas to focus on while we loaded our people at different location in the same village. That was, of course, just a thought, and we knew how complicated it was going to be.

In the meantime, we weren't able to acquire a contract with any agencies. Still we just couldn't stand by and wait for things to happen. Manh and I planned to spend a few days in Rach Gia to learn more about the surroundings and the city of this province, which would also give me the opportunity to visit my family.

We took a small sampan with an outboard motor to navigate throughout the river and canals of the province, and we also looked for potential loading areas. There were many areas that had no houses or population along rivers or canals, but it was impossible for people to reach because they had to walk over a vast, open rice field or muddy land. We found some good locations with high, dense bushes that could serve as hiding places, but they were too far from the mouth of the river and would force us to pass many checkpoints before we could reach the sea.

I asked Manh, "What about the location you used to load your relatives last time?"

"It is impossible. The police and guerillas watch over that location like a hawk. They would merely arrest anyone who isn't a villager at this location."

"How do you know?" I asked.

"A friend of mine still living in the village told me," he said absently.

"Can we bribe them?" I suggested.

"Probably. They would accept your money, but we can't bribe every single one of them. The ones who get your money will ignore you, but the ones who don't will arrest you. Anyway, we don't have enough money to buy diesel and food, so where can we get the money to bribe them?" he said perfunctorily.

"Yes, I understand," I said, disappointed.

I wanted to go to the sea to get an idea of how rough it was, so Manh navigated the small sampan underneath the bridge to the river mouth; the troops didn't stop us because they knew that we would not get far in the tiny boat. However, we still spread the fishing nets and fishing tools all over the surface of sampan to show them that we were only two poor fishermen looking for a meal. The sea was calm this time of the year, especially close the shore.

Once the entire horizon unfurled in front of my eyes, an overwhelming feeling of freedom surged, seeming to assume control over my mind and body. The urge to escape the life I knew under this oppressive regime reached a new pitch of urgency.

After spending half an hour navigating along the shore, we decided to go back to the city of Rach Gia using the same route. We left the sampan at a friend's house and then borrowed a bike to ride to the city. I had been to the city before, but this time it looked totally different. It seemed to me that the atmosphere of the city was heavier, and I had a vague but inescapable feeling that everyone was looking at me with a very unfriendly and inquisitive air. Despite the uncomfortable atmosphere, we went almost everywhere in the city, from east to west and north to south. We even entered the slum, where all the poor people lived in huts made of coconut leaves. From there, we went to the old steel bridge, and we stayed there for almost thirty minutes to look down at the river below. This section of the river was very busy, with many farmers selling firewood and women in traditional Southern black clothes and conical hats paddling their boats laden with rice, coconuts, pineapples, duck eggs, and all kinds of food. All of this produce was controlled by the agricultural cooperative, but the farmers still tried to hide some of what they had produced in order to bring it to the market to earn extra money.

Eventually, we walked from the steel bridge toward the white concrete bridge spanning the main river leading to the sea, and along the way we saw a coffee shop. It was small, but it appeared to be clean and organized, and it seemed that the owner had good taste in decoration. It had several big ceramic pots in front of the shop with beautiful water coconut plants and a couple of tables with a few chairs underneath of the blue canopy.

We had been walking for many hours and were getting thirsty, and this looked like a very nice place to sit down for a glass of cold coconut water. We went in to sit at a table next to the coconut plant. Before long, we were greeted by a very fashionable, beautiful young girl who looked to be about twenty.

She greeted us with a big smile. "Hi, gentlemen! What would you like to drink?" she asked.

"What would you like to drink, Brother Hai?" Manh asked me.

I wanted to quench my thirst, so I asked for something that would help cool me down a bit.

"Coconut water with ice," I said.

"Café au lait with ice for me," Manh ordered.

"Please wait for a few minutes," she said.

After she left, Manh remarked, "Brother Hai! Where in the world did this girl come from?"

"Yes, she is not only beautiful, but very fashionable also," I said. "I have only seen farm girls in this city. This is the first time I've seen a girl in designer clothes."

She brought our drinks and seemed to be interested in talking to Manh, probably since he was a charming young man and dressed in very neat clothes, with a crisp white shirt tucked into dark trousers. He also wore leather sandals, an expensive item which only a few people could afford.

Manh and the girl exchanged a few jokes, and they seemed to like each other's company. We finished our drinks and went on to walk toward the white cement bridge, and then we stopped on the bridge for a few minutes looking toward the sea.

It was about five hundred meters from the bridge to the river's mouth, and both side of the river from here on were full of high and thick bushes, blocking our view of the banks and the mouth of the river. There were two high towers on each side of the bridge, each of which was guarded day and night by a naval police trooper.

Their job was to stop boats suspected of carrying contraband or bringing people to the sea to flee the country. While we were standing on the bridge, we saw a few boats being stopped and searched by the troopers.

They searched the boats very thoroughly, but so far they hadn't arrested anyone. It appeared to me that the operators of these boats knew this section of the river and the sea mouth very well; they kept clear of the sandbar on left side of the river going out to the sea.

On our way home, Manh asked me, "What do you think of the girl at the café? Isn't she beautiful and hot?"

"I think she is beautiful," I said.

"You want to stop by this shop again sometime?" Manh asked with a smile.

"Maybe," I said.

However, I told Manh that I needed to visit my family and spend a couple of days with them, suggesting that he should do whatever he needed to do alone over next few days.

After spending two quality days with my family, I felt relieved to know that my wife and children were doing fine, although my kids wanted me to stay at home with them longer. However, I had a very critical mission to accomplish, so we all had to sacrifice for now. I hoped I would have time to make it up to them later.

After getting back to the city, I stayed at Hien's house. This was the house where I had once stayed temporarily to avoid the police raid when I was on the first failed trip, and where Huong and I had met Manh.

Hien's older brother was a friend of Manh and was now living in the Australia; he had left with Manh's relatives about two years

172

ago on the boat Manh and his family had built, and because of that close relationship, this family had been doing everything they could to assist Manh in this risky endeavor.

Hien was about twenty years of age, and she was also a very active member of our team. Her job was to keep track of all the logistics for our trip and her house was storage for all our equipment, such as the naval compasses, binoculars, military uniforms, and even the diesel we had recently acquired. She also watched over any suspicious activities of strangers around her house or neighborhood, and she would let us know not to come back to the house if she detected any signs of unusual changes. Her backyard was relatively big, larger than those of the neighboring houses, and it had many big fruit trees such as sweet star fruit, rambutan, milk fruit, and mango trees, with very thick leaves covering the entire yard. There was an underground bomb shelter that had been dug during the war in the middle of the yard, providing protection for her family, and its entrance was inside a fenced chicken coop and covered by a camouflaged concrete lid. We kept all our stuff inside this shelter.

Manh had been living at this house most of the time since the date his friend left the country, as the brothers and sisters of his friend considered Manh as their older brother. Manh also planned to have Hien and her two younger brothers go with us on this trip. Hien was a very nice and hard-working girl. She did all the grocery shopping and cooking for the family and didn't even mind washing clothes for Manh when he was out working on the trip. She called me Uncle Hai and was always friendly and nice to me, even though she had only known me over a few months. I ate and slept at her house when I was in Rach Gia most of the time, and Manh and I only slept at other houses when she told us not to show up at her house.

Manh was born and raised in this area, so he had a lot of friends who were working for the government in different capacities. Some were officers in the military or police, some were working for various government agencies, and some were working for the state-run farm. Most of his friends were his high school classmates or the people who had lived in the same village at a young age. He went out to the café with these friends and acquaintances very often, and that was how he had sufficient inside information on the time and location of police raids.

Living in this house off and on for a few months, I had seen that Hien always cherished Manh's presence and joyously talked to him, and she appeared to be very concerned for his well-being. Sometimes I noticed her looking at him in a way that could only be described as passionate. They seemed to enjoy each other's company, and he even bought her small gifts occasionally.

One hot day, Manh rushed into the house, complaining. "It's damn hot out there. Look at my shirt. It's all wet."

She then immediately ran to the closet to get him a towel and a clean shirt and said, "Take your shirt off and let me dry you off so you can put on a clean one." He complied, and she dried him with the towel.

"Don't take a shower now. Wait until you cool off a bit. Otherwise, you will catch a cold," she said.

She pampered him with care and love and affectionately treated him like her older brother. Manh had helped to get her older brother out of the country, and now he was trying to help her and her younger brothers to get out. I thought that might be the reason she went out of her way and risked her life to do impossible things to assist him.

We were all plagued with stress dealing with the daily issues relating to the trip, especially Manh, who had to make the decisions to get problems solved. Many times he came home with anxiety written on his face. He would go directly to bed to lie down and think about whatever problem needed to be solved, and Hien was always there, sitting next to him, holding his hands and comforting him.

It was a very small thing, but I had noticed that Manh always enjoys a glass of pickled lemon on ice on hot days. Hien knew Manh's favorite drink, and although she didn't know how to make pickled lemon, she tried hard to learn from others. She put herself through quite a bit of work to make him and her family a big jar of this drink containing so much pickled lemon juice that it lasted for at least six months.

A few days later, while walking along the riverbank on the other side from the café having the beautiful girl, Manh suggested stopping by the café to have a drink. I agreed, and we turned around to walk toward the old steel bridge, which spanned the river close to its mouth. We then walked all the way to the end of the bridge and turned left toward the café. Her shop was halfway between the old steel bridge and the white concrete bridge and sat right next to the riverbank. If customers preferred to watch boats going by in the river, they could choose to sit at the rear of the shop looking at the river, but if they loved to watch people walking by, then they could sit in front of the shop under the canopy. It was situated in a convenient location that could be reached either by walking or by boat.

This time, we chose a table at the back of the shop where we were able to watch the boats going by. I didn't know how many times Manh had visited this place since the last time I had been with him, but it seemed to me that the girl and Manh were very friendly. They laughed and joked with each other from the time we walked into the shop as if they had known each other for years, even though it was probably just a little more than a week.

There were only a few customers in the shop at this time, so she was able to spend time talking to us. She sat in a chair next to Manh, and he pulled out a small package from his pocket and gave it to her. I found out later that the box contained red Revlon lipstick. She didn't refuse the gift like other Vietnamese girls might, but accepted it with gratefulness. I was totally surprised by her reaction, since most Vietnamese girls were very shy when someone they had just met offered them a gift or even a compliment.

Well, as usual, I ordered a glass of coconut water and Manh had a glass of pickled lemon juice with ice. Today, Manh introduced her to me and said that her name was Dzung. She had just finished high school, but she couldn't go to college because her father had connections with the former regime. Instead, she quit school to work for her sister at this shop.

She turned to Manh, asking about me, "I have seen this man with you twice. You guys have any relationship?"

"Oh, Brother Hai, my oldest brother, he is a farmer living in Giong Rieng, and he came to visit," Manh said.

"You mean a remote farming region of our province?" she asked.

"Yes," I said.

"Hai Ruong," she bluntly joked. I didn't take offense even though the word meant a farmer who lived in the very remote farmland in primitive conditions.

Manh came to my defense, saying, "Well, even though he is a farmer, he does have some schooling."

"First grade?" she laughingly asked.

"I can read and write, too," I ironically pitched in.

I didn't blame her for calling me Hai Ruong, and I was sure that others would have given me the same nickname when they saw me. I did wear worn-out, wrinkled pants that were too short, my green shirt was old and faded, and I was barefoot. Furthermore, my feet were not dirty, but since I had walked barefoot in the muddy soil for so many years, the skin of my feet was dark and thick and my toenails were long and blackened by the mud as if I didn't wash my feet before going to bed. I really did look more like a farmer than someone who worked in the office at this time of my life. Whether she looked down on me, I really didn't know, but she just focused on talking and laughing with Manh and stolidly ignored me.

It was good that they left me alone because it enabled me to focus on observing this area, and from this position I was able to clearly see the riverbank on the other side, although the river was quite wide, at least two hundred meters.

We had walked on the street at the other side of the river and passed by the police station quite often, but I hadn't realized that it was directly across from the gas station until I had a chance to sit at the back of the coffee shop to see it. This was the police headquarters of this province. I didn't know how many people were working at this facility, but it seemed to be very busy; I saw many people walking in and out of this station during the time I was sitting at the coffee shop. Both banks of the river were the same height, so that if we were able to see them, then they were probably able to see the coffee shop clearly from the station as well, especially from their guard booth.

Manh met this girl, Dzung, a few times, and they became good friends and exchanged a little of their personal stories. I learned from Manh that this building was originally a gas station and had belonged

176

to Dzung's father before 1975. After the Communist regime took over the country, they confiscated the gas station and divided the building into two halves. They returned this side of the building to her father, and her sister turned it into a café. The other half was still being used as gas station to provide services to boats and other vehicles for the state-run farms and cooperatives.

Upon taking over the building, the government locked the door connecting the two sections of the building; however, it still could be used to go back and forth between two sections when the door was unlocked. Like all other government facilities, this one was also managed by a Communist cadre, one who had come from North Vietnam about two years ago. He had had nothing when he first got here, but after two years managing this gas station, he became wealthy, relative to the current living standards of the Vietnamese people. We didn't know what his ranking was, but he had his own brand-new Russian jeep called a Molotova and an assigned chauffeur who worked for him twenty-four hours a day.

Every day, boats from the state-run farms stopped by early in the morning to get gas before they were sent to the field. There were many state-run farms in the province, so this gas station was particularly busy early in the morning until around nine or ten.

While Dzung was talking to Manh, a group of soldiers walked in. She turned around at their entry and said to Manh, "Excuse me, I have to serve those guys. They always want me to be the one to serve them."

She immediately stood up and walked over to the table where the soldiers were still milling around. Even though they had already seen her approaching them, one of the soldiers pretended not to see her and flippantly said, "Where is beautiful Dzung?"

"She is no longer working here," she said with a smile.

We didn't want to have any trouble with them and we had just finished our drinks, so we stood up and walked out the door without even looking at them.

Hien's house was on the other side of the river, and the way would be shorter if we turned left on the street in front of the shop to reach the white concrete bridge, but we decided to turn right instead towards the old steel bridge farther from the sea. We stood on the steel bridge for a while looking at the river underneath. We then turned right at the end of the bridge, walking towards the white concrete bridge along the street on the other side of the river.

Upon reaching the police station, I looked at the coffee shop from this side of the river, and I could see people sitting and walking at the rear of the shop.

We both kept quiet from the time we left the old steel bridge. I didn't know what Manh had in his mind, but for me, finding a location for loading our people occupied my mind and soul all the time, even while I was at the coffee shop.

When we reached the white concrete bridge, we turned onto the main street to go home. Manh suddenly got close to me, asking in a low voice, "Brother Hai, have you come up with an idea as to where we can load our people?"

"Not exactly, but I have a suggestion," I said.

"Where?" he asked.

"Can you tell me how close you are with Dzung?" I asked carefully.

"Well, I met her a few times while you weren't here and I met her a couple of times with you, and I like her," he said.

"That's great, but what I wanted to know is whether she likes you."

"I don't know for sure whether she likes me, but she's nice to me and she was happy to see me, as you saw today."

"Tell me honestly. Did you guys go out to get something to eat, walk along the beach, or go shopping?" I asked. He was startled and looked at me closely.

"Brother Hai, are you my father?" he said discontentedly.

"No, I'm not. It is, however, very important for me to know so I can tell you my suggestion," I calmly stated.

"What does that have to do with selecting a location?" he unhappily asked.

"Just take a deep breath and we will talk about that more in depth, but for now please answer my questions," I insisted with a smile.

"Are you going to poke into my personal life again? Hien was very angry, asking me the same questions the other day when she saw me spending time at the coffee shop. Did you and Hien talk behind my back?"

"No, no, we didn't, and in fact I didn't know that Hien asked you those same questions either. I'm sorry you took it that way," I said.

"If it was not a conspiracy to corner me, why did you guys ask me similar questions on the same issue?" Manh angrily asked.

"It was sheer coincidence, and I am sure we don't have the same motive," I said apologetically.

"I don't feel comfortable talking about this at the moment. We can talk about it another time," he said.

"Manh! You misunderstood me. I didn't intend to interfere into your personal life but what I wanted to find out was for the good of the people who put their trust in us," I persisted.

"Oh! I see, you and Hien think Dzung will distract me from doing my work," he scornfully said.

"Well, I think we need to think this over and we will resume our discussion with a fresh mind later," I said.

"If you want," he grudgingly said.

The discussion became testy and distracted by our debate on this hot topic. We somehow passed Hien's house without even noticing until we saw the Three Gateway Entrance. We then realized that we were a few hundred meters away from her house. We walked back without saying a word to each other, and by the time we entered the house, I saw Hien quietly sitting on a chair at the table in a corner in deep thought.

She said to me, "Hello, Uncle Hai," but she didn't say anything to Manh. Manh walked directly into his room and lay down without saying anything to Hien either. She then looked at me and said, "Meals are ready. Are you hungry, Uncle Hai?"

I didn't feel like eating after what we had been through, so I said, "Not really. Thanks."

"Let me know if you want to eat," Hien said.

"Thanks, I will."

I went to the backyard and sat on an old wooden stool underneath the shade of a big tree. It was much cooler here than inside the house. I lit a cigarette.

I agreed with Manh that I had no right to tell him what to do in terms of his private personal life; I didn't have that intention. However, I had to work with him for the benefit of our relatives and friends.

Although there was no serious dispute between us, I felt tension in the air, so I wanted to get out of this place for a while by going home to spend a few days with my family. I knew that time was essential to us now. The longer we dragged this out, the more problems we were going to face later, but I had to let things quiet down and I didn't want to discuss anything important with Manh when he was not in good mood.

On the second day at home while I was helping my wife cook, I heard a voice coming from the door of our rented shack. "Hi, Brother Hai."

Turning around, I saw Manh standing at the doorway with a bag in his hand, and to my surprise I didn't have time to open my mouth to say hello before Manh said, "I brought some ripened mangoes for the kids. They are very sweet."

"Come on in, have a seat. Sorry we don't have a chair, just sit on the bed. Thanks for the mangoes," I said.

"Where is everyone?" he asked.

"We just bought some fish. My wife is cleaning them in the canal. The children are in school," I said. "How did you get here?"

"I took the bus! Oh man, it was so crowded," he lamented.

"Stay and have lunch with us."

"I'd love to stay, but I have things to do and I need to get back."

"Something important you want to talk about?" I asked.

"I am sorry for the misunderstanding we had," he said.

"It's not a problem. We work together every day. It is normal that we may have conflicts or misunderstandings, but the main thing is we know how to iron them out for the good of our common goal. Constructive conflicts make progress," I said.

"Can you go with me now to the city?" he asked hopefully.

"Would it be okay if I get there this evening? I'd like to spend some time with my kids when they get home from school," I said.

"Okay! I will say good-bye to Sister Huong and then I will take off," he said.

"See ya later," I said after him as he walked toward the canal and disappeared.

After eating lunch and spending a few hours of quality time with my children, I took the last bus to the city. Being the last bus, it was very crowded and therefore steamy hot. I couldn't get a seat, so I had to stand all the way to the city, but it wasn't a big deal for me since I was used to it. On the other hand, the strong smell of people's sweat made me feel nauseated, and my neck was hurting since the bus wasn't tall enough for me to stand straight.

I got off the bus and walked directly to Hien's house to meet Manh as planned. By the time I knocked on the door, it was already eight o'clock in the evening. The lights were turned on, and Hien answered the door. Under the dim yellow light I saw Hien's sullen face. She didn't bother to even say hello.

"Hien! What happened?" I asked.

"Nothing, Uncle Hai," she said mechanically.

"Is Manh home?" I asked, at a loss.

"He was here earlier, but I don't know where he is now," she hesitantly said then walked away.

Though her behavior left me feeling uneasy, I couldn't figure out what was going on. I decided that it was not wise to make things worse at this time, so I went directly to the small room Hien's family gave me for temporary stay and sat on the bed, pondering. Almost immediately, Manh walked in and quietly waved at me to follow him.

He whispered in my ear while I followed him to the front door, "I want to tell you something."

"What is happening?" I nervously asked.

"I will tell you. Let's take a walk," he said.

Pulling me close to him, he began in a low voice, "Two days ago after you left, I spent some time walking along the harbor thinking about the questions you had asked me when we were walking home from the coffee shop. I thought deeply about it…yes, deeply, and ultimately I didn't think you were trying to stop me from going out with Dzung or that you were poking into my private life."

"Oh! No, no, I didn't have that intention. Not my job," I agreeably said.

"I have been working with you for a long time and I know you are very open-minded person, but I was too quick to jump to conclusions. I am sorry."

"That is fair," I said.

"Dzung and I became very good friends, I would say even more than friends. I once tested to see how she would react by mentioning to her the idea of leaving the country," he said.

"How did she respond?" I was very curious.

"Well, she's always busy during the day, so I had to wait until the shop was closed, which was about nine o'clock in the evening. I left the bike I had borrowed from Hien in front of the shop and spent about two hours talking to Dzung inside her kitchen," he said.

"Did you tell her anything about our trip?"

"No, no not at this stage," he said. "I asked her why she didn't leave the country. Many people in Rach Gia have done so. And she told me that the Communists confiscated her father's gas station and she hates them, and though her family wants to get out, they don't have the means.

"I left at ten and some son-of-bitch stole my bike and I had to walk home," he ruefully continued.

"Oh my goodness!" I said.

"Hien was still awake waiting for me when I walked into the house, and I had to tell her the truth. She was very upset and she told me, 'Even at this stage of the project you don't devote your time to get the job done. Instead you still go out flirting with a girl.' She said, 'You are so infatuated with Dzung that you don't have any clue of what's going on. If you still go to the coffee shop and spend time there, I will throw everything you have in this house on the street and report your plan to the police.'"

I was stunned. "Really! This is serious!"

"Despite my best efforts, I still failed to convince her," he sadly said.

"What you want me to do?"

"I don't really know what you can do now, but at least you are here," he said.

"I don't think Hien was angry because you lost the bike, she was upset because she was fearful of losing you," I said.

"What…what did you say?" he asked me, his voice raised.

"Did you notice that she goes out of her way to do things for you? Do you see the romantic love in her eyes when she looks at you and the way she takes special care to comfort you when you are under stress? Have you seen her sitting in a corner of the house quietly waiting for you in the middle of the night? She loves you, or in a better term, she is infatuated with you," I said.

"She is my friend's sister. I consider her as my sister, and there is nothing more than that," he insisted.

"You don't feel romantic love for her, but she does love you. She was afraid of losing you and she would do whatever it takes to keep you," I said.

"You are kidding, right?"

"No. I am serious based on what I have observed."

"So, what should I do?" he asked.

"Obviously, I don't ask you to love her romantically, but you need to give her more of your attention, treat her better, and buy her a little gift here and there to show her that you care about her," I told him.

"Yes, I will," he said, shaken.

"On the other hand, I will explain to Hien the reasons why you and I were spending time at this coffee shop. Let me tell you now honestly that I had thought about using the coffee shop as a location for loading our relatives and friends," I said.

"Great minds think alike!" Manh gave me an enthusiastic hug.

"The idea of using this location came up when we both were sitting at the back of the shop looking at the boats going by," Manh said.

"Great!" I said with a smile.

We both realized that it was as yet just an idea and it would take a lot of work and effort to turn it into reality. In the meantime, I had the frightening task of explaining to Hien the reasons why we spent a lot of time at the coffee shop and persuading her not to do anything too drastic that might damage our unity and hard work and could get to the point where we would all go to jail or even be executed.

Although Manh needed to frequent the coffee shop more often to bring his relationship with Dzung to a more intimate level, in the next few days he had to refrain from making Hien angrier by spending less time at the coffee shop until I had the opportunity to discuss matters with her.

Our top priority within the next few days was to calm Hien down and to convince her that we had good reasons to frequent the coffee shop, but I had to choose the most suitable time to discuss it with her in the absence of Manh.

In the interest of getting Manh out of the house for a few days, we talked in front of Hien about a trip to An Giang to sign a contract for carrying goods for a government agency. Manh volunteered to go there for a few days. Despite being upset at Manh, she still packed some clothes for him and made him some glutinous rice with sesame and salt to carry on the trip.

Having lived in this house for quite some time, I knew Hien and her work schedule well. She was very hard-working, disciplined, and not materialistic; and even though she was a very well-groomed person, she had never put on makeup or fashionable clothes. She was a typical shy Vietnamese woman and more on the introverted side, but that didn't mean that she would keep quiet when she was jealous of love.

By her behavior, I knew that she loved him a lot, and I needed to understand her better so I could effectively convince her and channel her energy toward a more positive support of our goal, rather than her current destructive path that would jeopardize everything we had worked so hard for the last several months. Usually she had some free time in the morning before going to the market to buy food and returning home to cook, so I took advantage of this time to have a little talk with her.

I knew she usually sat at the table in the kitchen in the morning to write down items she needed to buy for the day, so I tried to wake up early to get my morning routine done before walking into the kitchen to talk to her.

"Hi, Hien…how are you?" I said amicably.

"I am fine, and you, Uncle Hai?" she said with a smile.

"I am fine, too. You have some green tea?"

"Yes! Uncle Hai, let me make you a cup."

"Thanks, let me make one for you and one for me. Don't you remember I am a tea farmer?" I said with a grin.

"Tea expert, be my guest," she joked.

I put the kettle of water on the traditional wooden stove and stoke the fire before putting a teaspoon of green tea in the teapot. While waiting for the water boil, I looked for a way to indirectly bring up the conflict she had with Manh.

"Green tea is very good for your health," I said.

"I heard that it has antioxidant properties," Hien agreed.

"How do you know?"

"I learned this when I was in my science class in the last year at high school," she answered.

When the water began to boil, I poured a small amount of water into the pot to rinse the tea and then filled the pot with boiling water. Waiting for the tea to dissolve, I sat down in a chair across from her and said, "Hopefully, Manh is able to secure a contract with the local government so we can bring our boat down here soon."

"I haven't seen the boat yet, and I want to see what it looks like," she said.

"It is a river boat, so its bottom is curved and not flat as a sea boat, and it is quite solid because we just had it reinforced with thick and stronger ribs."

"We are going to have many young women on this trip, and I am really worrying about their welfare. Thai pirates are very savage," she said.

I poured tea into a cup and slid it toward her side of the table before I filled my cup. "Enjoy," I said. I cautiously took a small sip of tea since it was still hot.

"Manh and other team members already have a plan for that. However, there is an important thing that we need to look into at this time. The location to load our people."

"Did you, Manh, or other members of the team have any ideas?" she asked.

"We learned through members of our team who infiltrated the government that the local authorities have their informants almost everywhere, especially along the coast and riverbanks. Now, for us to find a suitable location is harder than for a camel to go through the eye of a needle," I said. Hien frowned and kept her silence.

"However, we won't give up easily. We have been working so hard to this point. We are able to almost see the fruit of our labor," I added.

"A few days ago, I saw a group of people in tattered clothes on the beach being dragged by the police to a bus," she said.

"Horrible and scary! That is why we are diligently searching everywhere. There is still one place which Manh and I thought is a good location for our purpose," I said.

"Where?" she curiously asked.

"The coffee shop," I answered cautiously.

"Which one?"

"Dzung's coffee shop."

"Uncle Hai, What are you talking about? On the other side of the river, directly across from the shop, is a police station," she warned.

"They would never, ever think that someone would dare to load people right in front of their noses. Secondly, there is a short distance from there to the sea mouth," I said.

"You also have to go underneath of the white concrete bridge to get to the sea. There is one guard booth on each side of the bridge to watch boats going in and out. Are you aware of that?" she asked uneasily.

"Yes, you are right, and we are aware of that."

"Uncle Hai, it is so dangerous…very risky…you guys think about it again," she nervously said.

"As I said, it is just an idea, there are so many unknowns. We have no concrete plan to use this location as yet. We are still searching," I said. "If you have a suggestion, let us know. We will look into it."

"What about the location where Manh's relatives were picked up on the last trip?" she said.

"Manh had brought me to this location once. It is no longer safe. Our friends living in the area informed us that the police and local officials watch over this area closely," I said.

She frowned and let out a long sigh.

"Hien! We have looked into many different places, but the location at the coffee shop appeared to be promising, so Manh and I spent time visiting this area to learn more about the people, the surroundings, and a big question: whether we can use it to load our friends and relatives," I slowly said.

"Uncle Hai, you think that it is justifiable for Manh to stay at the shop until one or two o'clock in the morning?" she asked sharply.

"I understand that you have reasons for concern, but Manh is doing this for the benefit of our group. Sometimes we need to look beyond ourselves to support one another for the noble cause of our group. We need to stay calm to tackle the complicated problem we are now facing, and a hot temper is not the best way to get things solved. The French used to say, 'Il faut *tourner sept fois* sa *langue* dans sa bouche *avant* de *parler.*' If our neighbors have even a slight suspicion of our activities, then we would be in absolute disaster."

"What does it mean?"

"It simply means we have to think carefully before we do or say something," I said. Thinking for a few seconds, I continued, "I wish I could play Manh's role, but Dzung doesn't even want to talk to me, and as a matter of fact, she called me Hai Ruong. Given the situation we are in, I am pleased that my disguise can fool her."

"She is not a nice person," Hien said.

"I understand that, but we have a higher goal to accomplish," I said.

CHAPTER

8

Gift Giving

While Hien and I were talking at the kitchen table, Manh walked into the house. He had been gone for two days. He arrived with a bag full of green sour mangoes in his hand, which he put on table, then said, "Brother Hai, Dien said you like to eat the sour green mango dipped in spicy hot fish sauce with condensed sugar, so he picked some from his backyard and asked me to bring them to you."

"That's nice of you," I said.

"Hien, is your mouth watering yet?" Manh teased. "Hien, well, I have something special for you, and it isn't sour, but very sweet!" From the front pocket of his shirt, he produced a small gold chain with a jade Buddha pendant. He carefully dropped the necklace in his right palm and closed his hand, then asked Hien to open her right hand for him to drop it in.

She shyly and tentatively opened her right hand and laid it palm up on the table. With a smile, he dropped the necklace into her palm and said, "While I was looking for a propeller to replace the one we had for the outboard motor, I saw this chain displayed in a merchant's tray. I thought it was beautiful, so I decided to buy it for you."

"Try it on, I think it will look nice on your white, slender neck," I encouraged.

She ducked her head to hide her smile. "Thanks...I will put it on later," she said, blushing profusely, then dropped it into her pocket before fleeing to the kitchen.

Manh watched her retreat and chuckled. He told me that while in An Giang, he was able to get with Lam to secure a contract for carrying fish sauce for the school.

"Despite the fact that they told me that they still had enough fish sauce to last until the end of next month, I still convinced them that I would be able to get good quality and cheaper fish sauce for them." Rubbing his forehead in concentration, he continued, "Dien would represent us to sign the contract, and all the details would be clearly spelled out in the written contract. After the contract is signed and we get the travel permit, either you or I would have to go up there to bring the boat down here.

"So that's good news, but on the other hand, we urgently have to learn all the facts about the coffee shop," he concluded.

"Agreed," I said.

After Hien left the house for the market, he asked me, "How about going to the coffee shop with me this afternoon?" He pulled out another gold chain from the pocket of his pants.

"This one is for Dzung," he said.

My eyes widened. "Be careful, don't let Hien know this," I warned.

"Brother Hai, I am in a very fragile and difficult situation," Manh said defensively.

"We need both of them on our side. Use your charm and wit to win their hearts, but please, be careful!" I said.

"I am treading on thin ice. I can't just turn the switch on and off on these girls, they are human beings too," he said.

"We have no choice but to deal with this sensitive matter head on. I have explained to Hien the reasons why you and I had frequented the coffee shop and she seems to understand it," I said.

"How come she still had a sullen face when she saw me?" he asked.

"It takes time. She is only human," I said.

"Let's walk to the coffee shop," he urged.

"I think we should stick around to help Hien prepare lunch and eat lunch before we go," I suggested.

We walked to the coffee shop around three o'clock in the afternoon. I still wore the same clothes that I had on the first time I was at the shop with an old pair of rubber flip-flops. Even though my clothes were old, worn, and wrinkled, they had been washed so they weren't smelly. Manh wore a neat pair of trousers and a tucked-in white shirt with a pair of leather sandals. He carefully put the necklace in his pocket.

Dzung met us at the entrance and walked us to the rear of the shop, where we chose a table at a corner so we could see people but they couldn't see us. She then asked Manh, "Your brother, still here?"

I didn't know what she had in her mind, but to me, it seemed to be very rude. I thought to myself that I shouldn't be too finicky about this girl because she was more of the extroverted type of individual. It could be that she didn't want to see a poor farmer brother walking around her would-be boyfriend to dampen his image.

"The rice paddy fields have already been harvested. He has a few months free, so I wanted him to stay here and help me with a few things," Manh said.

"Is that right?" she said.

After we all sat down, Manh pulled out the necklace, handed it to her, and said, "This is for you. I hope you like it." Holding the necklace in her hand, she laughed excitedly.

"Beautiful! It is gold, right?"

"Yes, it is pure gold," he said.

He stretched out his hand and said, "Let me put it on for you." While putting on the necklace, he caressed her beautiful white, slender neck.

She seemed happy with the gift, and while fingering the gold necklace, she asked Manh whether he wanted to meet her sister. Manh agreed.

This was the first time I had the opportunity to meet her older sister. It was difficult for me to guess her age because she had a good layer of makeup on her face. She was tall to begin with and looked much taller in her high heel shoes. She wore a pair of jeans with a light yellow shirt, and like her sister, she was pretty.

She showed us a kind of offensive attitude of superiority when we were introduced to her, barely glancing at me and saying one word of hello. Then I guessed she pretended to be busy talking to Manh and other customers, because she didn't look at me or talk to me again the whole time. They treated me with derision. Through the way these girls behaved, it seemed to me that they were very materialistic and only wanted to associate or mingle with people who had money and status.

I learned from Manh that Dzung's sister had two young children with her husband, who was a non-commissioned officer of the former regime who had died during the war. She now was in an intimate relationship with a chauffeur named Than who worked for the gas station manager. The two of them were always together.

Than had also been a non-commissioned officer in the air force of the former regime. He had been working as a chauffeur for the high-ranking Communist cadre who was in charge of the gas station for about two years. His job was to drive the manager to his meetings or to wherever the boss wanted him to go. The boss usually went to Saigon for meetings or for fun.

At this time, the economic policy of the Communist regime was to prohibit the free flow of goods and commodities throughout the country. Therefore, people in the cities were in dire need of food such as rice, meat, fish, vegetables, and other necessities. This was especially true of Saigon, the capital city of the former regime.

The rural provinces were capable of producing rice, and Rach Gia was a fertile province that yielded a large harvest of rice and allowed for people to raise some chickens and pigs for their own consumption then sell the surplus on the black market. This province also lay along the coast, so the majority of people were fishermen. Taken as a whole, this province was very much self-sufficient.

The majority of the former ARVN officers or government officials were now in jail, and their wives and children now had a tough time making a living since they didn't have any land and they were faced with a lot of social discrimination from the new regime. They and other poor people had to find a way to survive by illegally transporting small quantities of prohibited items such as meat, rice, fish, vegetables, and other daily necessities from the rural provinces to Saigon to make a living.

It was almost impossible for me to imagine how people carried the so-called contraband. There was one time I was sitting next to a young woman on a public bus going from Rach Gia to Saigon. A rank, nauseating odor seemed to cling to her. By the time we got to the checkpoint, the agents stopped and searched everyone on the bus, and they found that she had a lot of thinly sliced pork wrapped around her thighs, belly, and chest areas; she probably was carrying almost half of a pig with her. It was very hard, I was sure, to have meat wrapped around her body in the extreme heat of the Mekong Delta area.

Another time I saw a very thin woman who yet had a big and full bosom; it turned out that she was wearing a big bra filled with two plastic bags of mung beans. The agents, of course, confiscated all the commodities regardless of how hard these women pleaded. The children of these women would go one more day without food.

These incidents had demonstrated to me how hard it was for normal people to carry prohibited items from the countryside to the cities. There were, however, still people who were able to transport a much larger quantity of contraband to Saigon without being searched if they had government vehicles with official license plates.

These were the people like the chauffer of the gas station and his manager. They collaborated to purchase prohibited items from Rach Gia and brought them to Saigon to resell for a profit; they made one trip to Saigon every week. Given the slow economy and widespread scarcity, these guys made a fortune. I learned that this was the reason the gas station manager had become so rich after just two years in this position.

Besides his salary, the chauffer also made a good share from the sale of the contraband on the black market.

Thanks to this money, the chauffer dressed in clean and up-to-date, fashionable clothes. His hair was always neat, sharp, and combed like the South Korean movie stars. There was one way in particular that he was different from the ordinary people: he always wore a pair of shiny black leather shoes. On the other hand, even though he was making good money, the manager of the gas station still always wore a pair of rubber tire sandals and old wrinkled khaki clothes like any other Communist official.

When he had first gotten the job as a manager, he smoked domestic cigarettes and drank rice wine, but now those items were no longer on the list for his chauffer to buy. He loved to drink foreign whiskey, especially Black & White Scotch whisky. He smoked only the English State Express 555 classic cigarettes. He also loved young women, and he emphasized clearly that he only wanted Southern girls when he'd send his chauffer to get him one. We didn't know why he didn't like the Northern girls; it could be that he had a bad experience with the women from his home in the North. It seemed to us that these two guys were getting along really well.

There were a couple of rooms adjacent to the coffee shop that were used as living quarters for Dzung's sister and her two children. The chauffer spent most of his time at the shop when he was in Rach Gia.

Manh wanted to spend more time with Dzung, so he stopped by the coffee shop more often and also purchased gifts for her, her sister, and her nephews. Their relationship seemed to grow to the point where they could confide the secrets of their life to each other, and he also spent more time staying with her overnight at the shop.

Manh and Than, the chauffer, became close friends, and now they considered themselves as members of Dzung's family. Through Manh I knew that Dzung and her family wanted to flee the country but didn't have the means, and they said that they were willing to assist Manh in any way they could that would include them in the escape.

The stagnant economy, the suppression of freedom, and especially the forcing of people to the new economic zones were factors that drove people to flee the country in high numbers. Many people from Saigon flooded the coastal provinces, mainly Rach Gia, because it didn't take a long time to go from the tip of this province to the

Gulf of Thailand with a decent boat. The local officials realized that this was a good opportunity to make money off the people who were trying to flee the country, so they positioned the police forces, local guerillas, informants, and plain clothes police everywhere to arrest them.

We were facing a tremendous amount of pressure to find a location to load our people, and given the high security along the coast and river mouths in this province, it would be almost impossible for us to carry out this task without the cooperation of Than, the chauffeur.

We knew that we needed to approach Than to find out if he was inclined to escape. We, however, didn't believe that he trusted us to the point that he would tell us the truth or cooperate with us. The storm season was rapidly approaching, and we still hadn't come up with a location. We absolutely needed Than's cooperation, but we didn't know what and how to approach him.

We desperately needed to find a location, but our hands were tied by the tight control and watchful eyes of all of the government agents, and we didn't know who would be able to accomplish the delicate task of approaching Than. We were at an impasse.

This issue was of the utmost concern. Manh and I dwelled on this for many days, and finally Manh recommended that Dzung sound out Than, even though her personality was not perfectly fit for this job. At this time, she knew Than better than anyone else on the team, so she seemed like our best option. Manh argued that Dzung was the best person for this job since she had lived in the same house with Than for almost two years, she knew him relatively well, they treated each other as family, and she had also promised Manh to assist him in all escape efforts. Above all, she was Manh's lover. He believed that she would do a good job. However, he wanted to give her a few instructions before she carried out this task.

After receiving the assignment, Dzung began looking for an opportunity to talk to Than alone and in private, but it didn't seem to be easy to find the time for this since he spent most of his time either with her sister or at the gas station.

On Sundays the coffee shop opened early in the morning, so Dzung had to wake up early to prepare coffee and food for the customers' breakfast, and she was very busy.

She was going back to the kitchen to pick up some condiments when she saw Than sitting in the nook in the kitchen alone, smoking. She immediately jumped on the opportunity, forgetting all about the condiments.

She approached him cautiously and smiled, hoping to start a conversation.

"Deep in thought, eh?"

He didn't respond, and it seemed like he was in another world. He took a deep drag and then blew smoke rings. He was looking at the circles without even blinking his eyes. She thought he was smoking pot.

"Hey! Wake up?" she said.

Without moving a muscle, he absently asked, "What?"

"Cup of coffee?" she asked. He nodded. She hastily left him, walking back to the shop to pick up a small yellow bag of coffee. When she returned to the kitchen, he was still sitting idly in the chair.

"This is special coffee called fox-dung coffee. It is so good that you will never forget it once you try it," she said pleasantly.

"Splendid idea, but how come you are suddenly so nice to me today?" Than said with a smirk.

"I have always been nice to you, but you didn't recognize it, you jerk," Dzung teased. "Let me make you a cup, it has a very unique taste. This coffee is very rare. My friend just brought it down from the Central Highland last night." While she spoke, she took a small, empty teacup from the cupboard and set it on the table. She then placed a coffee filter on top of the cup and carefully took one spoon of coffee and neatly dropped it inside the filter. She then filled it with boiling water from a thermos and covered the filter with its lid.

She pulled a chair to sit across the table looking at him smoking his cigarette. While waiting for the coffee to percolate, she continued. "Well, our friend dropped this bag of coffee last night. I asked her to stay here overnight, but she said she had to leave right away," Dzung said.

"It is difficult to travel from place to place nowadays because of the shortage of transportation. It probably took her a few days to get here from the Central Highland provinces," Than said.

"I didn't ask how long it took her, but it seemed that she was in hurry to catch a boat to get out last night," Dzung said.

He frowned slightly. "You mean fleeing the country?" he curiously asked.

Dzung didn't reply immediately. She removed the lid from the coffee and set on the table, then placed the filter on top of the lid. She then pushed the cup toward him and said, "You can add condensed milk or sugar to your taste." Dzung had to buy sugar and condensed milk in the black market for her shop; they were luxury goods for everyone, including low-level government officials.

"I just use a little bit of sugar so I can enjoy the real taste of it," he explained while adding some sugar. He stirred up the coffee and tried a sip.

"It is smooth and has a rich taste, no doubt it is special. Thanks, Dzung," he said pleasantly.

"What were you asking me earlier?" she asked.

He paused for a second to think. He raised the cigarette to his lips, took a drag, and let the smoke streamed out of his nose. Then he looked at her and said, "I remember now…she tried to escape, right?"

"With her two young children," Dzung confirmed.

"Risky, risky! Many people try to escape, but how many people successfully make it to their final destination?" he said, gesturing broadly with the cigarette.

"It is difficult, and my friend was aware of that. There are a lot of risks involved, but she said she couldn't stand staying in this country under the Communist regime," said Dzung.

"Why?"

"She said they confiscated her parents' coffee plantation and threw them in jail for not cooperating with the government. Her parents asked her to get out of the country with her children," she sadly said.

"Even though I have seen a lot of social injustices and my older brother is in prison for being an officer in the former regime, leaving the country is not an option for me," he said pensively.

"Why?" Dzung countered.

"Why? Did you ask me why? You know, firstly I don't know how. And boy oh boy, it would cost me an arm and a leg! I heard it is at least three taels of gold. Where in the world could I get that kind of money?" he said sadly.

"Would you go if somebody offered you a free seat in a boat?" she said with a smile.

"I'd have to be stupid not to go, but just think about it for a second. If that really happened, that person must be insane. Or it would be a joke, some kind of crazy prank, since I don't have any money to pay them or anything to give them in return. It could never happen," he said with a laugh before lapsing back into pensive silence.

Before Dzung could continue, her sister poked her head in the door. "Dzung, there are customers waiting for you!"

"Sorry! I'm coming!" Dzung said and hastily headed back to the shop, but when she reached the door, she halted and turned around to look at Than. "We'll see."

Once Dzung relayed the news that Than would also want to leave the country, we asked her to set up a time for us to meet with him in private to discuss the concrete plan and the tasks that he could do to assist us. However, he refused to meet with us. In his eyes, we didn't have anything to offer, especially me, a poor farmer. As he had said, he thought it was a joke. Escape was a very sensitive matter, so we did not blame him for being so cautious.

Moreover, he had been in this province for a long while, and he had seen quite a few people being arrested for illegally leaving the country. Than also had seen many bogus trips that aimed at milking money out of gullible people. Given the impossibly steep price people paid for a seat on a boat leaving the country, the idea that someone would come out of the blue and offer a seat for free was just a fantasy.

We also had to be very careful discussing our plan with him since he didn't have anything to lose if it turned out that he wasn't genuine, but our secret plan would be revealed and our hard work and lives would be in extreme danger.

He had once told Dzung that he had been a non-commissioned officer in the ARVN so he knew that the Communists only used him for the time being and would dump him when they didn't need him anymore. He knew that they didn't trust him.

We had only sketchy information about this guy and we wanted to know more about him. Manh was given the job of finding the facts since they met each other quite often and had routine casual conversations on different things.

One morning when Than was in town, Manh asked him to go to a famous local restaurant to have a bow of pho. Manh was willing to pick up the tab. This was a special Vietnamese beef noodle soup which most of the Vietnamese loved for breakfast.

Manh knew that this restaurant was very busy in the morning and wasn't an ideal place to discuss such an important and confidential issue as the trip, but he wanted to build a close relationship with Than so he could learn more whether Than really had a desire to leave the country. After enjoying a hot, tasty bow of pho, they both walked out of the restaurant. Than lit up a cigarette and took a long deep puff. He felt good. Even though Manh knew very well how long Than had been at the gas station, but for the sake of the conversation he pretended he didn't know.

"How long you have been working for the gas station?"

"About two years," Than said.

"It appears to be a good job, yeah?" Manh said.

"My wage is next to nothing, you know. I would go hungry without the money coming from selling goods on the black market. And you know, the son of a bitch gets most of that," Than said with rancor.

"Really? Who?" Manh asked.

"My boss. Manager of the gas station," Than said.

"I thought he liked you, eh?" Manh said.

"He just likes money. If I didn't make money for him, he would have kicked me out a long time ago. Without mercy." Than spat.

"Oh! Really?" Manh exclaimed.

"Working for the Communists I only know I'm making it day by day. They don't trust me, and I sure as hell don't trust them," Than said.

"I agree with you, I don't see a future here." Manh sighed. "My friends asked me to flee the country with them. I don't know if you want to tag along?" Manh asked him in a soft voice.

"I don't have any money to pay them," Than said. Though he didn't say it, his narrowed eyes revealed his suspicion.

"You don't have to pay, maybe you could do something to help," Manh suggested.

"Hey, buddy…you are kidding…right?" Than asked, stifling a giggle.

"This is not a joking matter…I am serious," Manh said.

"What…you mean you are serious? What do I have to do?" Than asked cautiously.

"If you are interested, we will meet with our friends to discuss?" Manh said.

We had tried every possible way to find out whether Than wanted to go, but there was no way for us to verify his trustworthiness. However, we had to move forward with our plan since time was short and we had no other choice. We decided to ask him for a meeting to discuss his role in the project, and thank God, we finally got his consent.

We asked Dzung to let us use the back room of her sister's living quarters the next day. Before entering the room, we asked Dzung to watch the area to make sure that there were no strangers hanging around outside the room where we were going to have the meeting. When Than arrived, I was surprised by how tall he was. This was the first time I had a chance to stand next to Than, and now I noticed that he was at least ten centimeters taller than I was. He wore a faded pair of blue jeans, a tucked-in white T-shirt under an unbuttoned blue-checkered shirt, and a big leather belt with a silver buckle. His hair was combed neatly, and he also wore a pair of beautiful Western black leather shoes that made him even taller. I wasn't certain whether he was charming with women, but I believed his outward appearance must be good to win the heart of Dzung's sister since she was very materialistic. I knew that Manh would have to use all of his powers of diplomacy to persuade Than to accept me and to convince him of all of the work we had done on the project so far.

Than looked annoyed upon seeing me with Manh at the meeting. In his eyes, I was only a farmer from an under-developed, remote village, an impression no doubt reinforced by Dzung and her sister. "What is this yokel doing here? You can't be serious?" Than sneered.

I didn't like how insensitively these people treated me, but I tried to brush it off. I realized that a confrontational approach wasn't the best way to get things done, and secondly, we were in need of his cooperation. I knew they judged me by the clothes I wore, my scrawny body, and my affected farmer's behavior.

Despite his condescension, I kept my calm. In order to break the ice, I immediately offered my hand to shake, and I tried to grip his hand firmly. He, on the contrary, just extended his hand and limply returned by handshake for just a second, not even looking straight into my eyes. While my hand was small, bony, and calloused, his hand was big but soft.

"I am glad that we have a chance to meet. I hope we can become friends. I will do my best to work with you," I politely said.

I thought that things were happening so quickly for Than that he might not completely comprehend the entire scope of the work that we were doing. He also wanted to show his contempt for me, so he dryly asked, "Working with you doing what? Raising pigs and farming rice?"

Upon hearing him say that, I knew that Dzung and her sister had told him something about me. I bristled at the derision in his condescending remark but as before, I still kept my cool, and I briskly said, "Yes, I am good at raising pigs, but we will probably work on something I am even better at." I sensed the change in his contemptuous behavior after he heard my answer.

"I see," he said. I thought that he looked intimidating.

Manh quickly broke the stalemate by interjecting, "We have a small boat, but it is reasonably stable, enough so to take us to sea. We have all that we need for the trip, and we are now looking for a place to load our friends and family members, and we think you have the means and capability to assist us in this area."

Than took a long puff of cigarette smoke and paused for a second, then carefully asked, "What do you want me to do?"

"You will pick up our relatives and friends with your Molotova jeep from designated locations and take them to the coffee shop in the early morning," Manh said firmly.

"How many people? And did you say one location?" Than asked.

"At this moment, we plan to have one location, but it may change," Manh said.

We heard a noise outside of the room, so everyone froze. We waited in tense silence, while Than quickly stood up and moved to a crack in the wall through which he could observe the outside alley.

"It's only Dzung walking outside," he said.

He then sat down again without saying a word. Than lit up another cigarette and drew a long puff. He sighed, releasing all of the smoke, and said with finality, "I want two seats on that boat."

"That's fine. In return, we need your cooperation," Manh said.

"I need to know the exact location and number of people," added Than.

"Of course, you will have all the required information before you pick them up," Manh said agreeably.

"As a matter of fact, one of the team members will work with you to watch over the location to let you know in advance if he or she sees anything that is suspicious," I said.

"We will have to discuss this in greater detail, but today's meeting is to confirm our agreement to work together on this important matter. Of course, we all need to keep this confidential," Manh said with seriousness.

We just wanted to get a firm promise of cooperation from the driver, and we didn't have much difficulty persuading him besides having to endure a few moments of his lofty and inconsiderate behavior. We held off for a few days before telling Than about what we were going to do or asking him for information about the activities and the habits of his boss because we wanted to observe his reaction after the meeting.

Two days later, Manh decided to visit the coffee shop in the hopes that he would be able to meet Than to ask for more information about the gas station so we could put together a plan for loading our people. Manh walked into the shop at around eight o'clock in the evening, while Dzung was sitting and talking with three young male customers. He smiled at Dzung and sat at a table in the corner.

Dzung was quite beautiful, and many young men wanted to date her. One of the young men at the table had asked her a few times to go out with him, but she had refused and also had told him that she already had a boyfriend. He wasn't too happy with the answer. He still frequented the shop, in spite of being explicitly rejected.

Dzung excused herself and walked over to the table where Manh was sitting. She asked if he wanted something to drink, but he answered that he only wanted to know if Dzung had seen Than around the last couple of days. She told him that Than had disappeared a day after the meeting, and her sister didn't even know his whereabouts. This concerned Manh greatly, but he kept his face impassive, not wanting to attract the notice of the other customers. He also had a few other important things to do, so he excused himself to leave. While Dzung was talking to Manh, these young men kept mischievously glancing at Manh and whispering to each other.

As soon as Manh approached the door, the tallest man in the group immediately stood up and blocked him from leaving the shop.

"Who the f—— do you think you are?" the young man burst out suddenly, throwing a punch at Manh with his right fist. Manh was able to dodge the punch, but he didn't fight back. Dzung saw the fight breakout, and she tried to get between Manh and the other guy to stop them and screamed for help. Another, shorter young man pulled a soda bottle off the counter and struck Manh with it on the back of his head. Manh fell down to the floor, and they started kicking and punching him repeatedly. Dzung cried loudly for help and begged them. "Please stop...stop please!"

"We have to teach this son of a bitch a lesson," one guy muttered.

"It will be worse if we see you come here again. Remember this lesson," another guy shouted at Manh.

They left the scene on their motorcycles right after the fight, and they didn't pay a dime for their drinks.

Blood and beer soaked Manh's shirt and spilled onto the floor, and shards of glass were strewn everywhere.

Dzung closed the shop early and brought Manh inside to care for him. He suffered a five-centimeter cut on the back of his head and a concussion. She cut the hair around the wound, cleaned it with hot water, and put a bandage on it. Manh asked Dzung not to call the police or report the incident because he didn't want police to be aware of a problem at this location.

Manh came home after one hour of rest at the coffee shop. He kept silent about the incident and wore a hat to cover up the injury. Hien would probably be the best person to clinically care for his wound, but he tried to hide the incident from her as much as he could since she would be furious if she knew that he had suffered the injury during a fight at the coffee shop and obviously an altercation would ensue. He was already in enough pain from the head injury and under enough pressure dealing with the project. He knew he didn't have the strength to withstand another blow because of the jealousy of a girl who loved him.

CHAPTER

9

Final Preparations

The boat was on its way to Rach Gia, and I was supposed to meet it at a confluence of two rivers and bring it to a location where it would be docked, waiting for the time to depart.

We had been searching everywhere for a suitable place to dock the boat, but regardless where we docked it, our boat had to pass underneath the old steel bridge before it could get to the gas station. This bridge was built by the former regime many years ago to connect two sections of the town for land travel while also allowing boats of different sizes to travel freely underneath.

There were a lot of civilian boats traveling in this section of the river, and ours was a riverboat, so we wouldn't arouse suspicion or stand out when we were mingling with other boats. We planned to have our boat travel to this part of the river from the dock to the steel bridge and return to test the water.

The portion of the river from the old steel bridge to the gas station wasn't a commercial site, so only a handful of boats traveled in this area except those from the state-run farms or very small fishing vessels. The police also had watchful eyes on boats traveling through this part of the river because from here, a boat could go underneath the white concrete bridge to the sea.

The distance from the old steel bridge to the gas station was about five hundred meters. There were civilian houses lying along the riverbank on the same side of the gas station, and most were supported in the rear by stilts that encroached at least fifty meters into the river with the result that these houses blocked our view of the gas station when we stood on the old steel bridge. This line of houses continued past the gas station about a hundred meters to the white concrete bridge. On the other bank, there was a street running parallel with the river from the old steel bridge all the way to the white concrete bridge, which was close to the sea. Houses lined this side of the river as well as the police station situated directly across from the coffee shop and gas station. Since our view was blocked, we had to walk on this street to count the number of houses starting from the old steel bridge to the gas station. This would help give us a relatively good estimation of where we were and when to stop, hopefully preventing us from speeding past the gas station.

There was a guard tower at each end of the concrete bridge with a bright floodlight mounted on top pointing to the river mouth. Beyond the white concrete bridge, tall bushes and overspreading trees grew on both banks all the way to the sea. We stood on this bridge many days and nights to watch the small fishing boats going in and out; we couldn't see anything under these bushes at night, so we assumed that the guards would probably not see anything either unless they had night vision goggles.

We also noticed that there was a big sand bar located on the left side of the river, which blocked almost the entire river; it left only a narrow channel on the right so the boats could go in and out. The sand bar shifted left or right somewhat depending on the tide and current, so we needed to know exactly where it would be at the time we took off to avoid being stuck on it.

Further complicating matters, the bottom of the bridge was built close to the water's surface with the intention of preventing relatively big boats from using this river mouth for going out to sea or coming in to the city. Standing on the bridge, I realized it was impossible to know how high it was from water's surface to the bottom of the bridge in the morning when the tide was low, unless we had a way to measure it, and fishing on the bridge was forbidden.

There was only one way to measure it—by going down to the bottom of the bridge. So, one early morning, I carried a big, dirty plastic bag over my shoulder filled with quite a few discarded plastic bags and empty bottles. In my other hand, I carried a long pointed stick with a rubber band wrapped around it to complete my disguise as a man picking up discarded plastic bags and bottles floating in the river. As I was climbing down the edge and approaching the foot of the bridge, I heard a man yelling with a Northerner's accent from one of the towers. I knew that the guard had discovered me, and it was all I could do to control my terror.

"Hey, you! What the hell you are doing down there? You can't go down there!" he barked, punctuating his command with a gunshot.

"Picking up the plastic bags, bottles," I screamed.

I looked up and saw that he was pointing the AK-47 at me.

"Get up here now! I will shoot at you," he ordered.

"So many bags here...I am going up...at once," I said while hurriedly measuring the distance from the water's surface to the bottom of the bridge and rapidly marking it with the rubber band. I also quickly picked up a few wet, dirty plastic bags and bottles and hastily dropped them into my carrying bag.

"You m——, get up here now...now!" I heard another shot.

I nervously climbed up and reported to the guard. He checked my bag, but he found nothing but the dirty plastic bags and empty bottles inside. He looked at me with contempt. I had only one flip-flop on my left foot; the other one had come off because the strap broke when I scrambled to climb up the slippery, steep edge of the bridge.

"You are forbidden to go down there, understand?"

"Many plastic bags, bottles down there," I insisted.

"God damn it! F—— stubborn" he angrily said and whacked my right shoulder blade with the butt of his AK-47. The blow knocked me to the ground, and my head hit the sidewalk. It caused me to grimace in pain, and I saw thousands of stars. It took me a few seconds to regain my consciousness and I tried to stand up, but I fell back to the ground again. He pulled me up by the collar of my shirt then kicked my butt and screamed at the top his lungs.

"You m——, get the f—— out of my face! Now! Now!"

This Northern soldier was trained to carry out his task without pity, and not because he had no heart, but because of the way he had been trained to be suspicious of everyone. I was lucky that I hadn't been killed.

As my head cleared, the first thing I looked for was my measuring stick, and to my surprise it was still in my left hand. I then tried to also pick up the bag. After the soldier's shattering blow, an acute pain lanced through my shoulder, and I couldn't lift my right arm to put the bag on my shoulder, so I dragged it along as I hurried away from the scene of the incident. The price I paid was very stiff, but I thought it was worth it since I had obtained a relatively accurate measurement that would let us know if our boat could pass under the bridge.

With the measurement I had collected, we were confident that the boat would have ample space to go underneath the white concrete bridge in the morning provided that we removed the temporary roof on top of the boat.

We had to go through all these hardships trying to sneak out under the white concrete bridge because we wouldn't be able to go through the official port. This city had only one official entry and exit port located in the city harbor; all regular boats coming into the city or going out to sea had to go through this port. The naval police had a checkpoint at this port to check permits for all boats, and they usually conducted a thorough search of boats that were suspected of carrying contraband or illegal passengers.

Obviously, no boats carrying illegal passengers could pass through this port unless the boat owners paid a huge bribe to the high-ranking officials of the city, and that was something we couldn't afford.

I had once sat on a bench at this harbor looking at the port, fantasizing that I was on one of those boats getting out of the country. Of course, that was just a dream.

Now I was almost turning that dream into reality. We were nearing our goal, but the next few steps were so perilous and difficult, and they seemed almost impossible to overcome. The level of risk and danger was tremendously high, the challenge we faced was more complicated than ever before, and we were under so much stress. We had a feeling that it was beyond our strength and capability, we were too exhausted, and sometimes we just thought about giving it up.

Besides the daily, routine problems, we had to deal with the internal conflict of the group members, especially between the two girls who loved Manh. They were always bickering about silly things when they had a chance to meet, even though we had tried to limit their contact. It seemed to me that the problem had been boiling underneath the surface all along and was even now just waiting for the right moment to explode like a volcano. If we couldn't take off soon, then this conflict had the potential to abort the project.

I didn't want to catch attention from people, so I didn't wear a sling, even though my right arm was badly hurt and I still had to participate in all the work that needed to be done for the trip. While we were standing on the old steel bridge to observe boats going in and out in this area during the day, I asked Manh with disappointment, "Did you notice the bickering between the two girls the last time they met?"

"Yes, so what you want me to do?" he asked.

"This is a symptom of a more serious problem, and I am afraid that it may run out of control," I said pensively.

"Well, I don't have one minute of rest. I have been working nonstop trying to get everyone out of this hell. So what in the world do they want me to do? What? What?" he growled through clenched teeth.

"Calm down…this is a very complicated and sensitive matter. You need to deal with these women tenderly, especially with Hien," I gingerly said.

"I treated them fairly, but I don't want to be blackmailed into loving someone who isn't compatible with me, and as I told you before, Hien is my friend's sister. I consider her as my sister as well," he said.

"Your point is well taken. But in the meantime, please understand that intelligently dealing with these women is an extremely important task now if you want us to get out of here safely." There was urgency in my voice.

"I am f—— sick of these women," he grumbled. Tensions were running far too high. I hoped we could finish our final preparations before everything blew up in our faces.

CHAPTER
10

Coffee for the Manager

A short while earlier, we had asked Dien to test the boat one more time to make sure the outboard motor propeller was working properly since it had just been recently replaced and all the mechanics who worked on our engine were in An Giang. One of the mechanics was willing to go with the boat to Rach Gia to assist us in case we needed some help. However, we hadn't yet told him about our intention of leaving the country, though on many occasions we jokingly mentioned about the good life and freedom of the Vietnamese people abroad compared to ours, and he also joked, "I work my ass off every day, so why do I keep getting skinnier?"

Originally, we had planned to send either Manh or me to An Giang to bring the boat down to Rach Gia, but now we had a volunteer mechanic, so we let Dien take care of this task and agreed that we would meet him at a designated location. We would then take the boat to a dock upstream relatively close to the gas station.

We had so much work ahead of us and so little time, including bringing our friends and relatives from Saigon and other provinces down to Rach Gia, finding a place for them to stay temporarily, preparing food for the trip, loading diesel oil to the boat, and acquiring weapons. The level of stress was mounting, and it showed on everyone's faces. On top of that, we also all had dark circles under our eyes from exhaustion due to overwork.

Than still hadn't shown up after he just disappeared without informing anyone, and we were very concerned. We wondered whether he was still with us or if he had already changed sides, abandoning his promise. We were in the dark, and we badly needed the information from him on the gas station for us to put together our plan of action.

We didn't know when he would be back, and the time we waited for him seemed like forever and pushed our group's tensions higher. However, we couldn't sit still; we had other tasks to do while waiting for him, and in case he didn't return, then we had to change to an alternative plan.

We had no way of knowing how long we would be at sea, so we prepared a lot of dried foods, especially dried rice. Hien had the responsibility to handle this task; she cooked a lot of rice and dried it in a wok. It took her more than three days to get this work done, and she had to do it with high level of concentration and caution to avoid ruining such a large quantity of rice. On the other hand, Dzung was asked to make a lot of lemon sugar; she went to the market and bought a bag of lemons, then she put sugar in plastic bags and squeezed the lemon juice into the bags. Since she had a coffee shop, people wouldn't pay too much attention to her work. We also contacted our relatives and friends, asking them to bring a small amount of food and informing them that they needed to be ready because we planned to leave within the next few days. We also told them that our member would meet them at the bus station and take them to undisclosed locations to stay temporarily for pick up.

The safety of our relatives and friends was very important to us, and I was especially concerned for the safety of my wife and children. We needed to protect them against the Thai pirates at all costs when we were in the sea. This fear was always in my mind, but I hadn't had a chance to talk to Manh about it.

This time of the year, the Pacific Ocean was relatively peaceful, especially around the area of the Gulf of Thailand. Since most of the refugees' boats were small and rickety, they usually chose this time of the year to leave the country. Thai pirates wanted to seize on this opportunity to rob them and they were also known to abduct and rape the young Vietnamese female refugees on their boats or on uninhabited islands. They therefore swarmed this area of the gulf like sharks waiting for prey.

One day, when Manh and I were walking along the road to our boat, I asked him, "I am concerned for the safety of our relatives and friends when we were at the sea, and I wondered whether you have a plan for this."

"Yes, we do," Manh said with firmness.

"What is it?" I asked inquisitively.

"We have four additional M-16 rifles, plus the one we captured, and a pistol," he said.

When I was raising money for the last trip, many people had promised to bring weapons just for the sake of getting onto our boat, and it turned out that they didn't have anything. "You already got them?" I asked seriously.

"Yes," he said.

"Where did you get them?" I asked.

He frowned and stopped for a few seconds to think, then said, "I will tell you later."

"We have enough ammunition?"

"Yes. It has all been loaded into the magazines," he said.

It wasn't my job to know, so I didn't ask any further. I was just happy that he already had a plan for this. He was a young man, but he had always planned everything out very carefully for all of the steps in the project.

Manh stopped for a few minutes then said, "We need to bring a few flashlights, a sickle, and a pair of binoculars, too."

"I still have the binoculars we had last time. A sickle for what?" I naively asked.

"If the propeller gets caught in fishing nets, we'll need to cut them," he said.

"Thanks. I see," I appreciatively said.

"I got a few flares, too," he said.

"Manh, you are really prepared, eh?" I said, feeling much relieved.

"We could use them in case," he said. "Who is responsible for the fresh water?"

"Dien," I said.

"Where did he get the water?" he asked softly.

"From a river in An Giang," I said.

"That is good," he happily said. "It would be lucky if we meet a foreign merchant ship when we are in the international waters. They may help us."

"It would be great. I pray for that all the time," I said.

Manh suddenly fell silent and put his hands into the pockets of his trousers, walking slowly alongside me, looking down for a few minutes. He seemed as if he was remembering something, then turned to me and said, "I had a severe headache the last few days. It was difficult for me think or focus."

"Did you take any medication?" I asked with concern.

"I took some aspirin, but it didn't help much," he sadly said.

"Slow down, you think too much about work," I suggested.

"Not really! Let me tell you, if you promise not to tell anyone, especially Hien," he said, putting his finger over his lips.

Manh then explained to me the incident that occurred at Dzung's coffee shop a few days ago and ruefully said, "I know Hien has very good and steady hands. She is very meticulous, but I just couldn't let her take care of my wound because she would freak out knowing that I got into a fight at Dzung's coffee shop. We need to avoid problems at all costs so we can focus on the upcoming trip."

I nodded understandingly. "Did you receive treatment at a hospital?"

"Don't you know that undercover police are everywhere in the hospital? I don't want to attract their attention," he said.

We were now walking along the dock, and although I had been with the boat this morning, now we couldn't find it because it was dark and there were so many boats docked at this location in the late evening. "Maybe we should call out to Dien," Manh suggested.

"Dien, where are you?" I yelled loudly, but there was no response; it seemed as if my voice was falling into the desert.

We kept calling several more times, and a few people in other boats started to complain because we were interrupting their sleep. We finally gave up and decided to see Dien and the mechanic in the morning when other boats were already gone; it would be much easier for us to find our boat then. The purpose of this visit was to talk to the mechanic and find out how he would react to the idea of his leaving the country. I would then be staying with the boat from then on until the date we took off.

While we walked back, Manh slightly tapped on my shoulder and said, "Let's stop by the coffee shop to see if Than has returned."

"Is it too late now?" I said.

"They usually close the shop at nine o'clock. It is only eight fifteen now, but we need to walk faster so we can get there before they close," Manh said.

Even though he wasn't much taller than I was and he also had the headache, Manh was moving really fast, and in order to catch up with him I had to run. I breathed heavily.

"Manh, you are walking fast," I panted. My shoulder was bothering me again.

"You have been working with me on the trip and you haven't had a chance to see your wife and children for a long while. I know you want to know how they are," Manh said.

"I miss them dearly," I said sadly.

"I understand, just hang in there a few more days," Manh said.

"God help us," I said.

"Hien's brother delivered a note to your wife this morning, asking her to be ready and telling her that we will let her know when she and the children have to be at the Three Gateway Entrance. Then our people will lead them to a location for pick up. They are fine." Manh comforted me.

"Thanks, and what time is it now?" I asked, still breathing heavily.

"We will make it," Manh said.

We got to the shop at ten to nine, and they were ready to close. We pushed the front door open, and walking in, and we saw Dzung sitting at a table with a woman whom we hadn't met before. Dzung introduced the woman to us as Than's sister who just came down from Saigon about a half an hour ago. Than was in the shower. We asked Dzung to tell him that we would be back the next morning to see him then we took off.

When we stepped out of the door, Manh said to me with a smile, "Brother Hai, Than must be serious since he brought his sister down here with him."

"I felt very much relieved seeing his sister," I agreed.

When we got home, we didn't talk about work; we said a good-night and went to bed.

However, I just couldn't sleep because there were so many things that kept swirling in my mind, and the pain in my shoulder was so persistent. I tried several times to count from one to one thousand, but I was just unable to close my eyes. It was still except the creaky noise of the bamboo bed under the twist and turn of my body. I could hear the buzz of mosquitoes outside the net. Now during the quiet and sleepless night, images of the police station on the opposite river bank, the white concrete bridge, and the guard towers started vividly rising up in my mind, and that made me really worry. Having time to think about the trip made me quite fearful since I realized that we had made a very bold and risky move by choosing such a heavily guarded place as a loading area. I suspected that no one had ever dared even to think about what we had planned, let alone to do it.

Besides that, I missed my family dearly. I wished I was with them at this critical juncture assisting them. I knew in the back of my mind that I was doing this for the future and the freedom of my children. I thought it was worth a try, and secondly, we didn't seem to have any other options besides relying on the gas station for loading our people.

I was very tired after the sleepless night, but we had already made an arrangement to see Than so I got up really early in the morning to brush my teeth. Then I went to a well at the back of the house to pull some cold water to douse myself, but my shoulder was still in pain, so I was only able to pull a few buckets; they, however, were enough to make me stay lucid and alert.

At around seven o'clock, Manh woke up. He didn't see me in my room, so he immediately started looking for me and he found me at the well, totally soaked.

"You woke up early, eh?" Manh asked.

"I couldn't sleep at all last night," I said.

"What bothered you?"

"Just one of those nights."

"I couldn't sleep well either, my headache really killed me," Manh said with a sigh.

After we changed, we went to the coffee shop quickly and chose a corner table at the back, away from everyone, to sit. Dzung was aware that we were going to have a meeting with Than this morning, so she asked him to wait for us in the back room of her coffee shop and she also kept her eyes out for any strangers loitering around. Manh pretended to go to the restroom then snuck back into the back room. I also stealthily entered the back room through the side door.

I knocked on the door, and Manh answered. Upon entering the room, I heard Manh talking to Than about his sudden disappearance, but they didn't talk about anything specific about the trip until we were all together in the room. I guessed that Than now understood the role that I had in the project.

I couldn't see clearly as I walked in the room because the light was dim and the room was full of cigarette smoke, and all of the curtains were drawn down. After a few seconds adjusting to the dim light, I saw Than sitting at a corner table smoking. I said hello and shook his hand. I still wore my usual wrinkled, worn-out clothes, but he seemed to be friendlier now than before.

"We met your sister yesterday. Did she come down the same time with you?" Manh asked.

"No, she took the bus, I didn't want to arrive together and arouse any suspicion," Than said.

"Where is she staying now?" Manh asked.

"With a friend of mine," said Than.

216

"Please ask her to refrain from talking to anyone about her leaving the country," Manh politely asked.

"I already mentioned this to her." Than nodded.

"Now, you know that we will probably leave within the next few days, and I just wonder whether you guys are ready and committed to this trip," Manh added.

"Absolutely," Than said without hesitation.

"Same here," I said with conviction.

"You both know that every task of this project is important, and now we are at the final step of loading people. This is extremely critical, and we need to get it carried out flawlessly," Manh insisted.

"What do I have to do?" Than asked again seriously.

"Generally, you will use your Russian jeep to pick up the passengers at designated locations and bring them to the coffee shop early in the morning. There are about sixty people altogether," Manh said.

Than frowned and immediately thought about the size of the small car, which normally carried a maximum of six or seven people. He smiled sarcastically and asked, "Sixty people? You guys are joking, right?"

"In that vicinity, including adults and children. No, we are serious," I said.

"Regardless of whether they are adults or children…it is impossible…impossible to fit that many people into this small car," Than seriously said.

"I understand it will be very tight even for just a half of that number. We will divide them into two groups of about thirty people each, and some of the young male passengers will be getting to the coffee shop by bike, so basically there will be about twenty-five people in each load," Manh said confidently.

"Well! You guys know the government informants are everywhere. I don't know if they are working at the time we had planned to pick our people up, but…fewer trips are safer," Than agreed.

"I agree with Than on this. We need to arrange so people could stay as close to the station as possible, and anyone who can use other means to get to the shop should do so," I suggested.

Manh stopped to think for a few seconds then said, "If you let people sit on each other's laps, some sit on the floor of the car, and some sit in the trunk, then you would be able to squeeze in twenty-five people. I will also arrange to have them converged at locations that are most convenient for you to pick them up."

"Other team members will work with you ensuring that it is safe for the pick-up. They will alert you, otherwise," I said. Manh and I had already talked about assigning a team member who was a local resident and knew the area well to assist Than on the reconnaissance.

"Than, trust me, I know how important and dangerous your task is. I assure you that we will do everything we can to assist you so it will be carried out as smoothly as we expect," Manh said sympathetically. Despite these assurances from Manh, Than realized that his task would be complicated by the fact that he wasn't a local resident, and he was also aware that most of the streets in this city were narrow, and he didn't want any mishap while picking up people. What he intended to do was to ride to the locations on his bike to observe them beforehand, and he wanted to make sure there was enough room for him to maneuver the car.

"Tell me the locations in advance," Than said.

"We will try to let you know as soon as we can, or at least eight hours in advance, unless there is an emergency and we have to move them to other locations," Manh said.

I was relieved that he had finally found Than and talked through this risky stage of the plan, but we still had many more complicated issues to be resolved, and we were also distressed over the discussion and resolution we had already discussed because they all related to the high-risk endeavor of dodging of the government security apparatus. Before we even brought people to the gas station, we needed to secure this area, which meant finding a way around Than's boss, the gas station manager. By then, the passengers could safely stay at the gas station until the boat arrived. Securing the gas station was a major hurdle since the manager stays at the gas station all the time when he was in Rach Gia. We either had to persuade him to go to another place or drug him into a deep sleep during the night we loaded our people.

Than had been working for this manager for almost two years now, and according to him, he was very conniving, suspicious, and highly aware of his surroundings. He wasn't reckless enough to just let anybody trick him into leaving the place; he was the king of his castle, and no one was allowed to get into the gas station without his permission, not even police officers. We were aware that he was smart and had a lot of experience in dealing with people who might try to take advantage of him, but we also believed that he had weaknesses that we could use to our advantage. We just needed to find out what his Achilles' heel was, and the one person who could provide us this information was our friend Than.

Like Manh and me, Than looked anxious and distressed after our discussion about the loading of our people, so we paused to let him smoke a cigarette before we continued our conversation.

Manh looked at Than and said, "We know that your manager is a very suspicious and smart individual, but he still has weaknesses. We will use these to our advantage. We want to ask you a few questions so we can put together a plan to deal with him."

"If we are not careful and wise, we will then become his victims instead," Than warned.

"Absolutely," Manh said.

I said to Than, "Actually, you are the one who will have to deal directly with him, since he already knows you, and I think you should behave the same way you had been behaving. Don't give him any suspicion or clue of what we are going to do."

"What does he like, what does he hate, and what time he usually go to bed?" Manh asked.

"He likes a lot of things, especially Black and White bourbon, and he is also fond of Southern girls," Than said.

"What does he hate?" Manh asked.

"Well, he doesn't say it, but by my observation he doesn't like Northern women," Than said.

"What is his daily routine when he is at the gas station?" I asked.

"He usually wakes up around eight or nine o'clock in the morning. I buy coffee and breakfast for him from Dzung's shop, or sometimes he wants a bowl of pho. He goes to lunch around one, and since he doesn't know how to drive, I have to take him. He has an afternoon nap, and he always enjoys sitting on the deck at the back of the gas station to watch boats going by at around six or seven o'clock in the evening, and while he's sitting there he has to have a cup of special dark coffee and a State Express 555 cigarette," Than said.

"Well, this guy knows how to enjoy life, eh?" I said.

"Does he frequently have guests staying overnight?" Manh asked.

"This guy is very suspicious of everything. He doesn't have a lot of friends. I have been working for him for two years now and I remembered seeing only two people staying overnight with him, and these people had come all the way from the northern part of Vietnam," Than explained.

"Does he have weapons?" Manh asked.

"He has an AK-47 but he has never used it. He doesn't even have any bullets in it," Than said with a smile.

"Does the gas station have a gas attendant?" Manh asked.

"The boat operators have their own keys. There's no attendant," Than said.

"Does he drink a lot?" Manh asked.

"He doesn't drink often or a lot, but when he has a good meal and free whiskey, then he knows how to enjoy himself. He goes to bed when he's had a few drinks or when he feels that he's drunk. He doesn't yell and make noise," Than said.

Manh thought for a few minutes then said, "I think we have enough information about the manager. You know that our people will temporarily stay at the gas station once we have it secured. I want to know your suggestions on how to deal with the manager." The entire room was silent. Than was smoking his cigarette. I was rubbing my hand, thinking deeply to come up with a suggestion, and Manh was chewing the end of a pencil. We didn't talk for about ten minutes. Then I broke the silence.

"Why don't we hire a young girl and bring him to the hotel with her on that night?"

"This guy is very cautious and astute. He knows that the police could raid the hotel but they can't enter his gas station. He doesn't want to get caught by the police, and I don't think he would go. He has asked me to bring girls to the station several times in the past," Than said apologetically.

"You have friends living here. Why don't you set up a party at a house of your friend, take him there for a drink, and then pull the spark plug to disable the car to force him to stay there overnight," Manh offered.

"Then who is going to pick up our friends and relatives?" Than asked wryly.

"You could leave him there and take the car with you when he goes to bed," Manh added.

"No...no...I wouldn't do this to my friends, I don't want them get in trouble...you know what would happen to them when I am gone." Than rejected the idea and stood right up when he talked as if he was stung by a bee.

"Relax, this is just brainstorming to find a solution, and I don't mean to hurt anyone," Manh said placatingly. I thought for a long while then came up with an idea that I thought it was brilliant.

"Why don't you put sleeping pills in the cup of his evening coffee?" I said.

"That is a good idea, but what if it doesn't work, and also where can we get the sleeping pills?" Manh asked.

"What do you mean if it doesn't work? They make pills strong enough to take down a bull. I can get the genuine article from a friend of mine who was a doctor," I said.

"I can put them in his coffee, but the sleeping pills have to be really strong to put him into a deep enough sleep for us to have enough time to load our people," Than said. "There can be no margin for error."

"What if he doesn't drink the coffee? I don't want to be negative...the possibility is there...this is just a hypothesis," Manh said.

I knew that we would have to do something to get out of this critical hypothetical situation, but I didn't really know what, so I just said from the top of my head, "In that case, we need to turn to the alternative plan immediately."

"I agree...what is the alternative plan?" Manh asked hopefully.

"I don't know yet…but we have to do something…right?" I said.

"Yes…yes! Absolutely…Than, you have any idea?" Manh added.

"I'm not sure, but I have another concern. Does the sleeping pill have a color, smell, or taste?" Than asked. "You know I've been working for this guy for quite a while, and like most Communists he's very suspicious and this guy especially has a keen sense of smell. In the past, he has on several occasions refused to eat food that I had bought for him because he said it had a different taste or smell than he is used to. He would refuse the coffee if the pills had any distinctive properties that might catch his senses."

Honestly, I had never tried anything like sleeping pills, drugs, or narcotics, and hadn't even tried cigarettes until I was so stressed working on this project that I smoked cigarette once in a while to release stress.

"I don't have any idea since I hadn't tried it yet," I admitted.

"Brother Hai, can you investigate?" Manh asked.

I gracefully accepted the assignment since I would have the job of picking up the pills anyway.

"When can we have the results?" Manh asked.

"I will let you guys know as soon as I find out, and I will also crush it into powder form for you to use," I said.

Even though the last portion of our discussion was relevant to the goal of our project, we should have focused on the alternative solution on how to deal with the situation in which the manager didn't take the laced coffee. After receiving the assignment, I started to think about what and how I would do the next couple of days to get the pills, test them, and crush them into powder to give to Than. In addition, I hadn't gotten any sleep the night before, so I was drowsy, and my anxiety was visibly annoying me.

Manh was not in better shape, either, since his headache constantly plagued him to the point that he struggled to have a productive and intelligent discussion, so he suggested, "You guys want to take a break or adjourn the meeting?" Actually, I did. I just wanted to take a nap for at least a half an hour. Than also agreed to take a break, and we decided that we would resume in about an hour. It was now eleven o'clock, and we agreed to get back at twelve noon. Than went back to the coffee shop to get something to eat.

Even though Dzung had been keeping an eye out for the intrusion of any strangers around the back room of the shop, she still didn't want Manh and I to leave the back room together. She gave a sign to let Manh leave the room first through the back door. I had to stay back for about fifteen minutes before I could get out through the front door of the coffee shop.

Manh and I then met at the pho place to have a quick bowl of beef noodle soup. I didn't really know what Manh was saying to me after we had lunch because I was so tired. I just looked for a bench in a secluded to take a quick nap for at least about thirty minutes or so before I had to get back to the meeting again. I found a wooden bench underneath a big tree; it was a wonderful place for me to lie down. Since I didn't have any money, I wasn't afraid of being robbed, so I just left one of my old leather sandals Manh had given to me under the bench then I lay down using the other sandal as a pillow. In just a few minutes I was already gone. I had no idea how long I had slept; I had no way to know what time it was.

When I woke up I figured that I needed to get back to the coffee shop for the meeting right away. I looked down under the bench for my sandal, but it was no longer there, and the one I used as a pillow had also disappeared. Somebody had already borrowed them and now I realized that I had been in a very deep sleep. I felt very sad because I had thought I was the poorest of the poor, but there were still people who were poorer than I was. I walked back to the coffee shop barefoot; for me it wasn't a problem to walk barefoot on the hot cement sidewalk or asphalt road because I was used to it, but it didn't look right walking into a coffee shop without a pairs of sandals or flip-flops on my feet.

I thought I was late, so I hurried back to the coffee shop. Manh, however, wasn't there as yet; we had to wait for him for about fifteen minutes. He didn't look refreshed; he looked very tired when he showed up. He told us that he tried to take a nap but he just couldn't sleep until the last few minutes, and then he had to wake up running to the meeting.

"You look tired. Are you okay to continue?" I asked.

"I didn't have a good nap, but I did have some rest. I should be fine" Manh said. Again, we knew that we didn't have much time to discuss all the issues in connection with our trip in one sitting, but in order to deal with situation where the manager refused to take the coffee mixed with sleeping powder, we needed to find a quick and effective solution.

"Any ideas, guys?" Manh prompted. My mind was totally blank, and I was having a hard time focusing my thoughts. I just couldn't come up with anything. My skull was absolutely numb.

"Guys, my brain doesn't work," I apologized.

"I couldn't take my mind off this problem since you guys left for lunch. I have an idea, but I'm not certain that it would work," Than said tentatively.

"What is in your mind?" Manh asked.

"If he doesn't drink the coffee, then I would buy him another cup," Than began.

"Then what?"

"I just pretend things are normal...I just carry out my duty as a chauffeur. Usually when we stay in Rach Gia, he always wants to have a female companion for a night. It would be good if we leave on Sunday morning."

"You mean this Sunday? Why?" I asked.

"Well, I don't know whether he ever married, but I haven't seen any woman living with him from the first day I worked for him. Since during the day he makes extra money from selling contraband in Saigon or secretly funneling diesel to the black market, he has a habit of bringing in a young street girl to the gas station on almost every Saturday night when he stays in Rach Gia. He doesn't want other people to know of his unethical behavior and he is also well aware that this is in violation of the Communist Party rules, so he always orders me to get him one. I hate to do it, but I have to earn a living," Than explained.

I immediately thought about Than's conspiracy with the manager to sell the foodstuffs on the black market, the fashionable clothes he had on, the shoes he wore, the money he spent, and the materialistic woman he associated with. But I stopped that line of thought instantly because I recognized that this wasn't the time for criticism or to work against each other, but it was a time to unite instead. If my mind was occupied with this unhealthy resentment, then I wouldn't be able to have a positive discussion that was badly needed at this critical juncture.

"It will be very dark this Saturday night. It is almost the end of the lunar month," Manh said.

"There will be no moon. It would help us elude the watchful eyes of police officers at the station on the opposite bank and also the guards at the bridge," I agreed.

"Let us get back to what I just said earlier. If it's a Saturday and if we know for certain that he didn't consume the coffee, then I would use his habit against him by hiring a young street girl, and then I would buy the good food that he likes and a bottle of Black and White bourbon…definitely…definitely…he would fall into our trap. This guy loves free things," Than said.

"You don't have to use your own money. I will give it to you for this purpose," Manh interjected.

"I know he will get drunk, and some sleeping pills in the bourbon will send him into sleep much faster. He would have a good night's sleep," Than said eagerly.

"I will be out to sea with a few team members on Saturday night to observe the area and make sure that there are no patrol boats nearby. Once you have everything under control, you would send somebody to inform Brother Hai," Manh said, and then he turned to me. "You bring the boat down to the dock of the gas station to pick people up."

I nodded. "What time you plan for the boat to leave in the morning?"

"It would have to be before four, or before a time when the merchant boats selling firewood and charcoal gather at the other side of the river. When they see us, the chaos of everyone trying to sell to us would inevitably alert the authorities," Manh said.

"How do you get people into the boat?" I asked.

"I am thinking we should use a wooden board as a gangplank. It has to be strong enough to hold at least two or three people at a time," Manh said.

"I saw a wooden board lying at the back of the gas station," Than said.

"Is it strong enough?" I asked.

"I don't know. I will check it and let you guys know," Than said.

"Let me know soon, and if it is not strong enough then I will use our sampan to slide another board to the back of the coffee shop the night before we leave," Manh added. "Brother Hai, you will go with me to see the mechanic, and you should probably stay on the boat until we leave."

"Yes...I will try to get the sleeping pills tomorrow too," I said.

"You will test it and turn it over to Than, right?" Manh asked.

"Yes," I said.

When we concluded our meeting, it was already four o'clock in the afternoon. Time had gone by so fast, and we all were very tired and anxious. However, Manh and I had to see the mechanic at our boat to ask him whether he wanted to go with us or back to An Giang with his mother. After talking to the mechanic about our intentions, he happily expressed his desire to go with us; he didn't think that he could help his mother much if he stayed back in the country under the current conditions.

Manh left after we had our conversation with the mechanic, and I stayed with the boat from then until the time we were to take off. Now we had three people on the boat and we all had to stay aboard at all times, except when we needed to go for business relating to the trip.

We decided to move the boat farther upstream where we would be able to take off early in the morning; we didn't want to get stuck between other boats and be unable to get out on time. The next day, we moved our boat a couple of hundred meters upstream where there were very few boats docked, and we immediately informed our team members of our new location.

While staying in the boat that night, I heard all kinds of noise from people singing folk songs along to the blaring of radios, drunken arguments, and the screaming, crying, and then the sobbing of a woman who was being beaten by her husband. The noise, however, died down after nine. It seemed to me that there was a whole different world for those who lived on boats.

Lying on the wooden board inside the engine room of the boat, I was again thinking about my family. I didn't know where they were or what they were doing now. Despite the trust I had in my teammates, I still had reservations. I didn't know whether my wife would be able to follow the instructions given to her by my teammate since she wasn't familiar with this area. I worried that she wouldn't be able to round up my kids for them to get to the designated location on time. What if they missed the bus? Thousands of what-ifs swirled around in my mind, resulting in another sleepless night.

I urgently needed a few sleeping pills, not for me, but for the manager of the gas station, and the only one way I could get them was from my friend who worked for the local hospital. Despite the dense population, this province had only one public hospital, so the line of patients waiting to see a doctor was very long and started early in the morning. I got up early to go to the hospital and registered to see a doctor, but I wasn't allowed to get a medical checkup slip because I was not technically a resident of this city and I didn't have a local family census book as yet. After spending a good chunk of money to bribe the nurse, I got a ticket and had to wait for more than two hours.

My friend and I had gone to high school together, and after graduation we went our separate ways. He went to medical school, graduating before 1975, and he opened his own practice. Most of the young men of our age had to serve in the military, but he wasn't drafted because he lost a small chunk of his right index finger playing with firecracker when he was a teenager. He volunteered to move to this hospital, which was located next to the coast, looking for an opportunity to leave the country, but he hadn't yet found one. He was glad to see me since we hadn't seen each other for many years after high school. I told him that I needed a few sleeping pills for me to use because I couldn't sleep.

He jokingly told me, "If you take all these pills at one time, you won't see me again." He gave me ten pills and asked me to take only one pill an hour before going to bed for ten days and then come back to see him.

I took the pills directly to Hien's house, where I borrowed a stone mortar and a pestle to grind a pill into very fine powder. Then I asked Than to give me a cup of the same coffee in terms of quality and quantity which he had usually bought for the manager to drink every evening. I had a sip without swallowing the coffee and I held it in my mouth for a few seconds then I spit it out. I put the powder from the crushed pill into the coffee, stirred it up, and let it sit for a few seconds before I had a sip of the coffee. It actually didn't have any different smell than the coffee itself; it slightly changed the color as if a tiny amount of creamer was added to it, and it tasted a little bit bitter. If this guy was as sensitive as Than described, then he would be able to recognize the difference, and obviously he wouldn't drink the coffee. I told Manh and Than about the results of my test, but we had no other choice but to move forward with what we had planned. I then turned the remaining pills over to Than, who said he didn't need the pills in powder form.

Having completed one of my most important assigned tasks, I now had to go back to the boat to wait for the final moment to leave the docking site for picking up our passengers. On the way back to the boat, my mind and heart were, however, with my wife and children. I wished I was with them at the critical time of our fateful journey. On the other hand, I had to focus on the task at hand since many lives, including the lives of my family, now depended on me. I couldn't be distracted at any moment for any reason from flawlessly carrying out my assigned responsibility. I have to focus. I have to focus—I pounded into myself.

CHAPTER

11

Gathering at a Secret Location to be Picked Up

learned afterward that my wife received a note around noontime on Saturday from a young man, one of our team members. The note had Manh's signature and advised my wife to be in front of the city public bus station at five o'clock sharp on Saturday afternoon so Hien's brother could walk them to a secret location to be picked up by a car later. Unfortunately, our children were not at home. They had each gone their own separate ways to play because today was Saturday and they didn't have school. Usually my wife didn't have to look for them; regardless of where they went, they always came home at around five or six for supper. However, she couldn't wait until then because it would take at least an hour and a half to get to the city by bus, and it might be longer with a three-wheeled *tuk-tuk*.

Huong immediately set out to look for the children, but she had no idea where they had gone, so she went everywhere from the marketplace to the riverbank, but she couldn't find anyone of them, and she lapsed panicky. She didn't have much time since she had to pack some dried rice, some warm clothes for the kids, and still have time to travel. She had no choice but asking the kids in the neighborhood if they had seen our children. One of the boys told my wife that he was with my youngest son picking up discarded fruit at the fruit stands in the market. My wife ran toward the market to look for him, but he was not there. She then started to sob. She couldn't leave without even one of our children, but she had no way to know where they were. She was completely in desperation, staggering home with tears rolling down her cheeks.

When she got home, my young son was there with a plastic bag full of partially rotten and damaged fruit he had picked up earlier from the market. She asked him whether he knew the whereabouts of his brothers. He told her that his two older brothers had asked him to come along to watch a woman drinking pig blood and dancing in a temple on the riverbank, but he didn't want to go because he was afraid. He led Huong to the temple to retrieve his two older boys, and she hastily brought them home to change clothes to be ready for the trip. My daughter, however, was still not home, but our boys said she usually played cooking at a friend's house, and they would run for her. Luckily the house was close, so they took her home quickly. It was already three thirty, and my wife had to hurry getting them ready to leave the house. Neighbors earlier saw my wife crying, and now all the kids were brought home to get ready, so they wondered what was happening. My wife just told them that they had to go to see their father who just got back to town after a long trip working far from home.

She finally managed to get them ready. Each carried a small plastic bag with dried rice, and she carried with her extra shirts for the children. She was very anxious to get to the city, so she nudged the kids to walk faster to the marketplace where hopefully they could catch a bus or a three-wheeled tuk-tuk for the city. However, she didn't see any transportation when she got there; instead, she saw of a group of middle-aged men and women standing on the corner of the open market under the scorching afternoon sun looking anxious. Each carried straw bags in their hands. She thought they also needed to have some sort of transportation to get to somewhere.

It was already four o'clock, and she knew she had no way to get there on time. Her mind was overwhelmed with fear of being late for the appointment.

Her heart raced with fear, but at the moment she didn't know what to do to get out of the situation. She thought that she had to get to the city regardless of how difficult or how many obstacles she had to tackle. After overcoming the initial emotional shock, she realized that something had to be done quickly, so she impulsively walked over to the group of people, asking, "Are you going to Rach Gia?"

"Yes, but there's no car."

"You live here in the hamlet?"

"No, Giong Rieng. We want to go to Rach Gia, not here. Where are we?"

"You are about twenty kilometers from Rach Gia. How did you get here?"

"A bus dropped us here and took off to get repairs." My wife didn't have enough money to rent a vehicle for her and our children, so she thought about asking these people to chip in sharing for the costs.

"How about renting a vehicle and we put money together to share for costs?" Huong asked. The youngest man of the group seemed to be more vivacious, turning around to discuss with others, and they all agreed with the option to rent a vehicle provided that it wasn't too expensive because they didn't have much money either.

"Yes, but we only have little money," the young man said.

"You guys stay here. I am going to look for a car." Huong thought of a woman selling rice at the public market. Her husband had a three-wheeled Lambretta to carry rice for her business. Huong found the woman, and after talking to her husband, she agreed to take them to the city at double the regular price because she said, "He'll make no money on his way back."

The three-wheeled tuk-tuk was brought to their location. It was an old and run-down vehicle, and now it had to carry almost sixteen people on a long trip. This vehicle was used to carry rice, so it didn't have any benches. Everyone had to sit on the floor, and two men were asked to sit on each side of the driver. At last the vehicle took off. Dark smoke came out of the exhaust pipe and underneath the car, and it somehow got inside the vehicle. The strong odor of incompletely burned gas made everyone nauseated, but even worse was the terrible, loud noise of the engine. Even going slowly, it still struggled on the road because there were so many potholes. It lurched up and down when it ran over big potholes like a frog jumping in a contest, and people had to hold on to whatever they could. My wife would have been thrown off the vehicle had she not held on to a metal bar for her dear life. Our children, on the other hand, especially the boys, were delighted when the vehicle bounced in the potholes.

After running for about nine kilometers, the engine of the vehicle started to hiccup then stopped running and coasted to a complete stop. Both sides of the road were rice field as far as the eye could see, and there was no house or people living in the area. While all passengers were waiting on the roadside, the driver took out a toolbox, lifted up the driver's seat, and then pulled out a sparkplug. He cleaned the ground electrode with a piece of sand paper, blew the gap several times, and then put it back into the engine. He kicked the kick-start pedal several times, but the engine refused to start. He swore ceaselessly at the vehicle. Visibly tired, his shirt soaked through with sweat he suggested a few strong people push the vehicle while he put it into the first gear. After running a few hundred meters, the engine started to cough a couple of times and then roared back to life. The driver put the engine in full throttle for a few minutes; the entire area was filled with black smoke pouring out of the broken exhaust pipe, and loud noise ripped through the air. He kept the engine running until he felt that it was back to normal, then he hastily asked everyone to get back to the vehicle, fearful that the engine would quit on him again.

It was now already six thirty. Huong had already missed the appointment with Hien's brother. It would take at least a half an hour before they could get to the city; she and the kids would not get there before seven. She was two hours late, and she was afraid that Hien's brother wouldn't stay there waiting for her since he had to meet other people to take them to the designated locations. Huong knew that he couldn't stay there all day waiting for her. She didn't have a penny left after paying the transportation costs; she didn't know anybody in the city; she didn't know Hien's brother's house address; and the worst thing of all was that she hadn't met Hien's brother even once, so she didn't have a slight idea what he looked like. That thought alone totally consumed her, and even though her clothes were wet with perspiration, an extreme chill ran through her spine. She sat on the floor of the vehicle stone-faced.

The vehicle kept jumping up and down for another forty-five minutes on the broken road before discharging them in front of the bus station. Huong quickly pushed the kids out of the vehicle, desperately hoping to see the young man whom they were supposed to meet, but she couldn't find anyone with the likeness of the young man as described in the note. It was already dark, and the faint rays of yellow streetlights only reluctantly reached the ground, adding to the difficulty of seeing anything at a distance. Although people bustled past on all sides, she felt as if she were stranded in the desert. In her desperation, she wanted to cry openly, and our children didn't make the situation better by asking so many questions about where their father was and when they could see him. Each of the simple questions from our children felt like an arrow penetrating her already wounded heart. She had to lie to them that "your father will come to get you provided that you keep quiet and don't ask too many questions."

My wife and children had left in a hurry this evening, so they didn't have supper, and the kids complained of being hungry. However, Huong didn't have any money to buy food for them, so she asked them to eat the dried rice they each carried in their bags and promised them that their father would buy them food when he got here. She asked the kids to walk with her on the right sidewalk along the main street to escape the attention of people passing by. While walking, she kept looking for a young man with a straw hat and a book in his right hand. They walked up and down for fifteen minutes, but she didn't see anyone who matched this description. Her eyes were flooded with tears. She couldn't withstand the high level of distress and anxiety, knowing that the opportunity to escape had already slipped through her hands. This combined with the lack of adequate food for the last few days to make her feel lightheaded and dizzy. She didn't have enough strength to walk farther, so she sat down on the pavement and put her face in her hands. The kids sat alongside her, clinging to her arms and eating the dried rice. She didn't have energy to cry or sob anymore.

While sitting on the pavement next to the Three Gateway Entrance for fifteen minutes, she heard a voice seemingly coming from far away. "Are you Sister Huong?" She thought she must be hallucinating. When she opened her eyes and looked around, she saw a young man standing a few meters away from where she and the kids were sitting.

She quickly asked, "Who are you?"

"I am Hien's brother," he said. She didn't believe her ears. She rubbed her eyes and looked at the young man again, and she saw that he wore a straw hat and he also had a book in his right hand.

"Yes....yes I am Sister Huong," she said faintly.

"I had been waiting for you since five o'clock. Now follow me," he instructed. "Remember, walk in one line. Don't walk together and don't talk. The youngest one first, must be five meters apart. Sister Huong, you are the last one."

After walking for about thirty minutes, they reached a house located in an alley, and he knocked on the door. A middle-aged man answered the door and let them in. They were immediately pushed into a small room containing one small bed and an oil lamp that cast a dim, flickering yellow light. They all sat on the bed awaiting further instructions. About five minutes later, their host brought them five rice cakes wrapped in banana leaves and an empty bucket.

He then quietly whispered into her ear, "You guys eat the cakes, don't talk, use the bucket if you have to go to the bathroom, and don't go out of the room until you are told."

She didn't know how long she and the kids were in the room, and she guessed it had to be several hours. Eventually, all the children were asleep.

After an eternity, the door slid open and the same middle-aged man told her to be ready. She woke all the children up and asked them to be quiet. They then were asked to go out of the house. A car was already waiting outside on the street, and under the streetlight she saw the car was packed with people. All of the kids were quickly shoved inside the car, where some sat on the laps of the adults and some sat on the floor. Huong was pushed into the trunk of the car. She saw that there were a few people already in there before the trunk door shut, and it became absolutely dark. It took less than five minutes for the entire loading process to be completed in silence. The car then sped away immediately without leaving a trace.

CHAPTER
12

Party at the Gas Station

Saturday arrived. It was a day off for the manager and for Than, his driver, as well. Even though he didn't have to work, Than still had to be alert and ready at all times to take the manager wherever he wanted to go. He was a driver, but he also unofficially served as a bodyguard for the manager.

It was around six o'clock and time for the manager to enjoy a cup of his evening coffee and a cigarette. It was a hot day, so the manager only wore his shorts with no shirt; he looked much heavier now than when he had first arrived from the North to take over the manager position of the gas station a couple of years ago. He walked out of his office directly to the chair sitting by the rusty steel hand-rail of the deck, as he did every evening when he was at the station. Right next to the chair was an old wooden table. He liked to sit at this place in the evening to enjoy his cup of coffee and cigarette while watching boats going by and reading his newspaper. He patted his pant pockets, searching for a pack of cigarettes, but he didn't see any. He frowned and remembered that he had run out of cigarettes this morning.

"Than, you have a cigarette?" he said aloud.

Than touched his shirt pocket and said, "Yes I do, Uncle Nam." Actually no one knew what his real name was, so they all called him "Uncle Nam."

"Can I have one?"

Than brought him a cigarette, which the manager accepted and put to his lips. Than then pulled out an old Zippo lighter to light it up for him. They both actually smoked the same brand of cigarette, British State Express 555.

"Give me a few minutes. I am going to get your coffee," Than said with a smile.

"Thanks," said the manager with a smirk. Than didn't know what was in the manager's mind, but he knew exactly what he had to do. The cigarette also vividly reminded Than of the first day when the manager got to his post. He had brought with him a bag full of tobacco made in the North and a book of thin wrapping paper. He had to roll the tobacco in the thin paper when he wanted a cigarette. He still had the tobacco and wrapping paper, but he only used them when he was at a meeting with other Communist comrades. He now adamantly refused to smoke this type of tobacco at home, and instead he only smoked British State Express 555 cigarettes. Than didn't blame him for this since he had a lot more money now and the British cigarette seemed to have a better taste and scent.

As the manager leaned on the handrail looking at the river, Than brought in a hot cup of coffee which he just picked up from Dzung's coffee shop.

"Uncle Nam! I put your coffee on the table," Than said. The manager didn't turn around but instead looked up, exhaling the smoke through his nostrils, and wheezed out a thanks.

After a few seconds, he turned around and assumed a cross-legged position the chair. He then slowly lifted the cup of coffee to enjoy a small sip. After swallowing it, he stopped for a few seconds to roll the remaining coffee around in his mouth, and then his expression darkened.

"Than, where the hell did you get the coffee from?"

"The same place, Dzung's coffee shop," Than said.

"What did they do? They put too much coffee in the filter or what, it is more bitter than usual," he complained.

"Really! Let me see," Than said, then he tried a small sip. "Yes, it is bitter…let me get you another cup."

The manager dumped the coffee into the river, saying, "Don't put too much ground coffee in the filter this time."

Than was by now very nervous, but he tried to maintain his composure because he knew what he had just done. He might have inadvertently dropped too much of the powder in the coffee. He knew from the previous experiences that this man had a keen sense of smell and taste, and it was likely that he would be able to detect any difference. The first plan had failed, and it wasn't the end of the world as yet, but it still gave Than a chill down the back of his neck.

Than knew that Manh had already gone to the sea early this evening with a few members of our team to find out whether police patrol boats or any government naval forces were out there close to shore. Manh wasn't available for consultation, so he decided to send a team member to contact me for advice.

It was only seven thirty, but it was already dark. I sat in the darkened engine room, my pulse beating in my ears as I waited for news of our progress. I then heard the sound of a paddle gently entering the water. I held my breath and listened closely to figure out where the noise was coming from, and then I felt our boat suddenly rock. A young man in black pajamas quietly jumped into the boat he crawled close to me. I recognized him as a member of our team. Breathing heavily from the exertion of paddling here, he whispered into my ear, "We failed…Brother Hai…we failed, he didn't drink the coffee…he dumped it all into the river."

"Where is Than?" I asked.

"He is still at the gas station, but I got the sense that he was sad when talking to me."

"I don't know what to do to help, and I can't leave the boat either," I said, feeling frightened.

"Manh has already gone, you know," he added.

"Yes, I know"

"Than wanted me let you know, and I have to get back right away," he concluded, looking at me as if for reassurance.

"We all need to be calm, especially me," I said. "Please tell Than to execute the second plan. Than knows what to do. I'll briefly tell you what we need to do. Than has to hire a young street girl right away to tire the manager out. Hien, your sister, needs to buy a dish called bird's nest stir fried noodles in Chinese plump sauce, which has a mixture of shrimp, squid, fish, and small bird eggs for him to eat. She can buy this dish at the Chinese food stand located on the north corner of the food court. He also likes *balut*. She can get the best balut from the woman who has a food stand opposite from Dzung's coffee shop. Please ask her not forget to get some Vietnamese coriander, he likes this herb with balut." I then reached down to a corner of the boat and pulled out a bottle of Black and White bourbon to give to him. "This bottle is authentic liquor. We bought it from the black market for him to use in case we needed to carry out the alternative plan. Don't forget to buy for him a pack of cigarette. I meant 555."

He nodded vigorously. "Anything else?"

"Than has to sit with him but tell him not to drink a lot. Also, ask Than to remember the powder," I said.

"What powder?"

"Than knows," I said. "Oh…by the way, tell Than that we need to somehow take out the flood light on the other side of the riverbank when he has a chance. It must come down." I was firm.

"Why?"

"The light points to the back of the gas station. With this light, the guard can see us clearly when we load people."

The messenger nodded again. "Just take out the light. Right? I can do that."

"We had planned to have Than do it, since he has a government vehicle. How would you do it?" I asked curiously.

"What if the police impound the car or detain him, you know?" I was flabbergasted! We hadn't even thought about a situation like this. It would make things more complicated at the last moment. I was baffled and didn't have an answer for this, so I thought for a moment. The messenger added, "In addition, he has so many things on his plate."

"How are you going to do it? And isn't it too late now?" I asked.

"Slingshot. I am very good at it. I hit the target nine times out of ten."

"But it is too dark out there," I protested.

"It's okay. I only need to see the light bulb. You know, it's good. After I hit the target, I just throw the slingshot into the river and quietly walk into an alley. Disappear, you know," he said confidently. "I've lived here all my life. I know this area like the back of my hand, you know what I mean," he added.

"Have you done this before?" I asked incredulously.

"No. But I shot a lot of mice and storks when I was at my father's rice field in the summer," he said.

"What do you use as shot?"

"I used small stones, but this time I'll use marble. More accurate, you know" he said. He continued fondly, "I'll bring twenty marbles with me, but I'll try to hit it the first time. I'll throw the bag of marbles into the river, too. You know I will tell you," he added.

"It's okay. You don't have to tell me. Just try to bring it down. I have faith in you," I said. I then scribbled a short message, which I asked him to pass on to Than.

The note said, "Sorry to change the plan at the last moment. Please let Duc take care of the light. You focus on your tasks. Thanks. Brother Hai." He carefully folded the note in half then put it neatly in the front pocket of his garment. I patted his back to say thanks. He smiled, shook my hand, and then quietly climbed out of the engine room. The faint sound of paddling grew faint until it completely disappeared.

Tonight was the end of the lunar calendar month; there was no moon, so it was completely dark outside except the areas illuminated by the streetlights. Our boat was docked close to the gas station so we could get there quickly in the morning and also avoid being boxed in by other boats. From this vantage point, I could see the light from the post on the other side of the gas station spreading out. This light was installed by the city public work for boats from the state-run farms to see their way in and out when they came to the gas station to get diesel in the morning, and even though it wasn't there for the guards at the provincial police headquarters on other side of the riverbank to watch over the boats but from their guard tower, they were able to see these boats very clearly.

The rice we had cooked for lunch was still sitting in the cooking pot left in the corner of the engine room. Neither of us could eat. I didn't feel hungry even though I hadn't eaten anything all day today. I felt very jittery about our plan to drug the manager because he had a keen sense of smell and taste, and also I felt we were putting too much work on Than's shoulders. Although I trusted my team member, I was still anxious to know how things were at the gas station. It was now already eleven o'clock at night, and if things worked out as we expected, then the manager should be in bed for a good and long sleep at this time. Most of our passengers should now already be in the coffee shop. It was almost midnight but it was scorching, at least about thirty-eight or thirty-nine degrees Celsius out there, and it was very hot and humid in our engine room. The two men who were waiting with me were wet with perspiration, but instead I had a chill running down my spine. I had goose bumps all over my body just thinking about navigating down the river under the watchful eyes of the guards at the police headquarters and the guard towers on both sides of the white concrete bridge.

I craned my neck to look downriver in the direction of the gas station. The light was still on. Maybe Duc couldn't bring it down with his slingshot. Maybe something had happened to him. It would be a dangerous undertaking to load our people when the light was still on since the guards at the police headquarters would see us, and they would alert the guards at the checkpoints on both sides of the white concrete bridge to stop or shoot at us. We would be doomed. Even though Duc was very young, I trusted him greatly since he had always successfully carried out his assigned tasks. However, as the hour approached midnight, my concerns grew. The light had to come down before twelve since the curfew hours were imposed at midnight.

My panic grew, and I was very afraid for both Duc and for our entire plan. He had only ten minutes to get the job done; it was now twenty minutes to midnight. It usually took me more than ten minutes to walk from the coffee shop to the provincial police station located on the street at the opposite river bank of the coffee shop.

He had to be close to the light, at least within ten to twenty meters, for the slingshot to be effective, and he had to walk back to the coffee shop after taking down the light. There were only two ways for him to get back to the coffee shop. He had to walk across either the old steel bridge or the white concrete bridge. If he was wise enough, he wouldn't use the old steel bridge because he had to walk right in front of the guard shed of the police headquarters, and it was highly likely that they would ask for his identification papers or question him about what he was doing in that area at this time of the night, all the more so because the light had been taken down. It was now only ten minutes to midnight.

I was highly skeptical that Duc would be capable of carrying out this risky task in just ten minutes. That meant our trip had to be aborted. I looked at my watch for every minute going by. While my mind was totally engulfed in this horrible predicament and disappointment, suddenly the entire area at the back of the gas station fell into darkness.

"He did it...he did it," I whispered to one of my teammates who was sitting next to me.

"What is it?" my friend asked.

"He brought it down," I said.

"What down?"

"Don't you see the darkness at the back of the gas station?"

"Oh...yes," he said.

"Thank God...he did it," I said with a long sigh of relief.

I then started to worry about how he would get back to the coffee shop since he couldn't run in the complete darkness. What if he didn't have enough time to get back? He would run into trouble walking across the white concrete bridge at this time of the night, and I was so afraid just to think about a situation if he would be arrested. We would have to face a terrible consequence. I hoped that he would safely make it back to the coffee shop. A few minutes later, I saw two bright beams of light from a car's headlights sweeping across the white concrete bridge. It didn't turn into the road leading to the gas station, but it instead ran directly toward the direction of the Provincial Administrative Headquarters, which was about a kilometer away.

The entire area was now cloaked in darkness, and I was so relieved to know that the guards wouldn't be able to see us picking up our people at the gas station, at least not without great difficulty. I began mentally counting the number of houses from the old steel bridge to the gas station and tried to remember all the images I had mentally captured when I had walked along the street on the river-bank opposite the coffee shop.

I muttered to myself, "The last house before I reach the gas station is…yes, it is the coffee shop. It has a blue canopy…then the gas station, the next house toward the sea is a house that has a coconut tree…" I also tried to remember where the sand bar was relative to the river and how far from the white concrete bridge it was situated. In my mind I drew a picture of our boat, without the top, quietly sailing down the river. In my mind's eye, it safely passed the guard towers of the police headquarters then passed several houses. While my mind was totally immersed in this exercise, I heard a man's voice seemingly from far away.

"It will be difficult for us to find our way around in the dark, eh?" I recognized Dien's voice. He knew that our boat didn't have any light besides a few battery flash lights. His voice brought me back to reality, and now I realized that I wouldn't be able to see anything in the dark. My head started to swim with this unforeseen problem.

I asked him, "What should we do?"

"I will sit at the bow using a flashlight to guide you through," Dien said.

"The gas station…you haven't seen the rear side of it as yet. Right?" I ruefully asked.

"No." I just couldn't absorb the notion that all my hard work walking on the street and standing day and night on the bridges observing was futile, so I mumbled, "It is too dark…impossible… impossible to see it."

"What about asking them to hang a lamp or lantern on the rear deck of the gas station?" he suggested.

"The houses encroach on the river unevenly, which would make it difficult for us to see the lamp. Once we see the lamp hanging at the rear deck, then our boat would have already almost passed the gas station," I cautiously said.

"What about using flash light to signal?" he persisted.

"That's better, but that will attract attention from many people, especially from the guards or informants. We want to catch them by surprise," I said.

I wanted to stay awake until it was time to take off, but I was mentally and physically exhausted after many sleepless nights, relentless stress, plus not eating anything today. I yawned repeatedly and finally fell asleep while I was still talking to Dien. At the back of my mind, I knew that the light was an important issue and we needed a solution before we took off, but I just couldn't keep my eyes open. I leaned my head against the engine and started to immediately fall into sleep. Dien knew that I was dreadfully tired, so he left me alone to have my quick nap.

I was in deep sleep when someone tapped on my shoulder. I was still groggy and half-asleep until I heard a hasty voice, "Wake up…wake up, Brother Hai…time to go." I immediately opened my eyes wide when I heard this urgent message. I rubbed my eyes several times to compose myself and to see where I was, but it seemed like I was living in another world.

I dreamily asked, "Go…where?"

"Brother Hai, wake up, we will be leaving in about thirty minutes," Duc said. I focused my eyes and vaguely saw three people standing around me, but I wasn't aware that Duc had already climbed to the boat. When I recognized his voice, there was something like a shattering lightning striking my mind, pulling me back to the real world.

"Are you okay?" he asked.

"Oh yes…I just had a quick nap," I said.

"Quick nap, eh? It was almost two hours," Dien said. I used water stored in a big clay jar to splash my face to refresh myself.

I asked, "What time it is now?"

"A little past three," Dien said.

"Listen, I've brought you two pairs of uniforms, two guerilla boonie hats, and most importantly two M-16 rifles and two magazines," Duc said.

I was kind of nervous when he mentioned the word *rifle*. "Are we going to shoot at them?"

"No...no...absolutely no shooting," Manh had said we just want to show them that we are legitimate Communist cadres of the state-run farms," Duc said promptly.

"How were things back at the gas station?" I asked.

"We are in good shape. The manager is in deep sleep. Everyone is now in the gas station waiting for us."

"How did you manage to bring down the light?" I asked curiously.

"Long story...I will tell you later...we need to move on quickly," Duc said. I didn't mind that he didn't answer my question; on the contrary, I had a lot of respect for this young man since he was a very responsible and punctual individual. He turned around and pulled out two pairs of dark olive uniforms from a wet nylon bag and softly said, "One pair for you and one pair for Dien. Put them on...put them on now."

"How come the bag was all wet?" I asked.

"Well...I put everything in the bag, tied the bag real tight so water couldn't get in. I dropped it in the water and dragged it along with a nylon string. That way they wouldn't find anything except a few baskets of fish in my sampan if they stopped me."

"Wow! Very clever...very clever," I said appreciatively.

"You have a belt? If not, I have some nylon string here. Waist of the pants was a little big, so try tying them up so it won't drop. Tuck in your shirt," he insistently said.

"I need a hat," Dien said.

"Just a second." Duc pulled out two boonie hats from the bag then gave one to me and one to Dien.

"You need to tie the hat strap under your chin. Tie it up. The wind is strong," Duc promptly reminded us.

We just did exactly as he told us, and then he carefully pulled out two M-16 rifles and two magazines from the same bag.

"Brother Hai…and Dien…Manh told me that you guys know how to use weapons, but please don't shoot. Remember don't shoot. We only need to show them that we have guns," Duc entreated.

"Don't worry, I won't shoot," Dien said.

"Me neither," I said.

"You can snap in the magazine, but don't load the gun," Duc added. "I will stay with you guys when we sail down to the gas station."

"It is too dark. I can't see a thing," I fretted.

"I have been back and forth a few times so I know the route relatively well, and I can help with guiding the boat," Duc said.

"I have no doubt that you are familiar with the route, but it is easier to maneuver the sampan. Our boat is bigger and the tide is low in the morning. I think the sooner we are able to see where the targeted location, is the better," I said gently.

"I agree. But…what should we do now? We don't have much time," Duc hastily asked.

"Have a sampan moored on the river directly on the opposite side of the gas station with a lamp hanging at a very easy-to-see place, I mean easily visible. Don't mingle with other boats," I suggested.

"Okay, I am leaving now. Don't take off right away. Wait for about twenty minutes after I leave," he said and then quickly climbed back down to his sampan. I heard him quickly but quietly paddling away.

After Duc left, I tried to stay calm so I could focus on operating the boat; I knew that all of our planning came down to this moment. I had a very heavy responsibility on my shoulders to take my family, friends, and others to sea. Realizing the extreme importance of this mission made me even more nervous, and my whole body started to tremble violently, especially my hands, which were shaking so badly that I couldn't even hold on to the rifle and the rudder control handle. My boonie hat and my uniform were soaked with perspiration as if I had just walked in from the rain.

Like a movie being rewound, images of guards leading the captured escapees tied together by a rope, walking from the beach to the waiting buses, ran through my mind. The guards repeatedly punched, kicked, and hit the slower escapees with their AK-47 rifle butts, and some of them had blood streaming down from their faces and heads, soaking their clothes. For a moment I thought about how they would treat us like this or even worse if we were caught leaving the country because we carried weapons with us. These images and the thought of being arrested tore at my soul, leaving me dazed and numb. I only had to wait twenty minutes, but it seemed to me like forever. The forced inaction of waiting and my state of fearfulness took over my faculties, making me absolutely incapable of reasoning or controlling myself any longer.

Noticing my undisguised terror, Dien tapped hard on my right shoulder and asked, "Brother Hai, what happened? Why are you shaking so violently? Are you okay?"

"I am so nervous and scared," I said, barely coherent.

"Me too," Dien said with empathy.

"I am afraid that I am going to screw it up," I continued.

"You are not alone and…honestly, I don't blame you for being nervous and scared, but you need to stand up because the lives of sixty people, including your wife and children, are now in your hands," Dien earnestly said.

"I know that, but somehow—" I said helplessly.

"You know, fear isn't all bad…but if too extreme, then it is not healthy," Dien said.

"Yes…I know…it is tough," I managed.

"We don't have much time. We will be leaving in ten or fifteen minutes, and as a matter of fact, we have already started the engine to get it warmed up," Dien said firmly.

"Well, I will try my best," I said grudgingly.

"Well, this is an extremely important matter. Your life and my life and lives of everyone else are in your hands. Your best in this situation is not good enough," Dien admonished.

I stretched my arms helplessly. "So what you want me to do?"

"You have to think positively. We have planned this trip very carefully. We have guns, we have uniforms. In their eyes, we are cadres working for the state-run farms. We know that they are Communist cadres. They think we are Communists, too. They wouldn't dare to shoot at us. You've said yourself that the most important factor was that we catch them by surprise, and that's what we will do. They would never, ever think that anyone would be stupid enough to load people going overseas right in front of the police station," Dien said with all the fervor of true belief.

"Go on," I said.

"What I said is not new to you...actually, you were the one who told me these things. Maybe you are too nervous now so you can't remember...but anyhow, if we trust our plan and ourselves and in our case we know the opponent too. Well, then we will win. Be positive and move on," Dien added thoughtfully.

"You think suppressing fear is as easy as snapping a finger?" I ruefully asked.

"No, it is not easy, of course. But we need to think at this moment and in this particular situation whether the fear out of proportion helps us or harms us," Dien insisted.

"I don't think it would help," I said.

"With the surprise factor plus all our careful preparation, we have the upper hand in this case. We will get out of here safely," Dien emphasized.

"I do hope so," I said.

Dien smiled then said, "You know, if a boxer is too afraid of his opponent, then he shouldn't go into the ring. If he does, he would definitely lose and be badly hurt. In our case, not just you and me, but our children, wives, friends, and the rest of the sixty people would also lose and be badly hurt as well. They put all their faith in us. We won't let them down." I kept quiet for a few minutes to think about what he had said, and I believed that he was right. I was convinced by Dien's thoughtful approach, and my entire perspective on fear changed. I gradually regained my composure and calm.

"I am with you…definitely, we won't let them down," I said with a smile.

He then shook my hand and asked, "Are you sure?"

"Yes, I am," I said. Despite the change in attitude, both of my hands were still shaky, but I tried to control them so that I could hold on to the rudder control handle. I stood up to stretch my arms, legs, and back. I took a few deep breaths and straightened my uniform, making sure the boonie neck strap was carefully tied and my rubber sandals were neatly on my feet. The gun strap of the M-16 was hung at my left shoulder with its barrel pointing upward for the guards to see. I then sat at the built-in wooden chair next to the rudder control handle at the stern.

Dien also tied his hat strap, fixed his uniform, and put on his rubber sandals, then he walked toward the front of the boat. He sat down at the bow with the M-16 clearly displayed on his lap.

The main engine had been running for a while, and it didn't seem to have any obvious problems. I turned toward the mechanic, asking, "How does the engine perform?"

"Good, no problem," the mechanic said.

"Water pump work?" I asked.

"Yes," the mechanic said.

"Engine has enough diesel?"

"Yes, I already checked," the mechanic said.

"Are you ready?"

"Yes."

"Let's go." I slowly pushed the gas pedal, and the boat started to move forward quietly in the dark. Dien only used the flashlight when necessary, such as for warning oncoming boats to avoid collision. The boat passed underneath the old steel bridge to enter the uncharted zone. In ten minutes, we were already in front of the provincial police station, which was on our left-hand side and under the yellow light I saw the police officer holding the AK-47 and looking at us. It was just only minutes, but how come the time went so slowly and it seemed to me as if it was thousands of years? We slowly moved close to the gas station. My heart was racing, but I tried to keep my focus since we would reach the gas station in a few minutes. I tried to look for the single lantern or lamp on a sampan on the left side of the river. I didn't see it, but instead I saw smudge of yellow light blinking a few times when we approached the gas station. I was nervous when I didn't see the lamp, so I turned to the right for any sign of lamp or lantern. I finally saw a lamp hanging under a roof covering the deck, but by the time we had seen the lamp, the boat had already passed the gas station.

"Brother Hai, Brother Hai, we already passed…we passed already…turn around…quick!" Dien yelled. I immediately turned the rudder control handle 180 degrees to go back for almost fifty meters before turning the boat around and swerving to the right to get close to the dock of the gas station. The current was strong running toward the sea, and the high temporary roof of the boat combined with my clumsiness in maneuvering caused our roof to come into contact with the dock roof, making a loud thud that caught the attention of the merchants selling firewood on the other side of the river. Some of them even talked aloud among themselves and I heard what they said.

"M——r…look…look…the dumbasses are leaving the country."

"God, they dare to pick up people right in front of the police station!"

Despite the noisy chatter from the merchants, Than and others quickly pulled the boat close to the deck and stabilized it. Then they quickly laid a thick wood plank to be used as a gangplank for people to board. In order to minimize the visibility of our activities to the police and others, Than used very limited amount of light, having placed one lamp inside the gas station and one small lamp at the roof of the deck. The escapees all quietly boarded in an orderly fashion under the guidance of our team members. Since the boat was small, no one could carry anything except a small amount of food and the clothes on their back. The lamp hanging outside didn't cast enough light and the wind kept swinging it, so it was difficult for people to see. The wood plank was bent down to the point that it almost touched the water surface under the people's weight, and it swung like a hammock because the boat was rocked by the waves. Two adults or four children were allowed to walk on the gangplank at a time. I hustled everyone to the cabin as soon as they reached the boat, and I constantly kept an eye out for my wife and children. They were almost in the last group to get to the boat. My children were walking in front of my wife. I counted them one by one, and I saw only three of my children.

"Where is our youngest son?" I asked.

"He was in front of me, just a few minutes ago," Huong said nervously. I started to call his name, but I couldn't yell because I was afraid the guards at the police station would hear. There was an adult who had the same name as my son answered, but I told him that I was looking for my son who was six years old. It took only five minutes to get everyone on board, and we had to take off immediately. I hadn't heard the sound of anything falling into water since the boat docked, which was somewhat reassuring. However, although we searched every corner of the gas station, my son was nowhere to be found. My heart was racing, and I was still in complete shock as the boat took off. I just wanted to stop the boat to continue searching for my son, but the lives of sixty other people hung in the balance. Just one wrong move and we all would be arrested. My wife began to quietly but incessantly sob, and the other women asked her to stop because they didn't want the guards to hear.

We now were on our way to the sea, but before reaching the river mouth, we had to go underneath the white concrete bridge. We knew in advance that our boat would have no problem going under the bridge provided that the temporary roof was removed. We had built the roof in such a fashion that it could be removed from the boat in just a few minutes. About three hundred meters from the white concrete bridge, four of us lifted the four posts of the roof from their holes and easily dropped it in the water. Then we sailed smoothly toward the bridge, and we passed underneath the bridge and bypassed the last police guard towers without an incident. We all felt relieved.

"Thank God we sailed through smoothly," Dien murmured to me.

"We are very lucky," I agreed.

I focused on maneuvering the boat to stay in the fast-flowing part of the current, and I also eased the gas lever forward to increase the speed. We were at about five hundred meters past the white concrete bridge, moving smoothly along the channel of water to the sea, when I suddenly felt a jerk as if someone pushed my head forward and the boat came to a complete stop.

"Oh my god! What is happening?" I blurted, my voice pitched loud enough for others to hear.

Despite my efforts to pull the gas lever and change the gear to move forward or backward, the boat didn't budge.

"What happened?" Than asked in panic.

"I think we are stuck on a sand bar," I said fearfully.

"What?" he asked again in horror.

"Stuck on a sand bar," I repeated in dismay.

Than knew from experience that when a boat carrying a heavy load got stuck on a sand bar, no one could pull the boat off by sheer human power. This very scenario was the reason many escapees from Saigon and a group of local teachers had been arrested by police in the past few months.

Than immediately urged his young friends to jump off the boat and swim to the shore to escape, since he knew there was no way we would be able to save our boat. I didn't think anymore but earnestly began begging them to help me push the boat off.

"Please don't abandon us…we still have a chance…we need to fight until our last breath." I then turned off the engine so that the propeller wouldn't accidentally activate and hurt somebody.

Some of the young men wanted to run, but most of them wanted to stay with me. They finally decided to jump into the water, and together we pushed the boat.

There were more than thirty young men on our boat, so when they all jumped off the boat it was much lighter. Our boat was also a riverboat, so it didn't have a true keel and the contact area between its bottom, the sand bar was not that large, the force of friction was not high and the water was rushing to sea in the morning. We were very lucky. Together we used all our might to push against the boat. With all those favorable factors, it finally budged; the boat was pushed clear of the sand bar and floated into deep water. As soon as the boat drifted away from the sandbar, everyone scrambled to get back aboard so we could get out of this area. I was at the rear of the boat pushing hard along with the others, so when the boat slipped off the sand bar I lost my balance and fell into a deep spot of water. I couldn't swim, and I was dragged by the current towards the sea. I yelled aloud for help.

It was so dark they had to use the flashlights to locate me. I heard everyone asking each other, "Where is he?"

Even though I didn't know how to swim, I fought hard to stay afloat, but I quickly began to tire. I couldn't yell any longer because I started taking on water. I still tried fighting hard to stay afloat, but in my mind I knew that this was the last moment of my life. But before I could drown, someone jumped in and pulled me out of water and back into the boat.

Even though I had swallowed quite a bit of salt water, I was still conscious but I just couldn't operate the boat. Dien had to take over this task while I sat leaning my back against the plastic water container next to him, panting. They started the main engine and headed toward the open sea. There wasn't a wave in sight; the water was still and calm, and we sailed out to sea smoothly.

CHAPTER

13

God Listening to Our Prayers

It was about four-thirty in the morning now, and it was still very dark, so we didn't see much of anything, except a few dots of light from small fishing boats going out to sea early in the morning. However, even in the darkness, the atmosphere on the boat was both relieved and jubilant. We used a flashlight to signal to Manh and other team members on the sampan that had gone out to sea a day earlier to let them know that we had made it to the sea. We followed our naval compasses, sailing northwest toward the Gulf of Thailand. After we had been at sea for more than an hour, we still didn't have any sign of the other group, but we hoped they would intercept us soon. They carried the bulk amount of diesel; the weapons and all of the bullets, which we had polished and loaded into magazines; and most importantly, the dried food and fresh water.

As the sun slowly rose behind us, the entire sky opened in front of our eyes. The sea reflected the golden glow of the sky, and both seemed to stretch on forever, without border or limit. With the fresh air and the rest, I gradually regained my normal strength, so I began to assist Dien in his efforts to navigate. We hadn't gotten too far from the shore of Vietnam, and while we merrily enjoyed the sunrise, Dien was experiencing something out of the ordinary. He turned to me, saying, "I hear some weird noise. And it seems like the engine is running but the boat isn't moving."

"Yes, I have the same feeling," I said.

"It seems as if the propeller is disengaged from its shaft," Dien said. I explained to the mechanic what we had noticed and asked him to dive into the water to find out what had gone wrong. After doing some inspection, he stuck his head out of water to let us know that the propeller had gotten entangled in a fishing net, and he needed a sickle to remove them. He submerged himself under the boat again for a few minutes to remove most of the entangled pieces of net. However, he couldn't stay too long under the water, so he stuck his head out of the water again to ask for help. Another young man got in the water to remove the rest, and he gave us thumbs up after spending almost three minutes under the water. I was very thankful for all the effort of our teammates. We had been working together very hard for many months and years to have this day.

The fishermen who owned the fishing net were aware that we had cut their net, so they chased after us using their sampan equipped with a strong engine. Their sampan was sliding on the water's surface like a bullet approaching us. We wanted to avoid a confrontation so we gave a warning shot in the air to ward them off, and they changed their course.

The sea was so peaceful. I felt as if we were traveling in a pond in autumn. The boat carried altogether about sixty people, including three two-week-old babies; with all the weight from the passengers, there was little leeway to the water. I was able to touch the water's surface when sitting down on the deck.

The vastness of the ocean also made me think about the fragility of our boat and the smallness of a human being in the sea. Combined with my fear of deep water, this really frightened me, leading me to think about the worst case scenario, in which just a small wave struck us, capsizing our boat. We all would be sent to bottom of the ocean or maybe be eaten by sharks. In this case, I wouldn't be able to do anything to assist my wife and children; we would all die together. It was a scary thought, but we had already mentioned the worst case before we committed our family to this adventurous trip for our freedom.

As we got farther from the shore, the water got clearer and gradually changed from light to darker blue. We had been in the sea for almost two hours, and we still hadn't seen Manh and the other teammates; we began to worry for their safety. In spite of their absence, we still had to move away from Vietnamese waters as far as we could, so we kept cruising at the boat's top speed toward the Gulf of Thailand. The sun rose high on the horizon, and we now were able to see things more clearly in the ocean. We used binoculars to scan across the surface of the sea for naval vessels and the sampan of our teammates, but all we could see were a few fishing boats at a distance.

Dien tapped on my shoulder and said, "With this speed, it would take us about two days to get to Songkhla refugee camp in Thailand."

I put my hands together and said fervently, "I pray to Jesus and Buddha that we won't run into Communist naval forces out there or have any problems with our engine."

"The main engine and outboard motor seem to be running fine," Dien added.

"I pray that we will meet foreign ships in the international water who are willing to save us," I said.

"We only have enough diesel oil to reach international waters. We will run into big problems if Manh doesn't show up," Dien lamented.

"Manh is very cautious. I think he will meet us when the time is right," I said.

"I hope you are right," Dien sighed.

I looked back at the sun rising over the coast of Vietnam. I didn't know when I could go back to visit my beloved country where I had so many good as well as bad memories, the place where my parents were buried, where I had spent all my young life with my family. This was a place where I was born and went to school from kindergarten to college and had a family with four beautiful children. And now, my youngest one had stayed back in that land, and I didn't know whether he was still alive or dead. All those stirred up in me a sense of nostalgia and sadness. I let out a long sigh.

We had been scanning the horizon for Manh's sampan since the time we got out of the river mouth. It had been difficult to see much in the dark, but it was now so clear. We agreed that they would probably have no problem seeing us and vice-versa. We believed that we would be reunited soon. Manh had told us that he and his teammates would put up a fight to the death, that he wouldn't give up. We didn't give up hope.

Dien used the binoculars to search the east side of the ocean, and on the glittering surface of the sea, he saw a sampan directly approaching us at a high speed. As a normal precaution, we got our weapons ready, waiting for it to get closer. As the boat drew nearer, we saw someone waving at us with a white shirt. We had no doubt that it was Manh and the other teammates. We shouted and waved back excitedly, but we still didn't slow down until Manh caught up with us in about fifteen minutes.

We transferred all six cans of diesel and all the foodstuffs to our boat. All four teammates climbed aboard, and before we sped away, Manh poked a large hole in the bottom of the abandoned sampan to sink it. We didn't want to leave any trace of our trip for the naval police. Manh and the other three teammates carried with them three M-16 rifles, so altogether we had five rifles and about three hundred polished bullets that had already been loaded into magazines. Manh told us that the reason he hadn't contacted us right away was because he had cruised back and forth to search for any naval vessels. He said he had scanned through the entire area of our itinerary for ten kilometers from the Vietnamese shore for almost two days and hadn't seen any government boats or camouflaged fishing boats.

We had been at sea for more than nine hours by now, and we started to experience slight choppiness as the sea got a little rougher. Even though waves were not too big, they were strong enough to make most people in the boat seasick.

Since the cabin was too small for sixty people, they were packed like sardines. There was no room for anyone to move around and we didn't have a latrine, so people who were seasick threw up freely wherever they could, and they also didn't have a choice but to urinate where they were sitting. The cabin didn't have ventilation, so after just a few hours it became so filthy and the smell was so strong that I wasn't able to stand.

It was about three o'clock in the afternoon of the same day, and we had been at sea for more than twelve hours. Manh decided to distribute some cooked rice and water to the people, but only a few wanted to eat because most of them were tired and seasick.

I didn't feel like eating either because I was exhausted after the trauma of the last few days, and also because of the waves, but somehow I was still one of only a few who didn't have seasickness. I needed to stay lucid to assist Manh, so I tried to eat a few spoonfuls of rice and a few pieces of dried fish. The rice wasn't evenly cooked because the boat was tossing left to right and up and down by the waves when the rice was being cooked.

While trying to chew rice, I heard a child crying loudly for his mother and complaining of being hungry. The voice was oddly familiar, so it right away caught my attention and I wanted to immediately find out who the boy was. I found him curled up in the corner of the cabin toward the bow of the boat. It was dark down there, so I couldn't see him well and I couldn't get to him because people were tightly packed in. My heart was pounding and racing to find out who the kid was, so I immediately asked people to pass him toward the engine area of the boat where I was standing. He was still crying for his mom while being passed on, and the voice was absolutely familiar! I was positive that I heard this voice before. After a few minutes, he reached me, all wet, and he was in my arms holding me tightly.

"Daddy, I am hungry," he said.

I could only utter two words, "My son," and tears started to flow freely from my eyes. This was the best gift I could have from God, and I promised to myself I would do the best for this trip until we got to safety. I fed him with the food we had and informed my wife at once that our youngest son was alive and safe. She cried out loud and wanted to see him right away.

He was shaking with hunger and cold. I took his wet clothes off and wrapped him up in my T-shirt. I hung his wet clothes on top of the engine to let them dry and also let him sit next to the engine to get warm.

We weren't aware that the cabin was full of water until my son was brought up to the deck, and we didn't know how long the people had been soaked in this filthy mixture of human vomit, urine, and salt water. The amount of water in the cabin was significant; we didn't know the cause of the flooding, but we needed to immediately get all the water out or they would all get sick. The leak must have been quite big for this amount of water to flood in within a short period of time. Even though it wouldn't be easy with the cabin filled with people, we needed to find out where the leak was so we could plug it.

Since most of them were seasick, Dien and I were assigned to this task. We didn't have a bucket, so we cut an empty plastic container for oil in half, and I used its bottom half to scoop the water. The water was thick, dark, and reeked, but someone had to do it. We took turns scooping the water out without ceasing for an hour, but the water level remained the same. We just couldn't keep up with it, and if the amount of water kept coming in at this level then the boat would definitely sink.

It was about five o'clock in the afternoon now and the sun was still out. We needed to get this problem resolved before dark. It was almost impossible to locate the leak because there was a layer of wood planks placed on top of the ribs for people to sit on and the cabin was full of people. There was no room for anyone to move around, and we tried in vain to locate the leak. In the meantime, other team members had to bail water as fast as they could.

"With this much water, the hole has to be very big. Did you guys see anything?" Manh asked.

"We tried to check almost everywhere, but we haven't found the leak as yet," Dien said.

"Have you guys checked the water cooling system?" Manh curiously asked.

"What about the cooling system?" Duc asked.

"Check to see whether the drain hoses are still intact," Manh suggested. Duc checked the drain hose and jumped up and down with joy.

"I found the culprit! The water is coming out of the hose…a lot…and I mean a lot," he said.

"Hook it to the pipe to redirect the water to the outside," Manh said.

"I need a pair of long nose pliers," Duc said with a frown.

"Let me take care of it," the mechanic said. He dragged the drain hose and connected it to the small metal exhaust pipe. Just like that, the water was now being channeled outside of the boat. I imagined that someone must have kicked the hose, disconnecting it from the metal pipe accidentally when they stretched their legs, but we didn't blame anyone for this mishap because the area was so crowded.

In spite of the small waves, our boat still moved forward at a relatively good speed. Tired and relieved, I lay down on the deck looking up at the sky to rest for a while. The sun started to go down, and I watched as the sunrays reflected on the glittering surface of the sea and one broad corner of the horizon turn golden red. It was magnificent. The night then set in. The entire sky faded into darkness until we couldn't see anything except the stars in the sky. It was so dark that I couldn't see my hand in front of me, and everything fell into silence, and all we could hear now was the monotonous hum of the engines.

We traveled in silence for many hours until at a distance we saw a bright spot on the horizon, and we didn't know what it was. It was already one o'clock in the morning by the time the light started to grow large. It looked more like an oil platform than a big ship; it had light everywhere and the entire area was lit up as if it were daytime. It looked like a small city. We didn't want to venture too close; we hoped we could just quietly move past it because we were fearful that if it were a Russian, Chinese, or Cuban ship or rig, they would tow our boat back to Vietnam. The sea was still very calm, and we cruised along smoothly all night until the sun again rose up at the end of the horizon. We all felt much better after a peaceful night of sleep, and we kept powering toward the Gulf of Thailand.

By now, we believed that we were in international waters, and we felt relieved that there would be no more Communist patrol boats in this area. The water was so dark that it looked black and very clear.

The waves began suddenly getting stronger than last night, and our boat started to rock up and down so much that it couldn't move forward, as fast as it was, and it also made everyone on the boat sick again. Manh, Duc, Dien, the mechanic, and I weren't seasick, but we were still very tired, and we tried staying alert in order to deal with any problems which might arise.

Around noontime, we noticed the sky over the southwest corner of the ocean turning dark. The sun quickly disappeared behind a black, heavy, and thick layer of clouds. The clouds crept lower to the sea's surface then rain picked up. We saw a waterspout running high up in the sky from the ocean surface that remained active for almost fifteen minutes. It was absolutely a miracle; it was so close, but the rain and tornado didn't move into our path. We all looked at the rain and the waterspout and prayed to Jesus, the Virgin Mary, and Buddha for help, and we believed that our prayers had been answered.

We traveled until three o'clock in the afternoon of the same day in the rough sea. The waves were getting bigger, and our main engine started to give us problems, only working intermittently. The outboard motor still worked normally, but it could only push the boat when it touched the water.

I was really nervous, so I asked Manh, "How long you think it will take us to get to Thailand at this speed?"

"With rough seas and current speed, it would take us at least two more days," Manh said.

"Does the mechanic know what the problem is?" I asked.

"He said the oil pump doesn't work. He has been trying to fix it all along," Manh replied.

Our boat was moving at a snail's pace, and it looked as if it was drifting. We were alone in the rough seas, and there was no one to call for help. We kept moving slowly for another half an hour, and then we saw at the end of the horizon a black dot. Manh pulled me over and pointed at that black spot and said, "I bet you that is a boat of Thai pirates."

"How do you know?" I asked with trepidation.

"Members of my family who left on previous trips told me about them," Manh said.

The Thai fishermen knew that the Vietnamese refugees sometimes brought gold or jewelry with them to leave the country. They also knew that this time of year, the sea was calm and the weather was peaceful, so it was an ideal time for the Vietnamese people to escape by boat, so they swarmed this area like sharks.

We tried to move away from them as fast as we could, but within a half an hour, a big yellow fishing boat twenty times bigger than ours was right next to us. Every woman who fled Vietnam by boat, and now especially the women in our boat, either tried to hide or to avoid contact with the notorious Thai pirates, but not Dzung and her sister. They said they wanted to see what the pirates looked like, so they climbed onto the deck to watch. I feared that what they were doing would entice the pirates to board our boat, and that would jeopardize the welfare of everyone else while also making things more complicated for us to deal with. I was very upset at their reckless behavior, so I growled angrily, "What are you doing up there? Get back. You are putting us all in danger!"

"We're here to see what Thai pirates look like," Dzung said flippantly, sounding unconcerned. They ignored what I had said because they knew that Manh was the boss of this boat.

Now the big boat was right next to our boat, side by side, and they were only about ten meters away from us. We were afraid that our boat would accidentally hit the Thai boat and break because the waves roughly rocked our boat. There were about thirty husky young men on the other vessel; they had head turbans, were bare-chested, and wore only short sarongs. I noticed with trepidation that some of them had machetes hanging at their hips. They all moved to the side of their boat that was next to ours, and their weight made this side of their boat lower and much closer to ours. There was also one man on the top of a watchtower, and I believed this man was observing the activities around their boat for police or Thailand naval authorities.

"Throw the rope over to them," Than said.

"Why?" I hysterically asked.

"No…no…don't give them the rope," Manh quickly said.

262

"They will pull us to the refugee camp," Than assured us.

"Are you sure? How you know?" Manh again asked.

"We would be in trouble if they pull us somewhere else," I warned.

"We have guns," Than said.

"We don't want to get into trouble...don't give them the rope," I argued.

Finally we all agreed not to go with them, so I tried to tell them in English, "We are looking for freedom, and we don't want any trouble." They, however, were preparing to jump over to our boat, so I yelled loudly again in English that we didn't want them to jump over to our boat. They either didn't understand or they just ignored what I had said.

Manh then told us that we had no choice but to show them that we had weapons and we meant business.

"Load the bullets into the chamber...point all rifles at them," Manh ordered. "If they don't stop and keep jumping over, then we have to kill them and kill them all."

When they saw the weapons, the pirates all ran to other side of their boat, looking for a place to hide, and the man on the top of the post immediately slipped down and quickly disappeared.

They now knew that we didn't have any intention to shoot at them, and we just wanted to defend ourselves in case of being attacked, so one of them on their boat held a compass in his left hand and pointed at it with his right index finger. Then he pointed us in the direction to go toward the refugee camp. They left us, and we went on our way, knowing that as this was the only the first boat we had encountered, and that we would likely face more like this for the rest of our journey.

With the only outboard engine working, we struggled to continue our trip in the rougher seas with our compass as our guide. Our boat was originally built as a river boat and wasn't equipped to go out in the sea. With a rounded bottom hull, it wasn't built to cut through the waves, so it was rocked constantly, making everyone sick including me and the mechanic. I had been fighting hard to stay alert, but now I gave up and lay down on the deck, motionless.

We had traveled for about two more hours when Manh saw two black dots on the horizon. He nudged me awake with his foot and said, "Brother Hai, I see two black dots at distance. I think they are the pirate boats."

"I am too tired," I mumbled.

"Wake up, I need you," Manh entreated.

"What do you want me to do?" I asked groggily.

"Just wake up to be with me," he insisted.

"Just move away from them," I said.

"Move away, eh? I am doing it now, but I can't move fast enough!" Manh said.

"Use the binoculars to see what they are!" I exclaimed.

Manh used a pair of binoculars we had on board to look at the dark shapes, and then he said, "It looks like a big ship, Brother Hai." I stood up immediately and took over the binoculars, looking at the object. It looked like a big ship and it was moving toward us.

"What country is it?" Manh asked.

"I can't tell, but it is clearly a big ship," I said.

"Wrap all the guns in plastic and get people to sit on top, covering them up," Manh advised.

He added, "If this is a Chinese or Cuban ship, then we will definitely be in trouble because they would tow us back to Vietnam. They have done this many times before." The ship was still far away, but we now could see it a little clearer. It was a massive ship, but neither one of us were able to recognize the country of ownership. Dien joined us on the side of the boat to watch the ship.

Since I was too tired, I didn't even attempt to stand up too long, and I just wanted to sit down or lay down so I told them, "Look for the flag. It will tell which country it belongs to." Manh turned the binoculars over to Dien, asking him to look for the flag on this ship.

"I see the flag flying, but it is too far away. I can't tell which country it is," Dien said.

"Very strange…why is it coming straight at us? Did you guys hide all the weapons yet?" Manh warily asked.

"We need to drop all weapons immediately in the sea if that ship belongs to one of the Communist countries," I ruefully said.

I took the binoculars from Dien and stared at the mysterious ship. Although it was massive, it didn't look like a commercial vessel, but it rather looked more like a warship. The structure of this ship reinforced my suspicion that it belonged to one of the Communist countries. I talked to Manh about my suspicion while still carefully focused on the ship. I looked at the lower deck of the ship then I slowly moved up to the upper deck, then I looked at the flagpole on top the ship, and I saw the flag flying in strong wind. To my amazement, the image of the flag was small but vivid, and although I couldn't consciously name it, in the back of my mind I felt a thrill of recognition. It was achingly familiar, and I knew that I had seen the flag before. I stared at the distant point until I was able to see it clearer, and I knew right away that it was the sign of freedom, and I had faith in God that our lives would be saved. I was so excited, I screamed for the whole boat to hear, "American flag! American flag!" A commotion broke out as people stood up to see the ship.

CHAPTER

14

Rescued by the United States Navy

"Please sit down, stay calm. The boat is very flimsy, and it will sink if you guys stand up or move around," I begged loudly. We tried to move close to the ship, and they also moved toward us but they suddenly stopped when they were about a kilometer away from us. Through the binoculars I saw them giving us a sign to stop from moving too close to them. I guessed they didn't want waves created by their ship to sink our little boat.

About fifteen minutes later, a rescue boat with five personnel on board from the ship approached us. The first question they asked was, "Do you have any oil left?" I was exhausted and a little seasick, and I hadn't used English for many years, but I still tried to spit out a few rusty and broken words of English. I was also just afraid that they would give us diesel and then push us out to sea again.

"Yes, but the main engine died, please help us."

"We are the American Navy. We will help you," an officer said. His words didn't register with me. "Please save us," I said again.

"We will help you. How many people do you have?"

I raised my hands showing six fingers, wracking my brain for the word, and managed, "Six…ty."

"Sixty?" an officer asked.

"Yes, sir," I confirmed.

"Any children?" he asked.

"Beaucoup," I said, accidentally switching to French.

"You have any weapons?" another officer asked.

"Yes," I admitted.

"You want to give us all the weapons?" an officer asked.

"Yes, we'll give you them all…please save us," I sincerely begged again.

"We will take you to our ship," an officer said. There was no word to describe how happy I was when hearing what the officer had just said and we knew now that our safety was assured. I turned around, telling everyone on our boat that the Americans would help us and take us to their ship. People cheered and cried and hugged each other. The escapees started to crawl out of the cabin to the deck, making the boat rock as if it was going to capsize.

"We need to stay calm, please sit down…we all will be moved to the ship…chaos will not help the Americans help us," I called out.

"Children will go first," the officer said. The navy boat and our boat rocked roughly like they were dancing because of the waves. It was a difficult task for the navy officers to bring the children from our boat to theirs, but they still remained patient and gentle with everyone. The officer had to carry many children from our boat to theirs because they were hungry, seasick, and so weak that they couldn't walk. My wife and some of the women were also too weak to walk; the officer had to assist with transferring them from our boat to the American boat.

I needed to stay with our boat until the last person because I had to assist the officers to communicate with people on our boat. Even though I was so tired earlier that I had been unable to stand, now I didn't know where I got the energy to spend hours working with the officers to accomplish the task of getting everyone moved off to the navy ship. The American boat took many trips to ferry people to the ship, and I finally got to board the last trip. When we got close to the navy ship, I saw quite a few people standing on the upper deck of the ship, but they didn't look like the officers or sailors, and I didn't know who they were.

My eyes were full of tears when I first stepped on the staircase of the ship. Now, at last, I knew that we were in good hands. Our lives were saved once and for all, and I felt as if I was walking up to heaven now that I was certain my family would be safe. We all were searched very carefully for weapons before boarding the ship, and as soon as I reached the stern of the ship, I saw that our boat was detonated and sank to the bottom of the ocean. Seeing the boat being slowly sunk, I was nostalgically remembering the beloved boat and all of the months of planning, danger, and hard work that had brought us to where we were now.

I learned afterward that the ship was a destroyer, USS *John Young DD-973*, and that the people I had seen earlier on the ship were the boat people who were picked up by the ship before us. The total number of refugees on the ship was about 350 people, including our boat. Less than thirty minutes after boarding the ship, I was contacted by a Navy Lt. Commander who asked for my help to organize people on the ship since there was no one on the ship who spoke both English and Vietnamese. I was more than willing to accept the request, but I told him that I hadn't taken a shower for many days and was very smelly and filthy, and I needed to take a shower very badly. The officers quickly brought me to the shower room and showed me how to use it, then showed me a pile of clean clothes that had just been washed and dried for me to select from. I was looking for a pair of pants and a shirt, but there were seemingly no shirts, so I just picked a pair of pants that fit me relatively well, and brought them with me to the shower room.

This was the first time in years I had a chance to take a shower with hot water and soap, and it felt like heaven. After finishing the shower, I put on the borrowed pants. The waist was much too big, so I had to hold on to the waistband with both hands to keep it from falling down while I looked for a belt or something to tighten it up. The officers were all choked up with laughter when they saw me walk back to the deck with both hands holding on to the pants.

They didn't have a belt that fit me, so they gave me a piece of nylon string to use for the time being. Since I didn't have any underwear, I tied the string as tightly as I could to keep the pants from accidentally dropping. It would be too embarrassing to bear.

One of the officers saw that I didn't have a shirt, so he gave me a navy T-shirt. It was too big, but that was all he could do for me in the meantime.

Unfortunately, when I started to mingle with people on the deck, a male Vietnamese-Chinese refugee approached me, saying that the pants I had on were his, and demanding that I give them back to him. I explained to him that I didn't know to whom the pants belonged, but the officer had given them to me asking me to wear, and secondly I didn't have underwear and couldn't take the pants off. I told him that I would give them back to him when I got another pair to wear, or he could contact the officer to get the problem resolved.

The navy fed the refugees very well. They gave each of us a whole roasted chicken, even though it was difficult to eat because they didn't give us any salt or pepper and we didn't dare to ask.

I assisted the officers to get people organized for showers and their meals. I also helped divide people into groups, and since they had to stay on the ship for three or four days, they needed a place to sleep. The refugees needed to follow certain rules when they were on the ship, and order had to be maintained at all times. There were a few fights that broke out between some men who were competing for the shower or bathroom, but otherwise things went relatively peaceful considering the vast number of people living in a very cramped space. Even though I was very tired and needed time to recuperate, the Lt. Commander couldn't work with the crowd without me, and the officers also needed my help with interviewing a few people, so I was constantly in demand. I only had a private moment at night when everyone was at sleep.

My family was given a corner on the open deck at the stern of the ship to sleep, and we loved this spot because from here we were able to look at the sea, and the view was magnificent. The water was so clear and dark, and the playful waves chased one after another until they gently hit the ship. At night we could see millions of stars in the clear sky, and to us it was a miracle that we were here tonight. The scene was so romantic that Huong and I felt like we were on our honeymoon again. It seemed to me as though we were in heaven compared to the time we had struggled to survive under the abominable regime back home, and I thought I would have a peaceful sleep.

However, in the middle of the night I had a nightmare in which I saw our boat travelling in a rough sea with towering waves. It was rocked violently and finally a big wave hit and broke it into pieces, throwing people everywhere. My wife and children were scattered in different directions, and while I was trying to help my youngest son, I heard a yell from my daughter, "Daddy, Daddy, help me!" But I couldn't get to her, and she started to sink. I screamed for help. I didn't know how loudly I had screamed, but I woke people around me up in the middle of the night, and the navy guard had to arrive to calm me down. I realized that it was just a bad dream and apologized to everyone for the disturbance.

One afternoon, I was standing alone leaning on a handrail on the deck, passively looking at the sea when I heard a female voice from behind saying, "Hi, Brother Hai." I turned around and I saw Dzung's sister. I smiled at her and said hello.

"How are you?" she asked in a friendly voice.

"I am fine, and you?" I said.

"You aren't helping the officer today?" she asked.

"I've worked all day today, and I just have a few minutes' break," I said.

She then moved to stand right next to me, holding on to the handrail and asked inquisitively, "Manh said you are a farmer?"

"Yes, I was a worker farming tea for a number of years," I said.

"You speak English," she said.

"Yes, few words here and there," I agreed.

"The officer brings you everywhere he goes," she pressed curiously.

"Actually, it's a long story, but if you want to know then I'll tell you. Before 1975, I went to college to study law, and then I worked for a US insurance company for many years, and now you probably know why I am able to speak English," I said.

"I thought you were a real farmer because you dressed up like a farmer and acted like a farmer. You fooled everyone," she said, sounding mystified.

"Fortunately, people also treated me as a farmer," I said with a smile.

"Well, you were a good actor," she emphasized.

"Thanks. Now I have to go back to report to the officer to see if he still needs me. See you later," I said. Even though I didn't have opportunities to talk to her in the past, I still considered her a friend.

We stayed on the ship for three days, during which time we ate well and recovered from our ordeal at sea, and on the third day the Lt. Commander informed us that the US Embassy in Thailand wanted to move everyone to the refugee transit camp in Phanat Nikhom, a district located north of Chonburi province. Before we left, the captain of the ship said a good-bye to me and gave me a captain's cap and a new pair of pants. I now had my own pair of pants and gave the borrowed pair back to the original owner. I had a captain cap on, wore the navy pants with a T-shirt and walked barefoot to the boat since they didn't have anything to give me for my small feet.

Several Thai tourist boats were used to carry us from the ship to shore. There were quite a number of Thai police officers standing on the beach waiting for us to disembark. It was a beautiful white sandy beach. I kneeled down to kiss the land of freedom three times to thank Jesus and Buddha for blessing us and all the benefactors who had helped us to this day. Manh was one of my biggest benefactors, and I would never, ever forget his help to our family.

From here we boarded buses to the refugee camp. It took us at least eight hours to get from the beach to the camp, and when we got off the bus, it was already dark. I guessed it was about nine o'clock. We had to stay in line for a roll call before we went to our designated living quarters, which was essentially a shack. It was very dark, and Huong and I had our hands full carrying our few miscellaneous possessions or leading our children. I thought that we must look as if we had fallen from the sky. We didn't know where we were or what to do.

Suddenly, someone pointed a flashlight at my face, dazzling my eyes, and yelled, "You are a f—— Communist. We will beat the hell out of you."

While I stood blinded, another guy came pointed a flashlight at my face and repeated the accusation. "I know you are a Communist, don't hide."

I was absolutely discombobulated and said, "I am not a Communist," and immediately someone shoved me to ground.

Finally, Thai officials arrived and took us to our assigned locations to stay. I was very concerned for the welfare of my family and friends since we didn't know who these people were or why did they shout at us.

As any refugee family, after living in the camp for about one week, we were scheduled for a prescreening interview with the officials of the International Organization for Migration in Thailand for them to determine whether we met the criteria for an interview with American Embassy officials in order to immigrate to the United States. Each family took turns to report to the IOM officials. All of the members of my family were lined up in front of a desk with three officers behind it, and they all were American, but one of them representing the American Embassy and a Vietnamese interpreter. I stood politely with both hands in front of me, and I kept my left hand holding my right wrist while I listened to the questions from the IOM officials. Since I didn't have any proper clothes, I wore the big khaki trousers the ship captain had given to me and a borrowed clean shirt from a neighbor, and my hair was rather long because I hadn't had the money to get it cut for a couple of months. No one in my family had a pair of shoes or flip-flops, so we had to stand in front of the officials barefoot. We didn't want to be disrespectful, but we actually didn't have proper clothes.

Then suddenly, a loud, flippant Vietnamese male voice pierced my ears. "You m——r! Disrespectful. Fold your arms up and kept them in front of your chest when you are standing in front of the advisors. Stand up straight, you understand?"

I thought this guy was an idiot, because to the American when you stood in front of them with your arms folded it was considered a challenge, but I didn't dare to say. I turned, looking at where the voice had come from, and I saw a man with a gangster face, standing and he looked at me as if he wanted to eat me alive. I didn't know who this guy was, what his job was, or why he used very abusive language toward a refugee when I hadn't done anything wrong. I had only been at the camp a few days, and I didn't want to get myself into trouble, so I did as he had ordered.

The US officer then looked at me with a reassuring smile before asking, "How many people in your family?"

"Six, sir, including me," I said in English.

He then showed me a piece of paper with my name printed on it and asked, "Is this your correct name?"

"Yes, sir," I said.

"Did you work for the US agency in Vietnam, can you tell me in detail?" he asked.

"I worked for the US Public Safety Division in Lam Dong province from 1967 to 1969 as an interpreter. I then worked for Pacific Architects and Engineers from 1969 to 1971 as supervisor of the insurance and claims department. My last company was American International Underwriters from 1971 to 1975 as manager, group health department," I said.

"Can you tell me the names of your supervisors at each company?" another officer asked.

"When I was at the US Public Safety Division, my boss's name was Gerasimos Nikas, at PA@E Company, my bosses' names were Don Farrens and Jim McCurley. They both were lawyers. And at AIG, my bosses' names were Patrick O'Rourke and Patrick Dutrey," I said.

"Do you want to migrate to the United States?" he asked.

"Yes, sir," I said.

"My last question is, do you want to work for the US Embassy in Thailand as interpreter to assist the refugees while you are in the camp? We will pay you ten bahts a day," another US officer asked.

"Yes, sir, I am happy to," I quickly said.

"Can you start tomorrow?" he asked with a smile.

"I would like to, sir, but I don't have proper clothes. Can I start when I get some clothes?" I said. I was thinking about asking my wife to sell her wedding ring to buy some clothes for me to go to work.

"I will get you some clothes tomorrow. What is your address?" he asked.

I gave him the address of my living quarters in the camp, and the next day he had a Thai woman come to my place to measure my waist, height, and weight and ask me a few questions about the color I preferred. She also noticed that I was barefoot, so she said she would bring me a small pair of flip-flops as well. In the afternoon of the same day, she brought me a pair of khaki pants, two short-sleeve white shirts, and a pair of flip-flops. I thanked her for the help, and just like that I was ready for work the next day.

I reported to office of the IOM in the camp for work, and they assigned me to work for a US officer who was given the unfriendly name of Fighting Cock by the Vietnamese refugees. The reason they called him that was because he rejected many applications from the refugees for immigrating to the United States, and they never found out the reason. From the date I started working for him, more applications were approved than before, and people were surprised and wondered why the Fighting Cock seemed to have changed.

After I had worked for the US Embassy for more than a week, I had some money to bring home so my wife and kids could go to the cafeteria to have a can of Coke or to share a bowl of pork noodle soup. I had craved a cup of fresh milk for many years, and this time I would treat myself with a big cup of whole milk. The milk tasted impossibly fresh and delicious, and I drank it to the last drop.

One Monday morning, when I was in the office earlier than usual to review some of the terminology with which I wasn't familiar, I heard a knock on the door. I was surprised since my boss had never knocked on the door before walking in to the office, and the refugees usually didn't show up this early in the morning. I answered the door and there appeared in front of me the Vietnamese man who had insulted me during my recent interview with the IOM officials. He shook my hand and introduced himself to me as Mr. Hiep. He was about forty, had dark skin, and was well groomed. His face was kind of plump, and he looked very healthy for a refugee. He had a big gold bracelet on his left wrist, a big gold chain around his neck, and a very big gold ring on his right ring finger.

"What can I do for you, Mr. Hiep?" I briskly asked.

"I just wanted to stop by to say hello," he said.

"I still have a few minutes, please have a seat," I said.

"I guess you like to work here. I had been in the camp for more than four years now and I know all of the Thai officials of the camp," he proudly said. I looked at his face once more and tried to remember whether this was the same person who had scolded me for not folding my arms before the IOM officials. There were many features on his face that bore a close resemblance to that man's face, but it now was much gentler than the criminal-like face I had seen at the time of my interview.

"Really…" I blurted.

"I am a former Lt. Colonel at Dalat Military Academy of the ARVN, and I left Vietnam by land, walking across Cambodia into Thailand," he said. I couldn't imagine a colonel of the ARVN behave as rudely as he had at my interview, and I dismissed that notion. I didn't want to have any further conversation with him, so I nicely reminded him of my duty.

"My boss is going to be here soon and we have to meet refugees referred by IOM in a moment. I hope to see you at another time." I stood up, shaking his hand to encourage him to leave.

"But…I want to discuss some important issues," he entreatingly said.

"I'd love to hear, but please at another time. Thanks," I said, and he left.

I learned afterward that he had actually been living in the camp for over four years and he was the head of a group of people who had the same immigration status. They came to this transit camp from Sakeo Holding Center where land refugees were temporarily held, and their applications for migrating to a third country had been denied so many times that they therefore ended up living in this camp for a long time. Since they had been living in the camp for so long, they banded together, protecting their own interests by working with the Thai officials of the camp. Mr. Hiep had met a young beautiful Vietnamese girl half his age while they were both living in this camp; they lived together and had a baby boy. I felt bad for them, but I didn't like the way they were making money by terrorizing and threatening the new refugees who had just arrived at the camp.

After a few weeks, I wrote a letter to my former boss, Mr. Patrick Dutrey, Chairman of the AIG in Vietnam, who was by then Chairman of AIU Thailand, informing him that I had just escaped from the Communists in Vietnam and was now in the Transit Center for refugees in Thailand.

A week after sending out the letter, I was eating lunch with my family on the cement floor of my shack when I saw a Thai man walking back and forth in front of my living quarters, talking to some refugee kids about a Vietnamese man he was looking for. He told the kids that he knew this person's name, but had never met him. He just knew that he lived somewhere in this area. He handed them a piece of paper with the man's name on it, and one of the kids then showed me the paper and asked for my help. I was amazed to see my name on that paper! After years of relying on anonymity in Vietnam for protection, I was wary about this stranger looking for me. I wanted to protect my identity until I knew that no harm would come to me or my family, so I proceeded with caution, inquiring politely why he was searching for this Vietnamese person. The answer surprised me. He told me that person used to work for AIU, Inc. in Vietnam, but was now a refugee living in this camp and that he had been searching for almost an hour for him. I was so delighted to meet him and told him that I was that person and asked how I could help him.

He wanted to see my identification, so I showed him the IOM badge that I wore for work. When he verified that I was the right person, he pulled out an envelope containing some money then said that Mr. Dutrey wanted him to deliver two hundred dollars to me as a gift and he wanted me to sign on a piece of paper so he could show it to Mr. Dutrey. I wrote on a piece of paper that I had received two hundred dollars from him and sending my many thanks to Mr. Dutrey. Though, two hundred dollars was absolutely helpful to our family at this time, we still shared some of it with my teammates who were in urgent need of help.

* * *

There was rumor floating among refugees that it was very difficult to enter the United States of America, and since our family's preferred destination for immigration was the USA, it made Huong very nervous for our future. Additionally, most of the people in our boat who had relatives living in Canada or Australia started to leave the camp one by one to unite with their families. There were only a few families including ours on the same boat who were still in the camp, and the rest were sent to refugee camps in either the Philippines or Indonesia to study English for two years before going to the country of their choice.

Huong became very antsy because she didn't know whether our family would be accepted to the United States of America and she understood that regardless of which countries we would eventually be admitted to, we would have to start our life in a new land from nothing and none of the members of our family could speak a word of English, except me. She knew that we would be faced with a great deal of challenge and if we had an opportunity she wanted us to leave the camp for resettlement soon.

The refugees had nothing to do all day, so they gathered around an area having the loudspeaker every day, listening to the announcement from IOM for a list of refugees having been approved for leaving the camp. My wife didn't miss a day in the last two months, and so far she hadn't heard our name declared, and she was very disappointed. I had to work every day so I didn't have a chance to look into the status of our case; my wife, therefore, now felt a little bit uneasy with me. After two and a half months of waiting, she could no longer keep her patience. She approached me asking questions when I just got home from work.

"Do you have any idea when we will be leaving the camp?"

"I wish I knew."

"You are working for IOM. Don't you have any information?"

"My job is interpretation, and I have no idea what people in other sections are doing."

"If we have to wait too long or it is too difficult to get into the USA, then why don't we look into going to other countries such as Canada or Australia?"

"I don't know how easy it is to go to those two countries either and whether we need to have relatives living there to sponsor us. I really don't know."

"Well…but at least we should try?"

"I agree with you, and all I am asking is to be a little more patient since we are here just over two months and we are no longer fearful of being snatched off from home in the middle of night or being hungry. There are quite a few people who have been staying in the camp much longer than us."

"That is it! Since I don't know how long we have to stay in the camp that is worrisome. We need to look to the future and our situation to make decisions. Our kids need to go to school. They had already missed many years of school and they have a lot of catch up to do and we do too."

"I am with you on this, but in our case; I don't think we will have to stay in the camp too much longer. However, I will check with the IOM office on this for you tomorrow during my lunchtime."

"Listen, this is not just for me, and don't you think this is an important issue for our family?"

"Your point is well taken. I will check it out," I said uneasily.

I understood that time was essential for us, but if it was for me I wouldn't be too stressful over this.

Before taking off for work, I noticed that my wife had already gone. I guessed she was now at the area having a loudspeaker with other refugees listening to the announcement. At lunchtime, I visited the IOM office, which wasn't too far from where I worked and as soon as I walked into the door, I saw my wife already sitting at a chair in the waiting room. I wasn't too happy with her assertiveness in dealing with this issue, but I kept cool by asking her a question.

"How long have you been waiting for me?"

"A few minutes."

"Did you eat anything as yet?"

"I am not really hungry."

"We will get a bowl of noodle soup at the restaurant next door after we get this issue taken care of."

There were few people who were ahead of us waiting for services in the IOM's office, so I picked up a ticket and waited for my turn to talk to the representative. The signs of anxiety were clearly written on my wife's face. Upon my turn, I explained to the representative the details of our case and asked him to see if I could change our preferred country of destination and whether my departure from the camp could be expedited. He asked me whether we had relatives living in Canada or Australia who were willing to sponsor our family but we didn't. He then told us that based on what I had just explained to him, he didn't think we had to stay too long in the camp but he also included a disclaimer that we shouldn't hold him accountable for his statement. He added that the approval for our family to go to the United States of America would be forfeited once we applied to go to other countries.

During the tense moments, I used to joke with my wife that "patience is a virtue," and it now became applicable in our particular case. My wife now realized that she would be much better to stay calm waiting for our papers to be processed; otherwise, she would only create unnecessary stress for the family. To date, we had been in the camp for exactly two months and fifteen days. I was still working for IOM, and as usual my wife still spent her time sitting at the location next to IOM's office to listen to the announcements.

Five days later, on a Friday—which was usually a relatively slow day—my boss wanted to interview as many families as he could. So he asked me to be at work an hour early. I left our living quarters directly for work without even stopping by the food stand to have a bowl of noodles. As soon as we got to the office, my boss immediately delved into the stack of files on his desk and refugee families scheduled for interview showed up continuously one by one. I tried to interpret as accurately as I could so the refugees interviewed by my boss would have a fair chance to relocate to the United State of America.

We didn't go to lunch. My boss ordered sandwiches for both of us, and we worked through lunch. We didn't stop work until at least five in the afternoon. I was really tired, and I just couldn't wait to go home to rest. My boss told me before we left the office at the end of the day that he would be on vacation the next two weeks so he needed my help today and he also told me that another US advisor would be assigned to take his place while he was gone. I left the office after wishing him a good vacation.

I needed some rest, but as soon as I stepped out of the interviewing room's door, I saw my wife sitting in the chair in the waiting room. Her face was glowing with a mixture of happiness and anxiousness. She stood up upon seeing me and immediately started asking a question.

"Did you hear our name announced today?"

"Really! When did you hear it?" I joyfully asked. We then walked out of the door together toward our living quarters among hundreds of refugees leisurely walking back and forth.

"About an hour ago. Can we go to the IOM office to check it out?"

"It is late. I think IOM office is closed now," I said.

"What are we going to do now?" she anxiously asked.

"We can't do much of anything now. We have to wait until Monday morning to find out," I said with a smile.

I was so thrilled with the good news and I thought we were so lucky that we didn't have to stay in the camp too long so I asked her a question. "Do you remember when we were first arrived at the camp?"

"I don't remember the exact date but I am sure that we have already been here two months and twenty days," she said firmly.

In retrospect, I said, "Two months and twenty days." I thought it meant nothing compared to the long miserable and painful years we had spent preparing for our escape. We worked very hard on those days, and of course we had hope but we had never ever dared even to imagine a day when we would step foot on American soil. I was totally immersed in the thought and I suddenly shut myself off completely from our conversation. She uncomfortably looked at me and asked, "What's the matter?"

Oh! Just a thought about our most happy day," I said gracefully.

"What is it?"

"Set our foot on American soil. Are you finally happy?" I asked with a smile.

"Absolutely! But we will have a lot of things to do ahead of us."

"Obviously but regardless of how much difficulty we have to face or how hard we have to work, we will make it given that God gives us our health. We experienced the harshest living conditions in Vietnam under the Communist regime, so I strongly believe that we would be able to survive in any society and especially in the United States of America."

As we reached the steps to our living quarters, a next-door female neighbor stood up from her living space happily yelling at us, "I heard your name announced today."

"Thanks, we are aware of it this afternoon," Huong politely said.

"When will your family take off?" she asked.

"We don't know for sure yet. We will check with IOM office on Monday to find out," I said with a smile.

"Where will you go? Philippines or Indonesia?" she asked briskly.

"No…we will go directly to America, the US advisor told us during our interview," my wife pleasantly said.

"How so?" she asked with astonishment.

"My husband has some command of English and he had also worked for several US agencies when he was in Vietnam," my wife explained.

"That was what we understand, but we need confirmation from IOM's office on this coming Monday," I carefully added.

"Congratulations," our neighbor cheerfully said.

"Thanks," I said.

I needed to get some rest and we also had to figure out what to pack for our trip, so we excused ourselves from further conversation. I was exhausted because I had to wake up early in the morning to go to work and spend long hours in the office. I just wanted to take a few minutes resting. I threw a plastic pillow on the straw mattress to lie down, trying to close my eyes for a few minutes. I, however, just couldn't rest. Blood rushed through my body with excitement, and it was impossible for me to think of the day we would all step on the American soil. It was absolutely a dream come through.

The first thing Monday, I notified my boss at IOM of my resignation. He asked if I could stay to work for IOM, and he would pay me three hundred dollars a month. It was a big amount of money for any refugee at this time, especially for me. I told him that I was very appreciative of his kindness, but I had a more urgent responsibility of sending my children to school since they had a lot of catching up to do and we also had to restart our life at an older age in a new land.

After talking to my wife, I realized that we didn't have any belongings of values except a few blankets my neighbors gave to us when they left the camp last month. We decided to leave them for our neighbor and the military duffel bag we received from IOM when we first got to the camp was sufficient for us to stuff a few pair of clothes for each member of our family, and there voila we were ready for the departure.

We had to stay in the camp for a few more days to get medical checkups, required vaccinations, and all the immigration papers completed including the signing of a promissory note to borrow money for our flight tickets from Bangkok, Thailand to our final destination. The total cost of our tickets was three thousand dollars, and we would have to pay it back in monthly installments after we were resettled in USA for three years. The IOM gave us a plastic bag containing all the important immigration papers for our family and instructed me very clearly not to remove any papers from the bag and to give the bag only to the customs officers at the port of entry in the USA.

Two day later, it was Wednesday, a big bus took us along with forty other refugees to Bangkok airport. Sitting on the bus on our way to the airport, I was able to see the immense rice fields and clusters of farmhouses with coconut trees on both sides of the road. I had a feeling of being mentally liberated. Besides, I knew with certainty that we were on our way to live in a most democratic and hospitable society where there will be a great deal of opportunities for us to better our lives. I felt really good. Until now, I really had only a few moments for myself looking back over those struggling years just to survive and I then closed my eyes leaning back to allow me to taste the sweetness of freedom, happiness, and inner tranquility I had lost for such a long time.

Suddenly, Huong slightly tapped on my lap, bringing me back to reality, asking, "Are we close to the airport as yet?"

Looking over to her, I saw she was holding the IOM plastic bag containing our immigration papers tightly close to her chest with both hands.

"It is supposed to be two and a half hours. We left at nine o'clock. I don't have a watch but I guessed we probably travelled for an hour already. We are almost halfway to the airport," I said.

"When the plane will take off?" she asked.

"Around three in the afternoon. We will have a few hours checking out the amenities in the airport," I said.

"I still have a small amount of Thailand baht. We can get something to eat before boarding the plane," she said with a smile.

"It is a good idea," I said.

Looking through the bus window, we started to see more cars, motorcycles, and tall buildings on both sides of the street and we knew that we were close to the city of Bangkok. Through the window, my kids were absolutely startled with their mouth opened to see the vastness, and the colorful, bustling city of Bangkok for the first time in their life.

Finally we arrived at the airport and we were led to waiting area of the designated gate where we would board the plane. While we were milling around the gate area, the IOM representative got us all together and advised us not to wander too far from the gate area since most of us weren't familiar with the airport terminal area and we might get lost. She also reminded us to get back to the gate area on time for boarding the plane.

We carefully wrote down the gate number and name of the airliner before setting out to take a walk looking for something for my children to eat. We were looking for a soup noodle restaurant, but I couldn't find any and instead we found many restaurants with strange name like McDonalds, Burger King, Chick-fil-A, KFC fried chicken, and etc., and we couldn't find any things on the menu that really appealed to my children's appetites.

We kept walking down a little further, and when we were almost at the end of the corridor, I was flabbergasted to see a man, a woman, and a child sitting in a plastic tent erected at the right end corner of the corridor. The man looked very much like Mr. Hiep, the man who was scolding me when we had an interview with the IOM officials. I didn't believe my eyes. I rubbed them a couple of times then I looked at him again and now I believed that person was Mr. Hiep. I thought that he and his family would probably take the same flight with us to USA.

I approached the tent and asked, "Are you Mr. Hiep?"

Instead of answering my question, he astonishingly asked, "Hi, Mr. Dai, what are you doing here?"

"We are taking a flight out at three o'clock today. And how about you?" I casually asked.

"I am working for IOM now. We are temporarily staying here until they get us a place to live," he said ruefully. Mr. Hiep and his family had been in different refugee camps for more than four years now, and though we were not friends, I still had a deep sympathy for his situation, especially his child.

"I hope you and your family will soon settle in a third country," I said with a smile. I then said good-bye and took off since we didn't want to be late for our flight.

We all gathered around the terminal area adjacent to the boarding gate, and after receiving instructions from an IOM representative, we all stayed in line waiting for our turn to get on the plane. It was a huge American Airlines jet. It carried almost five hundred passengers, and we had right window seats. Once all passengers were in their seats, a female flight attendant showed us how to fasten the seatbelt, instructed us to remain in our seat when the plane was taking off, and told us all other important rules to comply with when we were in flight.

The plane taxied down the runway and was moving forward at a fast speed and then it took off. Looking over at my children while the plane was taking off, I saw their hands and arms were tightly glued to both of the seat armrests. Their mouths were wide open, and the mixture of fearfulness and excitement were clearly written on their faces. They were absolutely thrilled.

We were served lunches and dinner during the flight. Between meals, my kids were thirsty and wanted to drink some milk or orange juice. I, however, asked them to refrain until the meal serving time since we didn't have any US money to pay for those extra items. I didn't know then that those items were free of charges.

15

Fired from My First Job

The plane landed in Anchorage, Alaska to refuel after many hours in the air, and we were allowed to get off the plane for about thirty minutes. We couldn't spend anytime outside because it was dark, rainy, and bitter cold.

The plane then took off again for California, and after about another five-hour flight, we landed in Los Angeles in the morning. All refugees were led to a big room with bright lights, enough chairs for everyone to sit, clean bathrooms and drinking water fountains. We were advised to get our IOM immigration paperwork ready for the customs officers to process, and we waited for our turn. I noticed that members of each family were sitting together neatly into a group, and we didn't talk too loudly either. We were all quiet, comfortably sitting in our chairs, waiting for our turn.

Our family was called into a small room to meet a young male officer; he smiled at us and invited us to sit down on the chairs against the wall in front of his desk. With a smile, he asked us to give him the plastic bag we carried with us. It appeared that he knew exactly what type of documents were contained in the bag. He took our pictures, fingerprinted us, and gave me and my wife some sort of identification cards. After the process was completed, we then were loaded into a bus and transported to an area about an hour's drive from the airport. This place was on top of a hill surrounded by a high fence and had many two-story buildings. We learned from the human service representative that this was an old army barracks and that each family was assigned a room with many beds, each bed had thick mattresses, white bed sheets, and a blanket. The mattress was so soft, the bed sheet and blanket smelled so well. We stayed here for two weeks, and during our stay, we were served three meals a day and were warmly clothed.

And to us, this was heaven and where else in the world were Vietnamese refugees treated with such kindness and hospitality. We remembered this for the rest of our lives.

We not only received food to eat, and clothes to wear, we were also sent to classes to learn about how the Americans go about their daily life and also American culture. It was very interesting to learn a new culture and new language, and we talked among members of our family that we would try our best to assimilate ourselves to this society. Our Vietnamese-American advisor told us that the city of Rochester, New York, where we chose to live was very cold, damp, and it had a long winter season with heavy snow. Hearing that, we were a little nervous.

We were booked on a flight for Rochester, New York on a Monday of the third week of October in 1982. Our advisor told us that the weather in Rochester wasn't too friendly. It was raining, cold with cloudy, and she warned us to dress warmly when we arrived at the airport. By the time the plane got to Rochester airspace, we saw through the window the light rain, fog, and layer after layers of thick, dark clouds. The pilot had to circle the airport a couple of times and descend slowly to look for an opening so he could land. We walked through the airport bridge and followed the signs to get to the baggage claim area, where we met my wife's uncle's family. They were waiting for us at the bottom step of the staircase. They all looked very healthy and dressed in nice warm clothes. Upon seeing us, Huong's uncle hugged me tightly and sobbed.

He said with a wavering voice, "If I met you on the street, I wouldn't be able to recognize you."

"We haven't seen each other for almost eight years now. Right?" I said with deep emotion.

"Just only eight years they had turned you from a young healthy man into a sixty-year-old person," he ruefully said.

"Not me alone! They had done a good job of making everyone in Vietnam look ten to fifteen years older," I said sadly.

They helped me locate our military duffel bag. It wasn't hard to find because I put a big red ribbon around it. He insisted on carrying my bag for me, and his wife pulled out from a big plastic bag she carried with her six old winter jackets and said, "You don't have shoes, hat, and warm jacket. You will be cold to death. At least you put on the jacket to keep you relatively warm for now."

They were quite big for us, but we needed them. By the time we walked out of the door of the baggage claim room toward the parking lot, I realized how bitterly cold it was, and it was windy, bone-chilling. We were all trembling from the cold as we got inside the car. It might not be too cold for people who were used to living in this weather, but not for us who just came from a tropical area with its temperature always at ninety degrees Fahrenheit.

They picked us up with two cars, and I was sitting at the front passenger seat with Huong's uncle. He cranked up the heat in the car real high to keep us warm. Looking outside, I was so impressed with the cleanliness and beauty of the road from the airport to his house, leaves from trees on both sides of the street had already changed color to yellow or red, except the pine trees.

"It looks like a huge multicolor picture," I said happily.

"Yes, trees start to change the outfit at the end of September each year. It is gradually getting colder until the end of April," he slowly said.

"How much colder is it?" I asked inquisitively.

"It starts to get colder from the end of November to around the end of March. It sometimes goes down to five below zero," he said.

"Wow! It is really that cold?" I expressed with concern.

"It isn't too big a problem. People have cars to travel, and they always wear warm clothes in the winter," he said with assurance.

It took about an hour to go from the airport to his house. I was impressed with his home, a beautiful two-story single house located in a section of town with well-manicured lawns. It had three bedrooms, three baths, and big basement. I knew that Huong's uncle didn't have any command of English before he left Vietnam, and neither did any members of his family but now he and his family managed to have a comfortable life after only seven years in the United States of America.

He looked for a government-subsidized apartment when he started the sponsoring process for our family, and we stayed at his house for two weeks while the apartment was being ready for the next tenant. We moved to the apartment at the end of two weeks, and he helped to pay for our first two months of rent. We didn't have many belongings. All we had was a military duffel bag with a few pair of clothes, and after throwing the bag into the trunk of his Oldsmobile station wagon, we hopped into the car and we went to our apartment.

Our apartment wasn't too far from his house, and it took only fifteen minutes to get from his house to our new place. It was a three-bedroom apartment with water and heat included; it was very comfortable for us though at the end of autumn weather.

We didn't have anything, and we were penniless when we moved to our new place. He gave us almost everything from a small bag of rice, a bottle of fish sauce, some old pots, pans, a kettle, a few rice bowls and a few pair of bamboo chopsticks, and one blanket. We knew that Huong's uncle and his wife worked very hard to earn money to support his family of six, and we were very happy with what we had.

The first night in our new place was really interesting. We cooked our rice in the pot and ate rice with the fish sauce he had given to us. We, however, were very happy with what we had since we had our own place to live and our children could roam the house without the fear of bothering others. At night, we slept on the floor of the biggest room. Since we had only one blanket, we all huddled together to keep warm and turned on the heat high.

Huong's uncle visited us at least once a day when he got out of work. I asked him that I wanted to work make some money to support our family. About two weeks from the day we moved to our new place, Huong's uncle and his wife sat me down to talk about what he had planned for us.

"When we first arrived in the US, we stayed with our sponsor in Naples, New York. We worked for them picking grapes to make wine for about a year. We then moved to this area where I got a job working as a machinist helper and my wife working for a publishing company until today, we didn't believe in the social welfare," he said.

"I do understand, but what about the medical health for our family?" I insisted.

"We will contact the United States Catholic Conference to find out what we can do about that, and in the meantime, we will try to get you a job, tell us what you can do," he said.

"I will do almost anything legally to assist my family," I firmly said.

"I know a farmer of an apple orchard located about five kilometers from here, and he needs a person to pick apples. You think you can handle that?" he asked.

"Yes, when can I start?" I asked.

"Tomorrow, I will stop by to pick you up."

Huong's uncle brought me an old pair of shoes and a winter jacket when he picked me up for work and then the farm's owner dropped me off after work on the first day. It wasn't heavy work, but it was cold and from there on I had to walk to work in the morning and walked home in the evening, though the owner sometimes gave me a ride when he had to do business in the place close to my home. One morning when I was walking to work, I saw for the first time in my life a frozen puddle of water in the open and I knew how cold it was the night before in this area. At the end of the workday, the owner gave me a few apples to bring home for my children.

* * *

In Rochester, New York, it started to get cold at the end of October; and though I wasn't used to the cold weather, I still tried to work hard to bring home some money to buy food for my family. I always climbed the trees picking apples and putting them into my bag. Other workers just shook the trees and picked only good apples falling onto the ground. The owner knew I was a good worker, so one day he brought me to a remote section of the orchard having Fuji apples and he wanted me to carefully pick them by hands. He brought me there by car and he said he would pick me up at the end of the day with the apples.

Unfortunately, it was raining hard on that day. I had no raincoat and I had no place to hide, so I was soaked with cold rain water. It was so cold that my hands couldn't even grasp an apple and I had to stay there all day until the end of the day when the owner picked me up. I came down with a bad cold and I could no longer work in the field picking apples.

I, however, made enough money to buy food for my children for one week and to buy a bike for me to go to work. It was hard work, but I was very happy with what we had because after work I went home directly with my family, and I wasn't afraid of being snatched away by secret police in the middle of the night or having our privacy invaded.

While I was at home recuperating, the parishioners of the Fairport Assumption of our Lady Catholic Church brought in a truckload of household goods and gave them to us. Until then, we were all sleeping on the floor. We will never ever forget the generosity and kindness of the parishioners of the Catholic church when we were in desperate need of help.

Staying home for a few days, I then got a job working for an Italian restaurant close to Huong's uncle's home as a dishwasher. I worked six days a week from Monday to Saturday and I took Sunday off to go to church. I worked hard cleaning pots, pans, and dishes for the restaurant all day, plus dumping trash and feeding his dogs. It was hard work but I wanted to keep it because it was a stable job and also I didn't have to work outside in the winter cold.

In the course of cleaning dishes, I had to dump the food scraps into a garbage can. There was so much food wasted. At the end of the day, I had to bring these food scraps to feed the owner's dogs living at his farm. These were the biggest and fattest dogs, and I wasn't surprised since their daily meals were full of thick juicy pieces of beefsteak and big pieces of fried fish.

I worked for this restaurant for about one week and at the end of my work week, which was a Saturday, the owner had the crew leader send me into his office. He sat me down on a chair and asked me with a smile, which I thought was good, "How are things?"

"It is alright," I said.

"Did you do what you are supposed to do?" he asked with a frown. I was kind of nervous, looking at the sign of displeasure on his face.

"Yes, I cleaned all the pots, pans, dishes, floors and then fed your dogs at the end of the day as instructed," I uncomfortably said.

"My chief cook said you are a hard working person. However, you aren't quite up to the par. I need someone who is quick to get things done right away." he said.

"I will try to work harder and faster for you," I said sincerely.

"I understand but I have a business to run and I need to get the things done. You don't have to come back next week, and this is your pay. Please count to make sure it is seventy-five dollars. Don't forget to dump the trash before you go home," he said coldly. I was shocked because I thought I was working hard for him.

It was almost five o'clock, and after dumping the trash, I rode on my bike home right away. It was just the beginning of November, but the sky was gloomy, dark, a few flakes of snow were flying in the air. It was quite cold and it seemed as if God also shared the sadness with me. I didn't feel as much cold as it used to be, and my mind was overwhelmingly occupied by the recent event. I was absorbed in a thought of what I should do to feed my family. This was the first time I tasted the bitterness of being fired from my job when I needed it the most.

My wife met me at the door. After putting away my jacket and hat, I pulled out an envelope from my pants pocket, giving it to her, and softly said, "You can use this money to buy food for the family."

"You don't look happy?" she asked with concern.

"Well, I got fired from my job for not being quick enough," I ruefully said.

"It is alright, you will get another job and I will work to help you too," she said softly and added with confidence, "We will survive."

I didn't know what to do as yet at this moment and I was planning to discuss with Huong's uncle this issue the next time I saw him.

Huong's uncle was my only oasis in this new land since I didn't know anyone. I had no car and was not familiar with the area. I needed him badly at the time and I was in the worst shape emotionally.

I knew with certainty that we wouldn't be hungry but the first thing was that I needed to get a job and hold on to it. I, however, always tried to think more positively by telling myself that things seemed to be difficult at the beginning but it would be easier once we pass the initial stage.

I called him the next day on my home phone, explaining to him my unfortunate situation and he gave me words of encouragement.

"Things will work out, nobody hungry in the United States if they want to work."

After having a short conversation, he stopped by my apartment. We had a lengthy discussion on the issue in connection with my family's welfare. I wanted him to understand that I didn't have any intention in absolute terms to be a burden to the society and I didn't want to hurt his feelings. I ruefully said, "You are my sponsor. I know you want us to work to support ourselves and I did work at least at two places, but it was beyond my control. I couldn't hold on to the job."

"I understand it's not easy to work in the kitchen as dishwasher," he compassionately said.

"I worked very hard but I know that I am not as strong and quick as other younger workers..." Thinking for a few minutes, I continued to say slowly, "The owner therefore has reason to let me go, I am not upset but I am sad."

"Well, there is not just the job but you guys also need medical care, let me contact the Monroe County Social Services and set up an appointment with them to see what they can do to help your family," he said.

"I hope you understand," I said.

"My plan was to let you work for a couples of weeks then I will make an appointment with the Monroe County Social Services to apply for the Medicaid for your family, but since it didn't work out, I will call them on Monday to make an appointment to look into those issues at the same time."

"At this critical moment of my life, I really need help to restart," I said.

CHAPTER

16

America—A Great Country

Two weeks later, we got an appointment with Social Services. We got there on time but we had to wait for about an hour to see the case worker. In order to receive $152 a week, I was assigned to work for the Monroe County Hospital where I had a job picking up trash around the complex of the hospital and county office complex.

I thought I was alone, but it turned out that there were about ten other healthy young men who were also assigned to do the same job that I was doing. I took a bus to leave home early to report for work at eight in the morning and left work at four in the afternoon. Though it was an easy job, I made more than when I was working for the restaurant or picking apples. I always showed up for work on time and I worked very hard to keep my assigned area clean and neat.

After two weeks working as a welfare worker, I was called into the office of the manager of the maintenance department as I walked into the shop to work on Monday morning of the third week. I thought I was working very hard and I didn't know why they called me into the office. I was very nervous since I didn't want to get fired again when I was badly in need of a job.

I didn't know where his office was, a worker had to take me there. He knocked on the door then a big, tall white man in a blue marine suit let me in.

He invited me to sit down in a chair in front of his desk. He then asked me why I worked for the state as a welfare worker and I explained to him the best I could with my broken English. He said he had an opening for a laborer position and showed me the job description consisting of cleaning the surrounding area of the maintenance department, picking up uniforms for employees in the laundry room, working two days a week in the incinerator room, and taking care of the yard work for the hospital. The job would pay eight hundred dollars a month plus all employee benefits, including medical insurance for the employee and his family members, pay for working uniforms, holidays pay, and this was a permanent job working for the Monroe County of New York State. I was so happy with this offer that I didn't wait to consult with my wife. I took the offer right away without hesitation.

"You start to work as of today," he said with a smile.

They took me around to show me the complex. This was a geriatric hospital treating the elderly and disabled individuals. I was also introduced to employees working for the department and there were a total of twenty-five people altogether. On the first week, I had to wear my regular clothes to work, and they paid me an extra twenty dollars for me to clean my clothes. I received four pairs of uniforms on the second week. When they were dirty, I gave them to the laundry department, and they washed and ironed my uniforms.

Since I worked almost every day, I always wore my uniform wherever I went and I didn't have to buy new clothes. Now I had enough money to pay four hundred dollars for monthly apartment rent, to buy food for our family, and all members of our family could go to doctors and the hospital when we were sick for free. Again, to me this was heaven.

I didn't have to struggle looking for odds and ends jobs. We, however, realized that with the salary I made, we had barely enough to make ends meet. My wife needed to step up assisting me. Huong wasn't able to communicate in English, and she didn't have any skills and all that she could do was to get some manual labor job.

I knew that she was very skillful with her hands and she had already worked on hair, and she liked this type of work. I advised her to take courses in cosmetology, but she was uncertain whether she was able to understand the course materials. I volunteered to stay late at night translating all the course work from English to Vietnamese for her to read and working with her instructors when needed. At first, though she was working hard and attentive, she couldn't keep up with the school workload. She usually stayed late after school to finish her assignments. She was in school for almost six months then.

One day, when I was waiting to pick her up in the school hallway, the headmaster sent for me to meet her in the office. She enthusiastically explained to me Huong's significant progress and every customer requested Huong to work on their hair. She graduated with honor after one year of attendance and received the Student of the Month Award. After graduating from school, she worked for a few local hair salons to gain experience and to help me paying our bills.

We didn't have a car yet. We didn't want to ask for help from Huong's uncle often, so our whole family worked on weekends, picking grapes for farmers in the Naples, New York area to earn extra money for a used car.

I worked hard by spending time to assist the carpenter of the department and finally he took me under his wing to work as his helper. I was no longer doing the yard work, burning medical wastes at the incinerator or cleaning the floors. I was given a cart with all the carpenter tools to do the maintenance work like repairing the hand rail, broken dry walls, fence for flower beds, building jewelry boxes and ramp for the patients. After one year working for the department, I was promoted to mechanic's helper making fifty cents more per hours, and that meant I made eighty dollars more a month, which was a big amount of money for our family.

We saved enough money to buy a washer, a dryer, and now we didn't have to dry our clothes on the electric heater any longer. After a few months of saving, I had enough money to buy a used car and started to go back to school after working for the hospital for six months. The Monroe Community College wasn't too far from where I worked, so I went directly to school after work and went home after school. I, however, needed to obtain a high school equivalency certificate before I could attend the school.

I took a course in data processing. I had difficult time understanding the computer concept. I had to repeat the course a couple of times for me to understand what the computer was all about.

I got an associate's degree in data processing after two and a half long years of school, and with the help from my wife's friend, I got an entry level operator job with Xerox Corporation. When a person at the human resources department of Xerox Corporation offered me a job with an hourly pay of eight dollars an hour, I was absolutely exhilarated and I had no words to describe how happy I was at that moment. The new job paid a higher wage, but my apartment rent went up significantly and we therefore had to buy a house.

With the combination of Huong and my wage, we were now qualified to buy a small house on the main street of Fairport, New York. The house had a big front room, and we got permission from the town to set up a one person beauty shop for my wife to work. It worked out very well. She had a high volume of customers, and we decided to rent a building across the street from our house to open a hair business for her. She then had a couple of hairdressers working for her.

After three years of resettlement, we had the obligation to pay back the amount of money we had borrowed from the IOM office for our airfare by installments. We were very lucky that my former employer, American International Underwriters, Inc., paid IOM the entire amount on my behalf. I wrote a letter thanking them for their support.

My children went to the local high school. They learned English quickly and they got admitted to the University of Rochester in New York. After graduating with a four-year degree, they went on to graduate school. The two of them got a doctor of pharmacy degree and started working for CVS as a staff pharmacist. My third son graduated with a bachelor's degree of science in biology from the University of Rochester also, but he ended up working as a computer programmer. He, however, didn't like sitting behind the monitor all day so he switched over to work with my wife as a hairdresser. He was a certified hair colorist and he now owns a very successful beauty shop.

I then continued my schooling at St. John Fisher College for my bachelor's degree in information management systems, and since I had to work on third shift, I could take no more than one course per semester. While I was working for the operations department as the operator, a group called Data Center System Development located in the same Building 300 posted a note on the bulletin board in the hallway looking for a system analyst/programmer trainee. I consulted with my supervisor, and he allowed me to apply for the position. I then worked for Operations for almost two years.

I took courses in COBOL, assembler programming languages, and system development when I was in college, so I had some basic understanding of how the computer systems work. I had an interview with the manager of the Data Center System Development group for the trainee position. Fortunately, she gave me an opportunity to get the training with this group for six months. I was also aware that there were a few other employees who got their training with this group before I had a chance. I realized that it was an uphill battle for me to get a permanent job with this group, but I didn't want to pass up a good chance to learn.

I worked diligently and I did ask my coworkers a lot of questions. They were very cooperative and helpful to me. I always stayed late until eight or nine in the evening in my little cubicle to get the assigned tasks completed while other had gone home at four or five. After two months, I was able to build a few simple systems using SAS, COBOL, and Job Control Language for the group. I kept learning and I was eventually able to build more sophisticated systems and helped the group to train users on how to use them.

I remembered one night when I was in my office, alone working on debugging a program and I suddenly felt dizzy and a sharp chest pain. The emergency crew took me to the hospital. After giving me an EKG and other stress-related tests, the doctor told me that my heart was working as the heart of an eighteen-year-old person and he concluded that the symptoms I had were due to stress.

When working for Operations, I was at grade 6 non-exempt. During my first two months of the training period in the Data Center System Development, I was promoted to grade 8 non-exempt. After I finished my six months of training, I was promoted to grade 10 non-exempt. Finally, the manager of the Data Center System Development finally opened the floor to select candidates for the system analyst/programmer position for the group.

I was lucky to be selected for fill the opening position. I was now officially an employee of this group with grade level of 6 exempt, which meant I had skipped grade 12 non-exempt and grade 4 exempt. My salary was now more than double the salary when I was working as an operator.

I thanked God for giving me the health, strength, patience and a little bit of intelligence to get to where I was within four years. Looking back, I remembered vividly four years ago when I was picking up apples in the cold field, burning amputated legs and arms for patients at the incinerator, and dumping garbage for the hospital.

Even though I did a manual labor job, I didn't feel inferior to anyone since I did the best I could for whatever job I had, and actually those jobs practically helped our family to overcome the initial difficult time. With patience, courage, and determination I was now working in the office as a computer system analyst/programmer. Obviously, I didn't have a strong command of English as other native-born Americans, my wife's English was even less skillful than mine, and we both still had decent jobs making good productive contributions to the society within a relatively short period of time. I, therefore, strongly believed that this country had a lot of potential and opportunity for anyone who yearned to make things better for themselves.

Though we worked extremely hard, without the tremendous support of this wonderful country for the past five years, we wouldn't have been able to get to where we are today. We will never ever forget the generosity of the American government and its people.

When we weren't in a melancholic state, we would comment that time seemed to flew by so fast, and that was true in our case. Looking back, we had been in America for almost five years now. Our dream of becoming American citizens finally became reality, and according to the US immigration law, any alien in good standing and remaining in the USA for five continuous years without interruption were allowed to take a naturalization test. I submitted the application for this test a few months prior to the five-year milestone, and we prepared for the test by reading test examples and all relevant materials.

It was a snowy day in November 1987. We drove to the regional immigration office in Buffalo for the test. We passed the exam the first time, and our children automatically became US citizens since they were under eighteen. We were sworn in a month later in Rochester City Hall to become American citizens. This was the best moment of our life. We now had the right to enjoy all of the privileges and obligations of being an American citizen.

I knew well where I came from. I, therefore, was always humble to learn on the job and to do the best job as I could for my company. I loved working for Xerox Corporation. It paid me for my education and it also helped me to grow professionally. I got my bachelor's of science in information management system at St. John Fisher College during the time I was working for the Data Center System Development Group.

Building 300 in Webster, New York was the global processing center for information of Xerox Corporation, and it housed the biggest IBM computer system. There were more than three hundred computer professionals working at this building.

The rumor had been floating around that the information management division would be outsourced, but we didn't know which company would take over until July 27, 1994. We were all dismayed when coming to work knowing that Electronic Data System Corporation, founded by Ross Perot, won the bid. The main office of Electronic Data System Corporation was in Plano, Texas. It had a big facility with thousands of employees working at this location, and it also had an office in Auburn Hill, Michigan.

EDS decided to transfer most former Xerox employees to these two locations. On my part, after a long discussion with my wife, I thought about moving to Plano, Texas. Weather was the main factor for our choice. We, however, wanted to make a trip to check out the area before we made our commitment. We flew to Plano, Texas and stayed at a friend's house for a few days to visit the main office, the facilities of this corporation, as well as the surrounding area. Its main office was comprised of many huge magnificent buildings located on a big flat piece of land with beautiful landscaping. I was impressed with the building structure of this company, but I didn't really care for the area of Plano, which had no hills or mountains.

After spending a few days traveling throughout the area, we weren't too keen on its flatness and lack of green trees. Returning to Rochester, I decided to stay at this city though I knew well that there were no facilities of EDS in this area to operate the IBM mainframe computer. I took a significant risk staying there because I knew that I had to look for a computer programmer job with other local companies that have an IBM mainframe computer.

As of June 27, 1994, we were all EDS's employees. We had two weeks to vacate our offices. While in the hallway hauling my personal items out of the building, I met the former manager of Xerox software group.

"Plano or Auburn Hill?" he asked me with a smile.

"No, I am staying here in Rochester," I said ruefully.

"Where you will be working?" he asked.

"I have no place to go yet," I said.

"You want to work in the client-server environment?"

"I don't have any knowledge or experience in the client server," I sadly said.

"You can take courses," he said. He had been the manager of the Software Group in Building 300 for many years. His office was close to ours, and he knew that I was a hard-working employee, so he wanted to take me under his wing.

"If you want, I will tell the EDS coordinator to move you to my group," he said cordially.

"Thank you so much. I would love to work for you," I said with a big smile.

I reported for work in one of the new buildings in Henrietta, New York hastily rented by EDS later on. It had no heat or desks, and we had to wear winter jacket working in this building. It took them almost six months to straighten things out and thank God during those six months I was in class most of the time, laboring through computer courses in C++, Visual Basic, relational database concepts, and Oracle Database. After training for about three months, I started to participate in the development of a client-server application, which would eventually replace several mainframe programs built earlier by Xerox's staff.

I had decent knowledge of a few Xerox mainframe applications and system development processes to give advice to developers working on the new application, so after one year working for this group, I was promoted to team lead/project manager.

Rochester, New York was notorious for snow and extreme weather. My wife constantly complained about the unfriendly weather of this area, She wanted to move to a warmer state. Talking about the bad weather of this area, I still remember the time when I was still working as an operator. As we walked out of the building at around one o'clock in the morning, all we saw was a curtain of heavy white snow. The ground was covered with two feet of fresh snow. Usually, it took me only twenty minutes to get home, but on that night I had to fight with two feet of snow to get home after more than two hours.

Fortunately, one of her clients working in Raleigh, North Carolina was kind enough to invite us to visit the area on holidays. As soon as we reached the border of North Carolina, I immediately fell in love with the area since it brought back to me fond memories of my young age. It had pines trees, creeks, small hills, lakes, the mild weather. The whole scenery appeared before me as if it was Dalat, my hometown when I was growing up from a child to young adulthood.

Upon returning to Rochester, I informed my manager of my intention of moving to a warmer place. He didn't like the idea for me to leave the group but he said he would support me if I decided to go. I contacted the installation manager of EDS's Raleigh facility and I was offered the job of team leader working on the Year 2000 project. I moved to Raleigh in November of 1997. After working for EDS about six months, I didn't feel comfortable with the company culture and the company management philosophy, so I decided to look for another job.

While searching for a new job, I found an ad in the local newspaper listing an opening for application development project supervisor in the North Carolina Department of State Treasurer. After reading the job description, I knew with certainty that I had the capability and knowledge to carry out the tasks they required, so I applied for this position. After a few face-to-face interviews with the management of the information management division, I was offered the position within two weeks.

I started to work for the Department of State Treasurer in the beginning of 1998 until my retirement in 2009. After working for more than twenty-seven years without interruption, I had a very comfortable retirement with income from Social Security, state pension, interest from our own investments, and I also had full state medical insurance plus Medicare.

Like any other American middle-income families in North Carolina, we had a relatively modern home in the suburbs of the state capital, Raleigh. After working for many years, I am now able to enjoy the fruits of my labor, retirement. It is great.

As American citizens, we could travel to any countries in the world where the United States of America has a diplomatic relationship. This magnificent country is very vast. It has many beautiful places that we haven't had a chance to visit as yet, and there is no limit to where we could go or stay.

We don't have to obtain travel permits from police or local authorities when we leave our house, and we don't have to report to them when we stay overnight at our relatives' home or a hotel.

Religious priests in this country don't have to submit their sermons to religious police for review prior to preaching to congregations in their worship places, and people could assemble at their home or worship facility to pray as long as they didn't interfere with the freedom of others.

America is a place where three branches of government are distinctly divided, and each has different, separate power and they are independent of each other. All officials of these branches are voted into the office by the people of the United States of America; they, therefore, have the responsibility to protect the rights of the people as stipulated in the Constitution. If they not do a good job of protecting the people's rights, then they would be peacefully voted out of the office and they therefore are accountable to the American voters and not to party bosses as under the Communist countries such as Vietnam and China. In the United States of America, people are allowed to do whatever the law doesn't prohibit them to do and they are also protected by a set of laws, which is very transparent.

I now have the right to vote or not to vote and I also have the right to vote for whomever I think would do a good job for our country. I have the right to speak my mind critical of the government. I have the right to have a peaceful protest to show the government of our disagreement with their policy on a certain issue. I have the right to travel and live anywhere I want in my country without being harassed by the police or government authorities. I don't have to bribe the government officials to open a business, and I don't have to lubricate the system to get things done.

There would be no police coming to my house in the middle of our dinner telling us what to eat and what not to eat. I feel absolutely safe sleeping in my bed at night without fear of being blindfolded and led away in the middle of the night.

It is, of course, not a perfect political and legal system, but on the other hand it gives me all that I need to have a comfortable and happy life. I hope that the Vietnamese people at home will someday have the freedom that we as Americans now enjoy in this beloved country.

Thanks to the American people and the greatness of this wonderful country.

Book Summary

I TOUCHED FREEDOM

Hai, an eight year old child growing up in the war-torn country of Vietnam in the 1950s, witnesses a devastating blow to his family when Communist agents kidnap his older brother. His older brother's long-time friend, a secret Communist agent is the villain behind this horrendous crime. Almost all of the Communist abduction victims vanish forever or their beheaded corpses are dumped at the edge of the thick woods in his poor little village. This incident creates a crease in Hai's mind about the Communists' grievous treatment of the innocent Vietnamese people.

With the full support of the Communist bloc, the guerrilla war initiated by the Communist North Vietnam escalated to a full-scale conventional engagement and ultimately the South Vietnamese government collapses in 1975.

The new totalitarian regime revokes all of the people's basic freedoms and creates havoc for the country's economy by establishing highly inefficient agriculture cooperatives and a moribund command economy policy. The oppression of freedom, collapse of the economy, the confiscation of people's properties and forcing them to the new economic zone pushes people to flee the country by any means imaginable.

Recalling painful memories from his own childhood and seeing nothing but a dark future for his children, Hai decides to flee the country.

Inflicted with poverty and the strict control of the government's brutal security apparatus, Hai and his friends work tirelessly in this precarious situation to escape Communist Vietnam. Their plan is dangerous, bold and risky but they successfully flee the country in 1981 by boat through the heavily guarded river mouth of Rach Gia province in the South of Vietnam.

Immigrating to the USA, the family works very hard to assimilate themselves in this wonderful country and they are now living a comfortable life in North Carolina.

ABOUT THE AUTHOR

Day Nguyen had put together a powerful and inspiring story of his memory when he retired after thirty years of working in the Information Technology as a Programmer, Developer and then IT Project Manager.

It is a riveting account of true events that Day Nguyen has personally involved from young age up to the heart pounding escape that he helped to orchestrate for him and a group of others and his now new life in the United States of America.

Dai Nguyen received his Bachelor of Science degree in Information Management System from St. John Fisher College in Rochester, New York and he was also a Certified Project Management Professional. He was actively participating in the activities of Raleigh, NC Chapter of the Project Management Professionals until the date of his retirement.

He had also spent time sharing his experience and knowledge about the Vietnam War with senior students of the Millbrook high school in Raleigh, North Carolina on the invitation of the history teacher.